# *Swami Purana*

By

स्वामी सत्यानन्द सरस्वती
Swami Satyananda Saraswati

Published By
Devi Mandir Publications

Devi Mandir Publications
5950 Highway 128
Napa, CA 94558 USA
Communications: Phone and Fax 1-707-966-2802
E-Mail swamiji@shreemaa.org
Please visit us on the World Wide Web at
http://www.shreemaa.org/


USA TX 3 868 605
ISBN 1-877795-17-8
Library of Congress Catalog Card Number
CIP 94-094303

*Swami Purana*, Swami Satyananda Saraswati
1. Hindu Religion. 2. Goddess Worship.
3. Spirituality. 4. Philosophy. I. Saraswati,
Swami Satyananda

## *Swami Purana*

### Introduction

The stories of the Swāmī Purāṇa comprise an anthology of the wisdom of the Sanātana Dharma -- the eternal Ideal of Perfection, a treasure chest of the folklore of ancient India, and a modern day application of these classical teachings. This collection represents a small bucket drawn from the immense ocean of spiritual wisdom. These stories originated from the Vedas and Upaṇiṣādas, were amplified in the Purāṇas, enhanced through the epics of Rāmāyaṇa and Mahābhārata, and explained in both the Śrimad Bhagavāt and Devī Bhagavatam. They have been arranged into a chronology from the Satya Yuga to the beginning of the Kalī Yuga, and are tied together by a lineage of events from the disappearance of Satī, the wife of Śiva, and the destruction of the God of Love, to the birth of King Janamejaya and the commencement of the Age of Darkness.

The stories are filled with many levels of meaning, and they are lots of fun. You will enjoy reading them aloud, acting out the parts, and sharing this heritage with your children and your friends.

May God bless you with Wisdom and Peace.

*Shree Maa and Swamiji*

# Table of Contents

Śiva Drinks the Poison 7
The Sons of Brahmā 8
Dakṣa's Boon 9
Churning the Milk-Ocean 10
Mohinī Tricks the Aśuras 11
Dakṣa's Daughters and Candra's Curse 13
The Birth of Satī 15
Dakṣa's Enmity with Śiva 16
The Marriage of Śiva and Satī 18
Śiva Sees Mohinī 20
Brahmā's Sacrifice 21
Nandi's Curse 22
Satī Tests Rāma 23
Śukrāchārya Performs Tapasya 25
Bhṛgu Muni's Curse 27
The Tapasya of Śukrāchārya 30
Bṛhaspati Becomes Guru of the Aśuras 32
Satī's Lament and Dakṣa's Yajña 34
Satī's Leaves her Body and the Śakti Piṭhas 37
Tārakaśura and the Celebration of Śivarātri 39
The Divine Mother Promises to Take Birth 41
The Birth of Pārvatī 42
Lord Śiva Burns Love to Ashes 50
Śiva Tests Pārvatī 53
The Marriage of Śiva and Pārvatī 54
Menakā Ascends to Heaven 55
The Curse of Jayā and Vijayā 55
Madhu and Kaiṭabha 57
Hiraṅyakṣa and Hiraṅyakaṣipu
and the Story of Prahlād 58

Ekāvīrya and Ekāvālī 62
Viśvarāth Conquers India 67
Vasiṣṭha's Cow 69
Viśvarāth Becomes Viśvāmitra 72
The Origins of the Solar Dynasty 73
Chyavana Muni and Sukanyā 75
The Story of Sudarśana 85
Sudarśana and Śaśikalā 89
The Story of Satya Vrat 96
Satya Vrat Goes to Heaven 103
Varuṇa Grants Hariścandra a Son 107
The Enmity Between
Vasiṣṭha and Viśvāmitra 118
The Examination of Hariścandra 120
The Story of Gaṅgā 141
Kapila Muni Curses Sāgar's Sons 147
Bāli and the Vāmaṇ Āvatār 150
Vedavatī Curses Rāvaṇa 155
Nārada's Curse 158
Rāma 161
Lavaṇaśura 172
Lav and Kuś 173
Mahā Biṣa and Gaṅgā 178
Viśvāmitra and Menakā 181
Śakuntala 184
Bhārat Gives the Throne to Śantānu 198
Śantānu Marries Gaṅgā 200
The Birth of Matsyagandha 203
The Birth of Veda Vyāsa 207
The Wisdom of Veda Vyāsa 210
The Birth of Śuk Deva 211
The Discussion on Marriage 213
The King and the Puṅḍit 215
The Debate Continues 217

Śuk Deva Visits King Janaka 221
The Marriage of Śuk Deva 227
Śantānu Reunited with Devavrat 228
Devavrat Becomes Bhīṣma 230
The Marriage of Vicitravīrya
and the Curse of Bhīṣma 235
Satyavatī Calls Veda Vyāsa 238
Pāṇḍu Marries Kuntī and Mādrī 241
The Curse of Pāṇḍu 244
The Five Sons of Pāṇḍu Return to Hastinapura 247
Yudhiṣṭhira Becomes the Crown Prince 251
The Marriage of Draupadī 253
Two Crown Princes 255
The ancestry of Kṛṣṇa 257
Nara and Nārāyaṇa and the Birth of Urvaśī 259
The Curses of the Ṣaḍgarbha 260
The Birth of Kṛṣṇa 261
The Incarnations of the Gods and Aśuras 265
Kṛṣṇa Raises Govārdana Mountain 266
The death of Kamsa 267
The Pāṇḍavas in Indrapraṣṭa
and the Rājaśuya Sacrifice 268
Arjuna Marries Subhādra
and the Birth of the God of Love 269
The Dice of Deceit 271
Arjuna's Tapasya 277
Bhīm Invites Hanumān 279
Arjuna Completes his Course 281
Arjuna the Dance Teacher 283
Draupadī and the Death of Kitchat 284
War! 289
Parikṣit and the Coming of Kali 292
King Janamejaya and the Great Yajña 297

## Śiva Drinks the Poison

There was once a class of demons called Hālāhalā (Deadly Poison), which appeared at the churning of the milk ocean. That was the poison which Śiva consumed in order to save existence from its deadly effects. The Gods, including Śiva and Viṣṇu, fought with those demons for over sixty thousand years. At one point the demons had conquered the three worlds, and made the Gods subservient, as has occurred on so many occasions.

Ultimately Śiva came forward and drank off the poison, whereupon His neck turned blue, and that was the end of those demons. Well, Śiva and Viṣṇu both went back to their wives boasting of their prowess in defeating the enemies. Their wives began to laugh at the egotistical chauvinism of their mates, and gave a gentle reminder that Śakti is the energy of all in everything, and that if anyone is deserving of praise for the victory, it is the wives who are made of Śakti. Even though the wives were sitting at home, they reasoned, it was they who gave their energies to their husbands by which the victory was accomplished.

The gentlemen took offense and became insulting to their wives, whereupon the Goddesses left. To teach their husbands a lesson in humility, they decided to become unmanifest, and that is exactly what they did. They sat in meditation and became imperceptible. Suddenly, the men felt themselves without energy, lusterless, without inspiration, and the entire task of creating, preserving and transforming existence fell upon the shoulders of Brahmā, who was the only one who had not antagonized his wife, and therefore, had the capacity to do something.

## The Sons of Brahmā

Brahmā had many sons; in fact, he is called Prajāpati, the Lord of all beings born. Nārada came from his lap; Dakṣa came from his right thumb; and Dakṣa's wife, Prasūtī, was born from His left thumb. Then came forth the four Kumāras: Sanāt, Sanāka, Sānanda, and Sanāt Kumāra; the four eternally youthful boys who taught the wisdom of the Vedas to the ṛṣis. They were eternally pure, crystal clear and radiant. Brahmā also gave birth to Vasiṣṭha, the wise one, and to Nārada Muni. One day Brahmā got angry and from the scowl of his forehead came forth Rudra. These were some of the more famous sons of Brahmā.

Each engaged in his respective course of action. Vasiṣṭha had the ability to teach wisdom. The four Kumāras taught the purity and clarity of the Scriptures. Nārada was the gadfly of all the worlds; he was always spreading gossip. Dakṣa, which means ability, the mind, mental energy, sought to become most powerful.

After spending some time creating, preserving and transforming the universe by himself, Brahmā began to grow weary. As he was busily engaged in his present efforts, he had no time to perform any spiritual practices for Himself. Therefore, he called all his sons together to see if they couldn't find a way to help him. He requested them to practice tapasya, spiritual austerities, in order to please the Divine Mother, and to request of Her to once again manifest as the wives of both Śiva and Viṣṇu, and to return the energy they need to continue their functions. Brahmā promised that who - ever among his sons could convince the Divine Mother to take birth in his house, would become the most powerful man in creation.

## Dakṣa's Boon

All the sons went off to perform austerities, and to propitiate the Divine Mother to make Herself manifest in creation once again. Dakṣa went with the others to engage in spiritual discipline, and he became extremely inspired. He wanted that Power his father had promised, and so he always gave a little bit extra. He stood on one foot and raised his hands into the sky. He chanted mantras while sitting in snow and in the rain and the sun. He never moved, never flinched and never swerved from this ceaseless, relentless vow of purifying austerities. For one hundred thousand years he sat in meditation, performing various severe austerities. He wanted the Divine Mother to manifest in creation again, and to marry Śiva to take the load from his father's shoulders, but most importantly, he wanted Her to take birth in his house.

Finally, the Divine Mother became pleased with those efforts, and appeared before Dakṣa and the other meditating sādhus. She told them that She was pleased with them and said, "Choose a boon."

Dakṣa immediately replied, "I want you to take birth in my house!"

The Goddess said, "All right, I will."

Then the other brothers said, "We want you to become both the wife of Śiva and of Viṣṇu again, and to give them the energy by which they can perform their functions of existence. Our father grows tired of creating, preserving and transforming this universe, so please give Śiva and Viṣṇu the śaktis by which they can do their share."

The Goddess said, "I grant you that boon. I shall take birth in Dakṣa's house and perform the austerities necessary to be accepted in marriage to Śiva, and My other manifestation will take birth from the milk ocean and marry with Viṣṇu. This will come to fruition when everyone begins to chant My mantra Hrīṃ."

## Churning the Milk Ocean

The munis, the great wise people of creation, were extremely pleased with the boons they received, and returned to their father to tell him. Then Brahmā instructed the Gods to churn the milk ocean in order to make the nectar of immortality. He told them to use the mountain Meru as a churning rod, and to enlist the aid of the aśuras, the people who always think of themselves, to churn the great milk ocean. With great efforts they all brought the mountain Meru to the edge of the sea to use as a churning rod. But alas! If they dropped the mountain into the sea, all of the milk would splash away. Viṣṇu came in his incarnation as a Tortoise to achieve the purpose of creation. "Place the mountain on my back, and I shall carry it into the sea," he instructed.

This was done and the great mountain floated out into the sea of consciousness on the back of the great Tortoise, Kūrma Āvatār. Thereafter Vāsukī, the King of Snakes, made himself into a rope. The snake wrapped himself around the mountain, while the Gods moved to one end and the aśuras to the other. They alternately began to pull, and the great mountain churned the infinite expanse of consciousness back and forth until its contents began to come out.

The Gods and aśuras churned the milk ocean, from which came out Mahālakṣmī, the Mūla Prakṛti, the primordial matter from which all of creation is born. The Gods raced forward to escort Her to Vaikuṇṭha, where Viṣṇu greeted Her with great delight and gentlemanly grace.

## Mohinī Tricks the Aśuras

Many other things came out from that ocean, all too numerous to mention. And then Dhānvantāra appeared, holding a bowl filled with the nectar of immortality. He was shining radiantly with the wealth of realization. His radiance beamed in every direction.

All the Gods and aśuras raced to get the bowl. Forgetting all propriety, they grabbed it from the deity's hands, and then a great fight ensued. Each wanted to be the first to drink the nectar. Aśuras fought with aśuras, Gods fought with Gods. At one point the Gods got hold of the bowl, but the aśuras stole it away. Because of the tremendous harassment they caused to one another, no one was able to drink.

Then the aśuras got hold of the bowl, and the Gods bewailed, "We are doomed! Now the aśuras will drink the nectar before us. Help us, Viṣṇu! Protect us! Come to our rescue! Please save us, Oh Lord!"

Viṣṇu, who is always prepared to save devotees, took the form of Mohinī. Moha means the ignorance of egotistical attachment. Mohinī is She who seduces Consciousness into the ignorance of egotistical attachment. This Mohinī was beautiful beyond belief. Everyone who saw her immediately became absorbed in gazing at her incomparable beauty, and the fighting came to an abrupt halt.

Mohinī asked innocently, "What are you arguing about?"

"We have obtained the bowl of the nectar of immortality, produced from the churning of the ocean of pure consciousness. Who shall be the first to drink it?" came the reply from both the Gods and aśuras.

"That's simple," replied Mohinī. "I'll portion it out to you. There is no need to fight. I will serve you. You just sit in two rows: the Gods in one line, the aśuras in another line, and I will give each the portion to which he is due."

"Sure, Mohinī. That's a wonderful idea. Here's the nectar," came the immediate reply from both the Gods and aśuras. The aśuras gladly surrendered the bowl of nectar to Mohinī.

Forming their lines, they all sat up straight and tall. "Okay, we're ready, Mohinī."

Mohinī took the bowl of nectar and walked down the line of aśuras, giving each one a cup of wine, and then she walked down the line of Gods and gave out the nectar while the aśuras looked on.

As she approached the end of the Gods' line, some of the aśuras realized that Mohinī was giving all of the nectar to the Gods. Seeing that now the bowl was almost finished without any portion for the aśuras, they became upset. Rāhū ran over to the Gods' line and sat down and began to drink a portion. Agni called out to Viṣṇu that Rāhū was drinking, and Viṣṇu immediately threw his discus and cut off Rāhū's head. The nectar had reached as far as his throat, so just Rāhū's head became immortal.

The Gods drank all of the nectar; the aśuras had been tricked. "That Mohinī is Viṣṇu's Māyā!" they exclaimed. "Viṣṇu always helps the Gods, the forces of unity! He never helps us aśuras, the forces of division! We were tricked, ripped off!"

The Gods were extremely happy, but the aśuras went home disappointed.

## Dakṣa's Daughters and Candra's Curse

Brahmā's daughter Prasūtī became the wife of Dakṣa. Dakṣa and Prasūtī gave birth to fifty daughters in their efforts to bring forth the Divine Mother. The first twenty-seven daughters were married to Candra, the Moon. Candra told his twenty-seven wives, "I don't want any difficulties among you. I am giving to each one of you thirteen degrees and twenty minutes of the heavens, and that will be your own region." These twenty-seven portions of thirteen degrees twenty minutes make up the three hundred sixty degrees of the heavens, and Candra, the Moon, moves amongst his wives. Every month he circumambulates the heavens to visit them all.

These are the names of the twenty-seven wives that were given to Candra: Aśvinī, Bhāraṇī, Kṛtikā, Rohiṇī, Mṛgśīrṣa, Ardrā, Pūnarvasu, Pūṣyā, Aśleṣā, Māgha, Pūrva Phalguṇī, Uttarā Phalguṇī, Hastā, Citrā, Swatī, Viṣākhā, Anurādhā, Jyeṣṭhā, Mūl, Pūrva Śādha, Uttarā Śādha, Śrāvaṇ, Dhaniṣṭā, Śattarā, Pūrva Bhādrapad, Uttarā Bhādrapad and Revatī.

They became accustomed to waiting for their turn to share some time with their husband. They gave him all their love, and in every way cooperated with each other.

But when Candra got to Rohiṇī's house, he stopped for a while and fell completely in love. All the other twenty-six wives started to complain and said, "Hey, Candra! You are supposed to spend an equal amount of time with each of us. Why are you staying only with Rohiṇī?"

Candra replied, "I will be with you in a little bit of time. Wait your turn." But Candra didn't move.

Then all the other ladies went home to their father, Dakṣa. They said, "Father, what kind of a husband did you give us? There he is having a special relationship with Rohiṇī, while he is ignoring the rest of us completely."

Dakṣa went to Candra and said, "Candra, you have twenty-seven wives. You better treat those twenty-seven wives equally. I am warning you."

Candra said, "Oh yes, Father. I will surely obey." But he didn't leave. He stayed there with Rohiṇī longer.

All the wives became angry and went back to their father a second time and said, "Father, he didn't leave! We are still waiting for our husband to come to us, and for each of us to have our fair turn. What kind of a husband did you give us anyway!"

Dakṣa went back to Candra and said, "Candra, I warned you. I told you that you had better treat all of my daughters equally. You gave them each thirteen degrees and twenty minutes of the heavens. Now why aren't you traveling around to visit each of them in their turn? You are only staying and enjoying with Rohiṇī? I curse you! Your body will wither away to nothing!"

Dakṣa threw some Gaṅgā water which struck Candra, and the Moon began to shrink. He got nervous as he started to get smaller and smaller and smaller. He thought, "Oh, what shall I do? I am shrinking away to nothing!" He kept getting smaller and smaller until he thought, "I must call on someone for help, and it had better be someone who will respond most quickly. Let me call on Śiva to help me!" He started to recite the mantra: "Oṃ Namaḥ Śivāya, Oṃ Namaḥ Śivāya."

Immediately Śiva came and asked, "Candra, how did you get so small?"

"It was Dakṣa's curse. You've got to help me, Śiva. You know I am very devoted to you. You've got to save me!"

Śiva said, "I can't withdraw the curse that Dakṣa gave to you. But I will give you a blessing, if you do something for me." Candra was desperate and said, "What shall I do for you?"

"You will become an ornament in my hair and from there

you will inspire pure devotion in the hearts of all devotees."

Candra said, "Certainly I will! Now save me!"

Śiva said, "Okay. Fifteen days of the month you will shrink, and fifteen days of the month you will grow again."

So that's what happened to the Moon. When he grows to his fullest, it is the full moon; and then he begins to shrink again. But Candra learned his lesson, and now he makes his regular pilgrimage around the heavens to visit all his wives in their turn.

Dakṣa gave his next thirteen daughters to Kaśyapa Muni. Kaśyapa is the Father of Creation, and the most famous of his thirteen wives was Aditi. From Aditi the twelve Adityas were born, the first twelve Gods known in Vedic times. From the other wives of Kaśyapa came forth the other forms of life in creation. Then Dakṣa gave ten more daughters to Dharma and he said, "Dharma, marry these ten girls." Dharma married the ten daughters of Dakṣa, and established them in the ten directions, whereupon he proudly proclaimed, "My Śakti fills the universe." Those were the first fifty daughters of Dakṣa.

## The Birth of Satī

One day Brahmā went to Viṣṇu's house in Vaikuṇṭha and said, "Viṣṇu, you know, it's so strange how Śiva is sitting up on top of his mountain, Kailāsa, all by himself, doing nothing. Some people are good for some things; other people are good for other things; but Śiva is good for nothing! He hasn't helped a bit since His wife left Him. We have to find a suitable partner for Śiva, to inspire Him and give Him energy so He will do something. I have been told that if we all recite the Māyā bīja, Hrīṃ, the Divine Mother Herself will manifest to marry Him."

"Let's ask Śiva to help us with the jāpa," suggested Viṣṇu.

Brahmā exclaimed, "That's a wonderful idea! Then when

the Divine Mother incarnates in a perceivable form, we will give Her to Śiva, so He will have a beautiful wife to inspire Him."

Feeling inspired, Brahmā went with Viṣṇu to Śiva's house on Mount Kailāsa. There they found Śiva sitting deep in meditation. Brahmā and Viṣṇu sang hymns and songs of praise to Him, after which Śiva arose from His divine trance and welcomed them with respect. "What can I do to help you, Brahmā and Viṣṇu?" Śiva inquired.

Brahmā replied, "Śiva, we need some assistance in chanting the Divine Mother's mantra, Hrīṃ. We are trying to propitiate Her so that She will grant welfare to the worlds. Śiva, will you help us?"

Śiva agreed and immediately began to chant the mantra. Brahmā, too, chanted the mantra, as well as Viṣṇu and the other Gods. Slowly all the munis began to chant, and then their disciples, and soon the power of the mantra spread throughout the three worlds. Then the Divine Mother knew that the time had come.

Dakṣa and Prasūtī had their fifty-first daughter.

When she came out of the womb, she was shining radiantly! Dakṣa said to Prasūtī, "This child is the embodiment of All Being. We will call Her Satī, True Existence." The child began to radiate the power of welfare in all directions, and Dakṣa was pleased.

### Dakṣa's Enmity with Śiva

Once upon a time the Ṛṣi Durvāsā went to bathe in the Jamuna River, where he had a vision of the Divine Mother. As soon as he saw Her, he began to chant the mantra of Māyā, Hrīṃ, and to sing to Her other hymns of praise. Mother was pleased and took from Her neck a garland of jasmine flowers, and handed it to the ṛṣi. The garland had such a sweet fragrance that bees were swarming around it, so he put it on his own neck and proceeded to return to his aśrama.

As he was journeying back to his residence, he happened to pass by Dakṣa's house, and decided he would pay his respects to the newly born child, Satī. Everyone knew that She was an incarnation of the Divine Mother, and it would be a great honor to see Her. When he arrived there, he greeted Dakṣa and bowed before the child, whereupon he noticed that Dakṣa could not take his eyes off the garland he was wearing. Dakṣa asked, "Durvāsā, where did you get that garland?"

Durvāsā replied, "The Divine Mother, Herself, gave it to me."

Dakṣa requested, "Please give it to me."

Durvāsā thought for a moment, "There is nothing in the three worlds that should be denied to the man whose austerities brought the Divine Mother to take birth in his house." Whereupon he announced, "Of course, you can have it."

He took the garland from his neck, which was still swarming with bees, and gave it to Dakṣa and then took his leave. Dakṣa was so pleased to have received the garland, he immediately took it to his bedroom, and kept it near his bed.

Well, in the night, when he went to sleep with his loving wife, he became extremely intoxicated from deeply breathing the fragrance of that garland. In that intoxication, he could hardly control his emotions. He began to behave with an unforgivable animalistic nature, during which he servely scolded his loving wife and used bad language. When he awoke in the morning, he realized his erroneous behavior, and was very confused and apologetic. Then he reasoned that one of Śiva's names is Paśupati, Lord of Animals. "If I committed any animalistic behavior, it was Śiva's fault, not mine," he argued. "Śiva is the Lord of animals."

Suddenly he blamed Śiva for all of the wrong-doing he had committed in the night. Even forgetting the desire of his previous austerities, to have his daughter marry Lord Śiva, he developed an enmity with Śiva and cursed him.

## The Marriage of Śiva and Satī

When Satī grew into a young child, the first word out of Her mouth was, "Śiva."

Dakṣa said, "Satī, Śiva is a naked fakir. He lives on top of a mountain all by Himself. Worship some other God."

From Her childhood Satī loved only Śiva. She would prepare Śiva liṅgaṃs, and She would perform pūjā every day. Very quickly she grew up into a lovely young lady, radiant with the bliss of Infinite Consciousness. One day She said, "Father, I am going to perform tapasya, to practice severe spiritual austerities, to get Śiva as my husband."

Dakṣa said "NO! Don't do that! Choose any God you like. Look at Viṣṇu; He sits in a palace of gold. Look at Indra; He rides on a big elephant. Śiva! Don't choose Śiva!"

Satī said, "My mind is made up. I will have only Śiva." She started to do tapasya. She would sit in the cold and the rain wearing only one cloth, and sing, "Oṃ Namaḥ Śivāya, Oṃ Namaḥ Śivāya." In the midst of the heat in the summer, she would enkindle four fires and sit in the middle between them with the sun beating down on her head, the sādhana of five fires, and she would chant, "Oṃ Namaḥ Śivāya, Oṃ Namaḥ Śivāya." She stood in the rain and in the snow. She went without food. She took only water, and then she stopped that and took only air. She continued in this way for many, many days.

Dakṣa was at his wit's end. "My goodness," he thought. "She is doing this tapasya to marry Śiva! Doesn't she know she will have a lifetime filled with poverty and misery being married to Śiva? Śiva doesn't have anything! She could choose any other God! Why Śiva? How shall I find a way to stop her? I must find the solution! I know, I shall call for her Svayambara, the ceremonial selection of a husband. I will invite all the Kings of the world and all the Gods of heaven above, except Śiva, and I will tell her she can choose anyone she wants!"

Dakṣa prepared the Svayambara. In this ceremony the bride has her choice from all the guests present. The Gods, kings, all the nobility of the three worlds were invited to the beautiful sacrificial arena. Everything was glaring with gold and flowers everywhere. Everyone was dressed in their finest clothes, hoping to make themselves appear the most beautiful, hoping in their hearts that Satī would choose them. In the Svayambara the girl is given a mālā of flowers and set free to roam in the sacrificial arena to examine all the candidates and decide upon whose neck she will place the wreath of victory. Whoever she would select will be her husband.

Satī took the mālā in her hands and looked all around for Śiva. But She didn't see Śiva. She felt such a tear of sorrow in her heart. "How can I choose?" She thought. "Śiva isn't here." She looked at every face in the room, but she didn't find the face of Śiva. Then she took her wreath, her flower garland of victory, and held it to her heart with a prayer: "If I am Satī, then this mālā will be worn by Śiva!"

With that prayer, she threw the mālā into the air. When she opened her eyes, standing in the midst of the sacrificial arena was Lord Śiva wearing the mālā of victory! Dakṣa swooned with pain, while Satī was so happy!

Dakṣa had no choice but to perform the marriage, so Satī and Śiva were married with full honors. Then Śiva took Satī back to Kailāsa, where they passed many beautiful days sitting in the bliss of infinite consciousness. They discussed the scriptures and meditated upon their contents, and shared all the bliss of their divine union.

## Śiva Sees Mohinī

One day Śiva and Satī went to Viṣṇu's house in Vaikuṇṭha and greeted Him with respect, "Hello, Viṣṇu!"

"To what do I owe the honor of this visit?" Viṣṇu was very pleased.

Śiva said, "Viṣṇu, I heard about how you tricked the aśuras and gave all the nectar to the Gods. I heard all about Mohinī, what power she has, how captivating she can be. Viṣṇu, can I see Mohinī? Would you show her to me?"

"That's not necessary, Śiva," Viṣṇu replied. "You don't need to see Mohinī."

"Oh, Viṣṇu, I heard the whole story. Mohinī is so wonderful that even the aśuras would give up the nectar of immortality just to gaze at her! Just once let me see her."

"Well, if you really want to."

Suddenly Viṣṇu turned into Mohinī. Śiva gazed in amazement. She was so captivating. Śiva forgot everything and became enraptured. He even forgot Satī, his beloved wife, who was standing beside Him. Mohinī was elegantly adorned with the finest ornaments, and her natural beauty was punctuated with a sheen of brilliance. She was clothed some - what scantily, with only a light silk cloth wrapped around her body. Every curve of her perfect figure was visible through the fine cloth she wore.

Mohinī was bouncing a ball right in front of Śiva. The ball slipped out of her hands and rolled off. She ran after it. Śiva ran after Mohinī. She began running hard and fast, and Śiva chased her close behind. Her cloth came loose and began to flap in the wind. Śiva became ecstatic to see Her voluptuous body. Mohinī ran faster, and Śiva ran to keep up.

Śiva was breathing very heavily, and suddenly he got so excited that He dropped His semen. When that semen of the Lord touched the earth, it manifested as gold and silver and all the precious wealth. As soon as His semen fell, He became startled. "How could this happen? Am I not a great yogi? How could I forget my own Self? What power this Mohinī has, that even I could forget my wife, Satī, forget all my years of tapasya, forget everything by seeing this Mohinī! Viṣṇu, I bow to your Māyā, and I bow to the power of Mohinī!"

Seeing Śiva's consternation, Viṣṇu took his own form again. "Yes, Śiva, no one can resist the power of Māyā. This Mohinī is all powerful. But because you asked to see her yourself, and because you realized the power of her nature of your own accord, today I am granting you a boon: henceforth, only you will remain free from Mohinī. No one in the three worlds but you, Śiva, will have the capacity to resist Mohinī. That is my boon to you."

## Brahmā's Sacrifice

Brahmā was performing a great sacrifice, to which Śiva and Satī were invited to attend. When Dakṣa walked into the hall of sacrifice, everyone in the room stood up to greet him. They all bowed with clasped hands: "Namaste, Dakṣa Prajāpati. With all of the Energy of Consciousness we bow to the divinity manifest within you. Namaste. Your tapasya has been victorious! You are shining radiantly and we know you are the one who made the Divine Mother take birth in your house. Prajāpati, you are the Pati, the Lord, of all Prajā, all beings born, the Lord of all beings."

Everybody stood up to show their respect. Only Brahmā and Śiva remained seated. Then Dakṣa thought, "Brahmā is my father, and there is no reason for him to stand up to greet his son. But everyone in the three worlds has stood up to pay me honor and respect, except Śiva. And he is my son-in-law. What kind of impudence is this? I can understand my father not standing up, but my son-in-law? I'm mad!"

Dakṣa walked over to Śiva and said, "Śiva, you no good uncouth, foul-behaviored person. You are the lowest of the low. You hang around with ghosts and goblins, you are always taking intoxicants. Now you are showing such disrespect to me? Śiva, I curse you! You live without a house and without a roof, and your devotees will be just like you. They will all be beggars, they will all be penniless, they will all be stoned freaks and hippies, every one of them. They will take intoxicants. They won't know how to pronounce Saṃskṛt correctly! That's the kind of devotees you will have!" And he took some water and threw it at Śiva. Śiva just sat there, and didn't react at all.

## Nandi's Curse

Now Śiva's friend and chief disciple is a devotee named Nandi, the bull. Nandi could not stand this outrage and insult to his Lord. He came over and explained, "Hey Dakṣa, do you know who you're talking to? This is not an ordinary hippie to whom you speak. This is not just one of the sādhus, nor just any one of the Gods. This is Mahādeva! The Deva of the devas, God of the Gods. He is the highest, the Consciousness of Infinite Goodness. He is the Supreme Consciousness, the Guru of all gurus.

"He didn't refrain from touching your feet out of disrespect. He did it because he didn't want anything bad to happen to you. Everybody knows that if someone who is very high touches the feet of someone who is very low, obviously something very bad is going to happen. He was trying to save you that disgrace. And now you see, he is so pure and free from anger, he has accepted your curse without reply. He didn't even utter one word back to you.

"I am a devotee of Śiva. I am not Śiva. I am not as self-controlled as Śiva, and when you cursed my Lord that way, I cannot help but to curse you back. Dakṣa, your followers may pronounce Saṃskṛt correctly, but they won't understand a word they are saying. They will preach the letter of the law, but they won't understand the spirit. They will sell their dharma, and they will do their pūjās only for money. They will all be well fed, well clothed and well housed; but their homes and their hearts will be empty. They will make a show of their faith to earn money. Even if they pronounce the mantras correctly, they won't understand divinity. And that's the curse I give to you!" Nandi threw some Gaṅgā water at him.

Dakṣa turned around and stormed out of the house. He went home saying, "I will show that Śiva, I will fix him!"

## Satī Tests Rāma

Satī and Śiva went back to Kailāsa, and there they continued to discourse on the scriptures, and to practice meditation. They enjoyed the bliss of their companionship in every way. One day Śiva looked down from Kailāsa, and his eyes moved toward Daṅdak's forest, where he saw Rāma and Lakṣmaṇ wandering in search of Sītā. Śiva grabbed Satī by the hand with the greatest of excitement, and said, "Look Satī, that is Lord Viṣṇu! That is Satcitānanda, the Infinite Bliss of Consciousness made manifest."

Satī looked down and said, "You know, I only see two men crying over the loss of Rāma's wife, wandering around searching everywhere. That doesn't look to me like Satcitānanda, True Existence, Infinite Conscious-ness, Pure Bliss. How can that be the Supreme Divinity?"

Śiva said, "Satī, the Supreme Divinity is both nirākāra and sakāra, without form and with form. When it is manifest with form, it must play the līlā, the drama, of the form that it has taken. But that doesn't change the fact that it is still Supreme Divinity made manifest."

Satī said, "Śiva, I see those two men down there wandering around looking and crying, 'Oh Sītā, Sītā! Where have you gone!' They are lamenting the loss of Rāma's wife, and it doesn't look to me like bliss made manifest. It seems like they are in a great deal of pain."

"Satī, if you don't believe me, go down and see for your - self. But I am telling you that is Satcitānanda, Infinite Bliss made manifest."

Satī replied, "I've got to see this."

Śiva said, "Go down and do any test you like. I am sure you will come back and agree with me."

Satī changed herself into Sītā's form, and put herself in the middle of the woods. Rāma called, "Sītā!" And Satī stepped out into a clearing in the forest. Rāma came running up to her and with folded hands said, "Oh, Satī, I am so glad to see you! Where is Mahādeva, where is Śiva?"

Satī was extremely embarrassed and replied, "Uh, uh, He is at Kailāsa. He just sent me down to say, 'Hello.'"

Lakṣmaṇ looked a little bit confused and asked, "Satī, why are you looking like Sītā?"

Satī replied, "Oh, I just wanted to show you how much I love Sītā. I really respect your wife, and I hope you will find her soon. I am sorry, but I have to be going now."

Satī went back to Kailāsa and Mahādeva asked, "Did you find out the answer that you sought?"

Satī said, "Oh, yes, Śiva. Mahādeva. That is definitely Satcitānanda. That is the manifestation of True Existence, Infinite Consciousness, and Bliss. Of this I have no doubt."

Śiva asked, "How did you come to that realization?"

Satī said, "Well, Śiva, I believed your words. I have no need to test the Lord, especially when you have said it. All I have to do is listen to your words and I have full faith. But, my Lord, how did Lord Viṣṇu become reduced to that state? What caused the Supreme Being to assume the form of a man in pain?"

Śiva sat down and closed his eyes in divine meditation, and saw the entire episode. He thought, "Is this the state of my marriage? My wife has lied to me. She didn't believe me and now she's lying to me afterwards? She went down there and tested Rāma, and now she has come back too embarrassed to tell me?" Suddenly a divine beatific smile came over His face.

"What are you smiling about, Lord?" Satī asked with incredulousness.

"Everytime I remember the divinity of Śrī Rāma, I can't help but smiling with joy. Even though I do not respect your swerving from the path of truth, I can never refrain from enjoying the manifestations of the Lord."

## Śukrāchārya Performs Tapasya

Long ago, while the Gods were fighting with the aśuras, there came a time when the aśuras were being badly defeated. The Gods had inflicted heavy losses upon them, and in great consternation, the aśuras ran to take refuge with their Guru, Śukrāchārya. "Oh Guruji, the Gods are severely beating us and causing us all manner of affliction. Please find a way by which we can defeat the Gods and make the aśuras victorious. Please tell us what we must do."

Śukrāchārya cast a horoscope, and seeing the positions of the planets, he instructed his disciples as follows: "Oh Aśuras, for every event there is an appropriate time and place, according to the circumstances and design of nature. Even still, all existence is required to make the best efforts possible to accomplish the ideals for which each individual strives.

Observation of the present circumstances indicates that the aśuras cannot become victorious right now. We need greater knowledge and assistance. I shall go to Lord Śiva and perform the discipline by which we can get that knowledge. I shall procure the mantra by which the aśuras can become victorious. Therefore, lay down your arms and weapons and desist from fighting until I return. Tell the Gods that you want to live in peace, and you have renounced fighting. Until I return, do not fight with the Gods under any circumstances. Without Śiva's mantra you will not be successful."

Śukrāchārya set out for Mount Kailāsa. Upon his arrival, he bowed deeply before Lord Śiva and said, "Oh Deva deva, mahādeva -- Oh Lord of all Lords of the Universe, I have come to you with all sincerity seeking refuge. I want the mantra by which the aśuras will become victorious over the Gods."

Śiva replied, "Greetings, Oh Guru of the aśuras, Śukrāchārya. Well you know it is impossible for me to turn away any sincere devotee who comes seeking refuge. However, it is very difficult for me to give the mantra by which the Gods can be defeated. To win such a mantra you will have to perform a difficult tapasya indeed!"

"I am ready to perform anything that you say," replied Śukrāchārya.

"Then stand on your head breathing smoke for one hundred years and do not miss saying my name even once, or you will not receive the mantra."

With great pleasure Śukrāchārya tied his feet to the limb of a tree and lit a fire on the ground beneath. He began to breath the smoke and chant, "Oṃ Namaḥ Śivāya, Oṃ Namaḥ Śivāya."

## Bhṛgu Muni's curse

When Indra learned that the aśuras' Guru was performing tapasya in order to get the mantra by which the Gods could be defeated, he summoned all the divine armies. "Come, we must attack our enemies while they are weak, or else we will have to fight a greater battle with them in the future. Their Guru, Śukrāchārya, is performing tapasya in order to get the mantra from Lord Śiva by which the Gods can be defeated. While they are pretending to be peace-loving citizens, they are in fact arming themselves for victory! It is our duty to attack them now!"

Indra and the deva armies swooped down upon the unarmed aśuras and began to attack. Then the aśuras began to cry, "We're doomed! Even the Gods have lost all honor! They are attacking unarmed innocents who are minding their own business and causing no difficulty to others! Oh who will save us? Quickly, let us take refuge in the aśrama of Bhṛgu Muni!"

The aśuras fled to Bhṛgu Muni's aśrama, with the Gods chasing close behind. The aśuras passed through the gates of the hermitage, slammed the door shut and bolted it before the advancing army of the Gods. The trembling aśuras immediately bowed down to Bhṛgu Muni's wife who stood before them. "Save us, Reverend Mother! Oh save us!" they called.

"What on earth is the problem, Oh Aśuras?" she asked.

"We were minding our own business, just as your son, our Guru, Śukrāchārya, had instructed us. We were not causing any harm to anyone. But those Gods will not let anyone live in peace. See! They are attacking us, even though we have committed no fault of our own. We take refuge in your aśrama, Reverend Mother! Please save us from those Gods!"

The Reverend Mother replied, "My husband, Bhṛgu Muni, is out in the forest performing tapasya. My son, Śukrāchārya, is also out of the aśrama performing a strict vow to propitiate Lord Śiva. Therefore, I alone must offer shelter to devotees who come seeking refuge. Oh Aśuras, I will protect you until my husband comes home. Then he will decide what is to be done."

Indra pounded fiercely on the door. "Open up in there! We have come to punish those aśuras! Open up in there!"

The aśuras cowered with fear, while the Reverend Mother stepped in front of the aśrama gate. "You cannot come in here, Indra. These devotees have taken refuge in this aśrama, and it is my dharmic duty to protect those seeking help! If you enter by force, you will have transgressed the laws of dharma!"

"These aśuras are making a pretense of being peace-loving, while actually their Guru is on top of Mount Kailāsa performing tapasya to become initiated in the mantra by which the Gods will be defeated. Now it is our duty to strike our enemy before he becomes strong. We know the pretense they are making by acting peace-loving. Open the door or we will break it in!" rumbled Indra.

The Gods began to pound on the gate, and within an instant the doors flung open, and their mighty armies entered into the sacred aśrama. The Gods drew their weapons and began to beat the aśuras. The aśuras cried out in fright, "Reverend Mother! You promised us protection! Save us! Save us!"

The Reverend Mother began to chant a mantra before the sacred homa fire, and suddenly all the Gods started to fall asleep. Seeing the Gods falling asleep in the middle of their battle formation, Indra became greatly alarmed. "Viṣṇu! Viṣṇu! You must protect us! Stop the Reverend Mother from putting our army to sleep. If we incur any sin for this, we can perform atonement later!"

Viṣṇu remembered his infallible discus. The discus began to twirl on his finger as he aimed it toward the meditating Reverend Mother. The discus took flight and severed the head of Bhṛgu Muni's wife from her body. Immediately Bhṛgu Muni rose from his meditation in the forest, and in great anger returned to his aśrama. "Indra!" thundered the Great Muni's voice. "You have no knowledge of dharma whatsoever! We can rely on you to breach all decorum. You have no scruples at all. You attacked unarmed beings. You ordered your armies to forcibly attack a muni's aśrama, a temple of God. You killed a Brahmiṇ and even killed a woman! Indra! You can do anything, and nothing that you do could surprise me. I curse you, Indra! Even though you are the King of the Gods, you will neglect the path of dharma at the slightest provocation, and in the coming ages there will be Gods far superior to you. People will even question the necessity of making offerings to Indra, and in many lands you will be forgotten entirely!" Bhṛgu Muni sprinkled Gaṅgā water on Indra to certify that the curse would come to fruition.

Then Bhṛgu Muni took some more Gaṅgā water in his hand and turned to Viṣṇu."Viṣṇu, I am surprised at you. You are supposed to be the upholder of dharma. You are supposed to be Pūruṣottma, the example of rectitude and piety in this existence. Here you are perpetrating this heinous crime of killing a woman, killing a Brahmiṇ, transgressing what is right! I curse you! Again and again, whenever righteousness recedes before unrighteousness on this earth, whenever dharma becomes weak while adharma is strong, then you will have to incarnate in the womb of woman, to be born upon this earth, to fight with the forces of iniquity, and once again establish the standards of morality and piety by which humanity is distinguished from the other animals! Even though you are divinity made manifest, still, as you wear an earthly form, you will be subject to all the pleasures and pains of manifested existence. Furthermore, since today you have caused me the pain of separation from my wife, you too will experience that same pain!" Bhṛgu Muni threw that water from the Gaṅgā directly at Viṣṇu, while the Lord Viṣṇu humbly accepted the curse.

And then Bhṛgu Muni walked over to the decapitated body of his beloved wife, picked up the body and said: "Now Gods and aśuras, I shall show you the power of my tapasya!"

He began to make silent repetition of the mantra. Suddenly to the surprise of all, the head of the Reverend Mother was attached again to her body. Then Bhṛgu Muni breathed life into her soul, and the Reverend Mother was revived to life. A great cheer of triumph arose from both the Gods and the aśuras to honor the tremendous spiritual power of Bhṛgu Muni. With great dejection, Indra and the other Gods returned to heaven.

## The Tapasya of Śukrāchārya

"What happened to Śukrāchārya?" Satī asked.

Śiva continued his story:

Ninety years had passed and Śukrāchārya had not missed a mantra. Indra became terrified, and he went to his Guru, Bṛhaspati, the Guru of the Gods, and asked for help. "Guruji, what shall we do? If Śukrāchārya is successful in getting the mantra, then the Gods will be destroyed! Who will protect the forces of dharma in the creation? We must find some way."

Bṛhaspati said to Indra, "Oh Indra, for every event there is an appropriate time and place according to the circumstances and designs of nature. Even still, all existence is required to make the best efforts possible to accomplish the ideals for which each individual strives. As it seems highly possible that Śukrāchārya may accomplish the object of his tapasya, then it behooves us to try to establish an ally in his camp. Send your daughter, Jayanti, to befriend him, and we shall look for an opportunity to deflect him from his path."

Indra called his daughter, Jayanti. "Jayanti, I am giving you to Śukrāchārya with the order to cultivate his friendship by serving him with the offering of loving devotion."

Jayanti went to where Śukrāchārya was performing his tapasya and began to assist the meditating muni. She would gather flowers for his pūjā, cook his food and clean his utensils. In the night, when he was finished with his meditation, she would massage his feet, rub his legs, and in every way became a partner in his life. For ten years Jayanti surrendered her loving service to her beloved Śukrāchārya, and her tender śakti was a tremendous inspiration in the difficulties of his tapasya.

At last Śiva initiated Śukrāchārya in the mantra by which the Gods could be defeated. He was so pleased to have attained the goal of his tapasya. He spoke to Jayanti with great appreciation, "Your sharing with me in the rigors of my tapasya has been a tremendous inspiration to me. It was your loving offering which motivated me in the pursuit of success in my most cherished goal, Jayanti, and I grant you the boon of your cherished aspiration."

"My Lord, my Guru, my father gave me to you with the order to cultivate your friendship by serving you with the offering of my loving devotion. As I served you by paying full attention to your every need for ten years, would you reciprocate and give to me your full attention for the next ten years?"

Śukrāchārya agreed. "But I can only stay ten years, Jayanti. After that I must return to the aśuras."

Śukrāchārya and Jayanti built a little hut in the forest, and began to enjoy the affections between two people solely attentive to each other. They were very happy and very much in love.

Meanwhile, Indra returned to Bṛhaspati and said, "Guruji, he has attained the mantra by which the Gods can be defeated! You must do something to help us!"

Bṛhaspati said, "Now I have no other course but to act for the assistance of the Gods." Immediately he disguised himself in the form of Śukrāchārya, and returned to the camp of the aśuras.

## Bṛhaspati Becomes Guru of the Aśuras

The false Śukrāchārya entered the camp of the aśuras, and all gathered round and bowed down with devotion in respectful welcome of their loving Guru. Śukrāchārya returned their loving greetings, and sat down upon the dais and began to teach: "Aśuras, I have returned from the difficult tapasya which Lord Śiva had prescribed for one hundred years, and I have attained success. The Great Lord has blessed me with the knowledge of how the aśuras can become successful in life, and how to attain our cherished goals. We can only become successful through clear definition, careful organization and regular discipline. It is totally wasteful for us to deplete our energies in needless conflict with others. Why not negotiate for the harmonious resolution of community goals, rather than for individual interests and selfish desires. Put away all enmity with the Gods. Let us cultivate peace and contented awareness. Let us study the philosophies and systems of Yoga, so we can pursue union with our cherished ideal."

The aśuras listened to him spellbound. What novel philosophy he had expressed, totally foreign to their thinking. For ten years the aśuras listened with rapt attention to the brilliant discourses of the Guru of the Gods in the form of Śukrāchārya, and sought to practice his every ideal. For ten years peace and harmony reigned on the earth, in the heavens and in the atmosphere. For ten years the real Śukrāchārya enjoyed his relationship with Jayanti.

After ten years Śukrāchārya took leave of Jayanti. The false Śukrāchārya was giving discourse when Śukrāchārya entered the aśrama precincts. He saw the false Śukrāchārya with great astonishment, and immediately recognized the inner being of his adversary. "Oh Aśuras," he called aloud. "Why are you listening to this false prophet! Do not believe him! He is really the Guru of the Gods. I am the real Śukrāchārya."

The false Śukrāchārya boldly proclaimed, "Aśuras, I have been here the last ten years, and have always endeavored to inspire within you the most noble conduct to which an individual can aspire. I came here immediately after my tapasya with Lord Śiva was completed, and have been sharing the wisdom by which we come into harmony with all existence and attain our highest potential. Where has that false pretender been, and what has he been doing?"

Śukrāchārya became angry, "Aśuras, don't listen to him. He is here to trick you. Don't believe him. I have the mantra from Lord Śiva, and it is I who will make you victorious!"

The aśuras became angry with him, "Where have you been the last ten years!" they scowled. "What makes you worthy of our trust?"

Śukrāchārya again spoke out in anger, "I am the real Śukrāchārya, your Guru. If you forsake your Guru, and pay him disrespect, I will curse you! You will never defeat the Gods!" He threw the Gaṅgā water upon the aśuras, who were shocked with confusion, and he departed from the scene.

After Śukrāchārya had gone, Bṛhaspati in the form of the false Śukrāchārya, stood up and bowed before the assembly of aśuras. "Aśuras," he announced. "It is time for me to ascend to my heavenly home." With that he assumed his real form and rose up into the heavens.

When the aśuras realized their grave mistake in trusting the false Guru, they ran after the real Śukrāchārya and bowed at his lotus feet. "We have committed error, our Father! We have committed error! We succumbed to the logic of divinity, and therefore, we were unable to recognize you. Please forgive us. Do not abandon us to a life of continual defeat!"

Śukrāchārya looked at his disciples with great compassion. "My disciples, there is nothing I can do. The curse has been spoken and cannot be revoked. Whenever devotion is strong enough to focus attention, there, duality will not be able to remain. The aśuras ultimately will be defeated. Any aspirant who persists in the practices of self-purification will ultimately become pure."

## Satī's Lament and Dakṣa's Yajña

Śiva concluded the story. He looked deeply into his own self and drifted into meditation. For fifty million years He remained still and motionless.

Satī was sitting outside looking at the meditating Yogi, thinking, "Oh, what I have done was very wrong. Will my Lord never come back from his meditation? Will he ever pay attention to me again? When will my Lord see me again? How could I have done such a terrible thing as to lie to the Lord of all Lords, the God of all Gods, being untruthful to my own husband. How could I ever trust anyone again, knowing that it is possible for even me to tell lies to my own husband?" Satī inquired of herself.

As the years went by, Satī became disgusted with herself, thinking, "I am unworthy of the trust of the Lord of the Universe. If there only was some way I could become purified, so I could regain his favor. I would rather not have a body at all, than a nature which is untrue to the Lord." And in this way for fifty million years Satī sorrowed and lamented over her bad behavior.

Well, about fifty million years later Dakṣa Prajāpati was ready to institute a new creation with which Brahmā had entrusted him. He wanted to conduct the greatest sacrifice of all time to initiate the procedure of creation, and he invited everyone who is anyone in heaven to attend. He invited all the Gods, all the kiṇaras, all the apsaras, all the Gandharvas and celestial beings, and all the divine beings of heaven and earth, except Lord Śiva. "I will show that Śiva," he said. "That Paśupatināth."

Satī looked out from Kailāsa and saw everyone adorned in their finest, racing off towards her father's home. She stopped someone and asked, "Where are you going?"

The reply was, "Don't you know? Your father, Dakṣa Prajāpati, is having the greatest sacrifice of all time! We've all been invited. He's giving away so many presents and so many gifts. What a sacrifice! There has never been a sacrifice like this in all of history!"

Satī went over to where Śiva was sitting and said, "Śiva, Śiva! wake up a minute. Śiva, please. Just come to me!"

Śiva opened his eyes and Satī said, "Oh Śiva, there is a great sacrifice going on at my father's house. Let's go."

Śiva replied, "We were not invited."

Satī said, "Oh come on, Śiva. It's my own father's house. What do we need with an invitation?"

Śiva said, "Believe me. We won't receive any respect there. We should not go."

Satī said, "Please, Śiva, can't we go? It's my own father's house, and I don't need an invitation to go to my own dad's house. What kind of a daughter needs an invitation to go to her own home? Am I just supposed to sit around here watching you meditate? Can't we do something fun in our lives?"

Śiva said, "We're not going."

By this time Satī was adamant and said, "Śiva, I want to go!"

And Śiva said, "Okay, if you want to go, go ahead. I will give you an entourage and transportation. Nandi, carry Satī to the sacrifice and let the whole army of ghosts and goblins, all my entourage, go with her and make sure she has no problem."

Satī mounted Nandi, the bull, and with Śiva's entire entourage went to her father's home. She walked into the sacrificial arena, but Dakṣa didn't recognize her. One muni, Dadichi by name, looked around the assembly and said, "Everybody has been invited, but I don't see a place for Lord Śiva."

Dakṣa said, "There is not a place for Śiva here. Śiva was not invited."

Dadichi said, "There can't be any sacrifice without Śiva. What kind of nonsense is this? Do you think you will be able to complete a yajña without inviting Śiva? Impossible! Dakṣa, be careful. I warn you! This sacrifice won't be complete until you invite Śiva. Please, go get Śiva. No sacrifice can be complete without an offering to Lord Śiva."

"That uncouth hippie! He hangs out with ghosts and goblins and takes intoxicants all day long. I am not inviting him into my house! He is no good, that Śiva."

Dadichi declared to the assembly of munis, "I am not staying at a sacrifice where Śiva is not invited, and if any of you want to take my advice, you, too, will get up and leave."

No one got up but Dadichi, and he walked out.

Satī walked over to her father and said, "What kind of a yajña is this anyway? What did my Lord do that you want to insult us like this, inviting everyone but your own daughter and her husband?"

Dakṣa said, "Daughter, who invited you here? If you want to stay, go into the inner apartments and remain with the women. I didn't tell you to come here. Don't you tell me how to run my sacrifice. That no good Śiva has no place here. That is all there is to it!"

## Satī's Leaves Her Body - the Śakti Piṭhas

Satī said, "Father, I am insulted to wear this body that was fathered by you. Now I am giving this body back to you!" She sat down in meditation and in the fire of yoga her Soul ascended to heaven.

Immediately Śiva, who was sitting upon Mount Kailāsa, felt his Śakti had dissolved. He pulled out a tuft of hair from his head and threw it on the ground. It broke in half, and out of one lock of hair came Vīrbhādra, the Excellent Hero. Out of the other tuft of hair came Mahākālī. He called all the armies of ghosts and goblins, all his friends: "Destroy the sacrifice and cut the head of Dakṣa from his body!" Śiva declared his order.

Śiva's armies immediately marched off to war. They marched right into the sacrificial arena, and all the Gods fled in terror. Mahākālī was there swinging her sword and Vīrbhādra attacked with his spear. They fought off all the defending forces. They put out the fire, stopped the sacrifice, and then cut the head of Dakṣa from his body. "The sacrifice has been ruined!" Brahmā cried. "What shall we do now? How shall we have a creation?"

Brahmā went to Viṣṇu and said, "What can we do so that the sacrifice can be completed?"

Viṣṇu said, "Let us ask Lord Śiva."

Viṣṇu and Brahmā along with all the Gods went to Mount Kailāsa and they said, "Śiva, we have to complete this sacrifice in order to evolve the new creation. Please forgive Dakṣa his wrongs and let the sacrifice be completed."

Śiva, who is as quick to forgive as He is to anger, said,

"Take the head of a goat and put it on Dakṣa, and say the mantra to let him come back to life. Let everyone be forgiven, and let the sacrifice be completed."

Then Śiva, himself, went and took the body of his Satī. Raising it onto his shoulders, he started to dance. He was dancing the dance of destruction. He was so intoxicated in this spirit, that the whole world started to quake. And the Gods said, "Oh, we are doomed! Śiva is dancing the dance of destruction. How are we ever going to make him stop? Viṣṇu, save us!"

Viṣṇu thought, "Well, what shall I do?" Then he took his bow, and cut the body of Satī into fifty-one pieces (the Devī Gīta names one hundred and eight) with his arrows. Śiva was dancing all around the cosmos. And here fell an arm, there fell a leg, there fell her eye, and when all the pieces had fallen from his shoulders, Śiva sat down and stopped the dance.

When he came to his senses, he felt very much alone and dejected, and in the greatest of despair he began to wander in search of the fallen pieces. Wherever he found a piece of the body, he would sit down and meditate. In his mind's eye he would put that piece back with the other pieces, and in this way he tried to reconstruct the body of Satī. That is why there are fifty-one Śakti Pīṭhas, or in some texts one hundred and eight. Wherever there was a piece of the Divine Mother's body, that place became a pīṭha. Wherever there is a temple to the Divine Mother, very near is a temple of Lord Śiva. There is a temple where the piece of Satī's body fell, and also a temple where Śiva sat to meditate.

## Tārakaśura and the Celebration of Śivarātri

Śiva was quite naked. He used to wear ashes, and especially since he lost his loving wife and housekeeper, he really had nothing else clean to wear. He was wandering around in this naked and intoxicated state, meditating upon the presence of the Goddess, when one day he came to a Brahmiṇ village. He walked up to the well of that village, where a number of the young maidens of that village were drawing water, and requested, "Give me some water to drink. I am thirsty."

The ladies looked at that naked fakir and screamed, and they went running into the village. When the Brahmiṇs came out to see what the commotion was about, they found Śiva standing by the well stark naked. They got very angry and said, "Śiva, you have no shame! You have no sense at all. Our young girls have been raised in the highest standards of purity and modesty, and here you are with no shame, walking stark naked into our village. What nonsense is this! We curse you, Śiva! Let your liṅgaṃ fall off!"

Śiva didn't say anything, but instantly his liṅgaṃ fell down. And when that happened, simultaneously all the passion was drained from the universe. All the animals stopped procreating, and all the plants stopped producing. Even the earth stopped rotating and the sun stopped moving in its course. There was no attraction to conduct any of the laws of gravity, and all the laws of motion became useless.

The Gods said, "What's happening on earth? Nobody seems to be making a sacrifice! We haven't had our food today. Nobody is feeding us! Do you know what happens when the Gods are not fed? They don't send the rain. If it doesn't rain, nothing grows on the earth. The men get weak, the Gods get weak, and creation can desist from existence. Who shall we call for help?"

Well, about this time, there was an aśura named Tārakaśura. Tārak means illuminator, and aśura means duality. Tārakaśura is the Illuminator of Duality. He did a severe tapasya, a great penance.

Then Brahmā came to him and said, "What boon do you want? Choose from me some boon, and I will grant you your desire."

Tārakaśura said, "I want to be immortal. I wish that I will never die." Brahmā said,

"That's impossible. Everything born must die at some time or other. Choose another boon."

Tārakaśura thought for a moment and then said, "If I have to die, then I want my death to occur only at the hands of the son of Śiva."

"Oh joy!" he thought. Śiva doesn't have a liṅgaṃ, and even if he got one, he doesn't have a wife. It will certainly be a long, long time before Śiva gets a son!"

Brahmā said, "Tatā-stu, I give you that boon!"

Then Tārakaśura, the Illuminator of Duality, conquered the entire earth and made everyone on earth servants of the Illuminator of Duality. He then marched straight up to the heavens and sat down on the throne of Indra. He threw all the Gods and Goddesses out of heaven, and became Lord of the three worlds. "I want everyone to serve the Illuminator of Duality. No one will worship the Gods. Don't waste time meditating. Just serve me. I will be the only one worshipped in the three worlds," he ordered.

At this news, the Gods were extremely depressed, and in that dejected state they asked one another, "What are we going to do about this? Śiva doesn't have a liṅgaṃ. Mother doesn't have a body. We need the son of Śiva in order to get rid of this wicked aśura.

Indra remembered the curse of Bhṛgu Muni, "People will even question the necessity of making offerings to Indra, and in many lands you will be forgotten entirely!"

"All of this is overwhelming! How are we going to combat such a state of affairs? Well, the first thing we have to do is to make Śiva capable of having a son. Let us ask him to put his liṅgaṃ back on," said the Gods.

Brahmā and the other Gods, along with all the Brahmiṇs, went to where Śiva was sitting, and said, "Śiva, please put on your liṅgaṃ."

Śiva said, "It wasn't my idea to take it off. In fact, it was the curse of these Holy Brahmiṇs that brought this about. Therefore, I am not going to put the liṅgaṃ back on until every one of you worships that liṅgaṃ with milk and ghee and honey. And bowing down with the greatest of respect, beg blessings of that liṅgaṃ. All night long you will sit up and chant songs of worship and devotion to that liṅgaṃ. After celebrating the Śivarātri, then I will put it on. But remember your promise to observe the vow of Śivarātri every year."

Then all the Gods and Brahmiṇs celebrated the Śivarātri in every meticulous detail. Śiva was pleased, and he put on his liṅgaṃ, blessing all creation with the capacity to procreate.

## The Divine Mother Promises to Take Birth

Then the Gods and Brahmiṇs, the ṛṣis and munis, all went to the Himalayas. There they began to perform various forms of tapasya in order to request the Divine Mother to make Her presence manifest. They recited hymns to the Goddess and sang the stories of Her manifestations. They performed fire sacrifices and yoga āsanas, prāṇāyam, mudras and kṛyas, jāpa and tāpa and in every way they knew they invoked the Divine Mother. They begged Her to please make Her presence manifest.

When they lost themselves in the ecstasy of devotion, the Divine Mother came and spoke to them. She said, "In what way can your desires be fulfilled?"

"Tārakaśura, the Illuminator of Duality has won the boon that only the son of Śiva can destroy him. With the strength of this boon he has been creating evil on earth. Therefore, we request you to come and manifest yourself in an embodied form. Please Mother, marry Śiva again, and give us the son that will lead the armies of divinity to victory in battle."

Mother said, "I accept your proposal, if Śiva will have me. I will try to fulfill your wish. I will take birth in the home of Himalaya, and I shall perform tapasya in order to secure Śiva's forgiveness. If he becomes gracious and so desires, I will marry Lord Śiva again, and when Śiva will accept me as his wife, we will bring forth the son that will lead the armies of divinity to victory."

Hearing this news, Himalaya began to cry. "Mother, what have I done to deserve the honor of having You take birth in my home? How should I act when I become the father of the Divine Mother? What kind of home should I maintain when the Divine Mother takes birth? What kind of tapasya should I perform? What should be my way of life? How should I speak? How should I act? How should I regard You? How should I serve You? How can I love You purely, so that Your mission can be fulfilled? Please explain this to me." The discussion of these questions of Himalaya, constitute the teachings of the Devī Gītā.

## The Birth of Pārvatī

After the Divine Mother gave Her promise to the Gods that She would take Her birth in the House of Himalaya, Himalaya went back to his home and awaited Her arrival with great anticipation.

Finally Satī was reborn in the house of Himalaya. As She was the daughter of the great mountain, Parvat, She was called Pārvatī. Pārvatī took birth in the house of Himalaya, and there was great rejoicing. Himalaya performed beautiful pūjās of worship and gave tremendous dakṣiṇas as gifts to the Brahmiṇs, to the poor, and the homeless.

From Her very childhood, the first word out of the Divine Mother's mouth was "Śiva." As She grew up, She loved making Śiva liṅgaṃs, performing their pūjās, and in many ways She increased Her devotion for Śiva. She learned all His mantras and all His songs, and in every way how to propitiate the Lord.

Pārvatī grew up to be a very devoted lady. She became master of all the sixty-four arts that any young lady, worthy of marrying the Lord, should possess. The following is a list of the arts that She mastered:

1. gītam
   Singing

2. vādyam
   Playing musical instruments

3. nṛtyam
   Dancing

4. nātyam
   Union of dancing, singing, and playing musical instruments

5. ālekhyam
   Writing and drawing

6. viṣeśaka-cchedyam
Tattooing

7. tandula-kusuma-balivikaraḥ
Arraying and adorning an idol with rice and flowers

8. puṣpastaranam
Making flower arrangements on beds, couches or upon the ground

9. dasana-vasanaṅga-rāgāḥ
Staining, dyeing, coloring or otherwise painting hair, nails, bodies, or teeth

10. mani-bhūmikā-karma
Fixing stained glass or gems into the floor

11. śayana-racaṇam
The art of making beds, or spreading cushions or car - pets for reclining

12. udaka-vādyam
Making vessels of water to sound musical notes

13. udaka-ghātaḥ
Storing water in vessels or cisterns

14. citrā yogāḥ
Making pictures, trimming and decorating

15. mālya-granthana-vikalpāḥ
Stringing of rosaries, necklaces, garlands and wreaths

16. keśa-sekharapīda-yojanam
Binding the hair with turbans, top-knots, or crests of flowers

17. nepathya-yogāḥ
Scene-making or stage representations

18. karṇa-pattra-bhaṅgāḥ
Making ear ornaments

19. gandha-yuktiḥ
Preparing perfumes

20. bhūṣaṇa-yojanam
Proper placement of ornaments, jewels, gems and adornments in dress

21. indra-jālam
Magic or sorcery

22. kaucumāra-yogāḥ
Quickness and dexterity in manual skills

23. hasta-lāghavam
Cooking

24. citra-sākapūpa-bhakṣya-vikāra-kṛyā
Preparing lemonade, sherbets and various drinks with flavor and color

25. pāṇaka-rasarāgasava-yojanam
Sewing and tailoring

26. sūcīvāpa-karma
Making flowers, animals, birds, etc., from yarn or thread

27. vīnā-dama-ruka-sūtra-krīdā

Solving riddles, enigmas, covert speeches, verbal puzzles, etc.

28. prahelikā

A game which consists of repeating verses, and as one person finishes, another person has to commence at once, repeating another verse, beginning with the same letter with which the last speaker's verse ended. Whoever fails to repeat, is considered to have lost and is subject to pay a forfeiture or stake of some kind. The art of proposing riddles.

29. pratimā

Making figures and images in clay

30. durvacaka-yogāḥ

Study of sentences difficult to pronounce like a limrick or tongue twister

31. pustaka-vācanam

Reading from books, including chanting and intoning

32. nātajakhyāyikā-darśaṇam

The art of mime and dance

33. kāvya-samasyā-pūrṇam

To complete the stanzas of poems composed by others

34. pattikā-vetrabāṇa-vikalpāḥ

The art of making coarse and common things to appear as fine and good as excellent silk.

35. tarkū-karmāṇi

Knowledge of spinning or spindle work

36. takṣaṇam

Carpentry and building crafts or trades, also the knowledge of cutting things

37. vāstu-vidyā

Architecture or the art of building

38. rūpya-ratna-parīkṣā

Knowledge about gold and silver, jewels and gems

39. dhatu-vādaḥ

Chemistry and minerology

40. maṇi-rāga-jñānam

Knowledge of the qualities of gems

41. ākara-jñānam

Knowledge of praise

42. vṛkṣā-yur-veda-yogāḥ

Knowledge of gardening, of treating the diseases of trees and plants, of nourishing them and determining their ages

43. meśa-kukkuta-lāvaka-yudha-vidhiḥ

Cockfighting, quail fighting and ram fighting

44. suka-sārikā-pralāpaṇam

To speak the language of the parrots

45. utsādaṇam

The art of speaking by changing the forms of words. It is of various kinds. Some speak by changing the beginning and end of words, others by adding unnecessary letters between every syllable or word, etc. like pig-latin.

46. kesa-mārjana-kausalam
Dressing, braiding the hair with unguents and perfumes

47. akṣara-muṣṭikā-kathanam
Understanding writing in cipher or code

48. mlechitaka-vikalpāḥ
The capacity to understand foreign languages

49. desa-bhāṣā-jñānam
Speaking in the dialects of a region

50. puṣpa-sakatika-nimitta-jñānam
Various flower arrangements, like baskets, etc.

51. yantra-mātṛkā
Preparing yantras or mystical diagrams, amulets, etc.

52. dhāraṇa-mātṛkā
Mental exercises, such as completing stanzas or verses upon receiving part of them; or supplying one, two, or three lines when the remaining lines are given indiscriminately from different verses, so as to make the whole an entire verse with regard to its meaning; or arranging the words of a verse written irregularly by separating the vowels from the consonants, or leaving them out altogether; or putting into verse or prose sentences represented by signs or symbols. There are many other such exercises.

53. sampātyam
The knowledge inspiring wealth and welfare, or success and accomplishment

54. kāvya-kṛyā
Composing poems

55. kṛyā-vikalpaḥ
Knowledge of the rules of society, and of how to pay respects and compliments to others

56. calitaka-yogāḥ
Knowledge of the art of war, of arms, armies, etc.

57. abhidhāna-koṣa-cchando-jñānam
Knowledge of using various vocabulary and rhythms in verse or speech

58. vastra-gopanāni
The art of disguising individuals

59. dyūta-viśeṣaḥ
Various ways of gambling

60. ākarṣaṇa-krīdā
The capacity to draw or attract to one's own self

61. bālak-krīdanakāṇi
Skill in youthful sports

62. ithihasam
Knowledge of history

63. vaināyikīnām vidyānām jñānam
Knowledge of good moral conduct

64. vaijayikīnām vidyānam jñānam
Knowledge which confers or foretells victory

Pārvatī became master of them all.

From Her youth, She had decided to perform tapasya, strong spiritual discipline, to attain Śiva as Her husband. She went to Her Mother, Menakā, and said, "Mother, I am going for the performance of tapasya. I am determined to have Śiva as my husband. Would you bless me?"

Menakā replied, "I am not so sure about your choice, but I bless your tapasya."

Wearing only one cloth, Pārvatī went off to sit on a glacier, where She chanted, "Oṃ Namaḥ Śivāya." She submerged Herself into freezing cold water that ran off from the melting glacier and chanted, "Oṃ Namaḥ Śivāya." She fasted on water, fasted on air, fasted without even taking air, and in many ways She deprived Herself as a sacrifice to show Her love for Lord Śiva.

## Lord Śiva Burns Love to Ashes

All the Gods were extremely anxious because of their desire for the son that would come from Lord Śiva to slay the wicked Tārakaśura, the Illuminator of Duality. The Gods convened together and said, "Let's find a way to help Pārvatī. Let's help Her in Her objective of marrying Lord Śiva."

In the assembly of the Gods, it was decided, "Kāma Deva, God of Love, take your flowered arrows and shoot them at Lord Śiva. BE ACCURATE! Make sure Lord Śiva falls in love with Pārvatī, and quickly accepts Her as His wife."

Kāma Deva said, "Certainly this is going to be the end of Me. I should shoot an arrow at Lord Śiva? Let Me shoot at anyone else! I'll be more than willing. But Lord Śiva? He is master of all passions. He has received the boon from Lord Viṣṇu that only He will be free from Mohinī. How can I inflame Śiva with the passions of love?"

The Gods said, "You must try! This is the only salvation for the Gods. We must give Pārvatī every available assistance. Now go! Take your wife, Ratī, the Spring, along with all of your accomplices, everyone who will aid and abet you in performing the arts of love. Take them all and go shoot your arrows at Śiva."

Receiving the orders from the assembly of Gods, the God of Love marched off in the performance of his appointed task. He saw Śiva deeply absorbed in perfect meditation, and the God of Love prayed for success in his task. All the Gods and Goddesses of heaven stood behind the trees watching the scene from afar. Ratī allowed the Spring to begin, and birds began to chirp and bees began to buzz. The air was scented with the fragrance of fresh flowers, and the stage was set for Love. The God of Love drew his bow, and he let loose his arrow. Whissh. The arrow struck Lord Śiva.

Śiva was awakened from his meditation. He looked at the arrow that struck him and said, "What is this? An arrow with a flower at the end! Do you think I am going to fall victim to the God of Love? Does he think he's going to make Me a slave to passion?"

Śiva got angry. From His third eye came a light, a radiant light of fire, and He beamed it right at the God of Love, who was immediately burned to ashes.

All the Gods exclaimed, "Oh, no! What have we done? Śiva! Now you have burned Love to ashes. How will there be any Love in the universe?"

"Was this your idea, Gods? Did you think that I, Lord Śiva, would fall prey to the flowered arrows of the God of Love?" Śiva inquired. "Impossible! That was a very ill-conceived plan!"

"But Śiva," answered the Gods. "Satī, your wife, has taken birth as Pārvatī, the Daughter of the Mountain. She is doing tapasya to marry with you again and have you for Her husband. You see, the wicked Tārakaśura, the Illuminator of Darkness, the Illuminator of Duality, has thrown all the Gods out of heaven. He became strong with the boon that Brahmā gave him, that only the son of Śiva will be able to defeat him. You see Śiva, we're dependent on you! We need you to marry Pārvatī and give us the son that will remove our difficulty!"

Śiva replied, "I am always ready and willing to help the Gods in any noble purpose. If marry I must, marry I shall; but not because of passion inspired from the arrows of the God of Love! I will marry for the noble purpose of protecting Dharma and not because the God of Love has shot an arrow at me to try to infect me with passion. If indeed Pārvatī is Satī, then most certainly I will agree to marry her."

Ratī, the Spring, wife of the God of Love, went to Śiva crying in desperation. "Śiva, today you have made me a widow. How shall I enjoy my life without my husband? How shall I pass my life as a widow? Is there any sadness greater that being bereft of my beloved husband?"

Śiva said, "I give you a boon. Your husband will live eternally, and he will be the strongest and most dynamic of all the Gods, but he will remain invisible. Even still, he will touch the hearts of every living being."

Receiving Śiva's boon, Ratī was pleased. She said, "Śiva, when will I ever be able to see my husband again?"

Śiva replied, "Spring, your husband will incarnate as the son of Arjuna and Subādrā, the sister of Kṛṣṇa. His name will be known as Abhimanyu. At that time you will take birth in the house of Matsyanareś, the King of Cheddi, and your name will be Uttarā. Uttarā and Abhimanyu will again embrace, just as Love and Spring do now."

Ratī was very happy with this boon, and in that happiness she praised Lord Śiva.

The Gods were pleased to have received Lord Śiva's assent. They immediately sent messengers to Himalaya:

"Himalaya, we bring you glad tidings. Lord Śiva has consented to marry Pārvatī."

Himalaya, too, was very pleased. But Menakā, his wife, was sorely distressed. She said, "Himalaya, Lord Śiva sits on top of the mountains naked. He is not a fitting groom for our Pārvatī."

Himalaya replied, "Menakā, you do not know who Lord Śiva is. Pārvatī has been doing tapasya just for this purpose, to get Lord Śiva to be Her husband. The Gods themselves want Śiva to be Her husband. Please accept it."

"All right," Menakā agreed. "Allow the wedding to proceed."

## Śiva Tests Pārvatī

Lord Śiva disguised himself as a native village hunter, and went to where Pārvatī was performing Her tapasya. He said, "Oh young lady, what tapasya are you performing?"

Pārvatī replied, "I want to marry Lord Śiva."

The village hunter laughed, "Ha, ha! Lord Śiva! Do you mean that naked sādhu who lives on top of the mountains alone and by himself, who sits the whole day in meditation, who associates with ghost and goblins, and who always remains intoxicated; you want to marry that Lord Śiva?"

"Yes, that Lord Śiva, the Lord of the Three Worlds!"

"Oh no! A young lady like you who is so beautiful and well skilled in all the sixty-four arts deserves a finer husband than that."

"Who could be a finer husband than Lord Śiva?"

"Me!" replied the village huntsman.

"Huh!" said Pārvatī. "You go away from here right now! Leave me alone! I will have no one other than Lord Śiva for my husband! I won't listen to your insolent insults! I will have no one but Śiva!"

When Śiva heard those words, He assumed His own form and said, "So be it. I accept."

## The Marriage of Śiva and Pārvatī

Pārvatī returned to Her home and messages were sent to Himalaya to complete arrangements for the marriage of his daughter. The entire city and all the palaces were gaily decorated and prepared to receive the groom's party, and the bride was adorned in glorious radiance.

The marriage procession proceeded. Śiva set forth from Mount Kailāsa accompanied by all His friends, the ghosts and goblins, and just as He reached the outskirts of the city He thought, "I'll play one joke on all those people."

Śiva made Himself into a contorted, twisted, ugly man, dancing wildly in the streets. The bridal procession marched through the city and towards the bridal canopy where the wedding ceremony would take place.

Menakā looked down upon the marriage party and exclaimed, "Who is that Freak down there?"

Pārvatī looked down and replied, "That is my Śiva!"

And Menakā said incredulously, "That is your Śiva? No way! Where is your father? Himalaya! We are not going through with this wedding! I am not allowing my daughter to marry that contorted Freak down there!"

Himalaya said, "Menakā, you stay out of this. It has already been arranged. We are doing the work of the Gods. Pārvatī, what do you say?"

"That is my Śiva!" replied Pārvatī. "I want to marry him!"

"Menakā," continued Himalaya. "You have nothing to say. If you want to participate, then stay here and be quiet. Otherwise, go to your room and close the door."

Menakā exclaimed, "My daughter! My only daughter! At least tell Śiva to put on a nice form and a crown on His head, and come to his wedding like any worthy God."

Himalaya went down to talk to Śiva and said, "Śiva, please assume a beautiful form just to please my wife."

Very accommodatingly Śiva replied, "Okay," and immediately He became very beautiful, decked with gold and jewels and exquisite silk and satin clothes, with the digit of the Moon as His crown.

All the three worlds rejoiced and celebrated at the marriage of Śiva and Pārvatī. And what a marriage it was! The conch shells were blaring and the drums were beating as the Vedic mantras were recited. All the Gods and Goddesses of heaven came to shower flowers and blessings upon the divine couple. And everyone awaited for the birth of the son who would free the Gods from the domination of the Illuminator of Darkness.

## Menakā Ascends to Heaven

After the marriage of Pārvatī and Śiva, Indra called to Menakā, "Menakā, you have completed your work in this world. You have given birth to the Divine Child, Pārvatī, and given Her in marriage. Now come back to live in the Indra Loka, in the heavens above."

Menakā was pleased that her karma in the world was complete, and she was happy to return to her retreat in the Indra Loka. With great pleasure she left her earthly body and ascended into the heavens.

## The Curse of Jayā and Vijayā

Once upon a time the four Kumāras: Sanāt, Sanāka, Sānanda, and Sanāt Kumāra, went to Vaikuṇṭha, the home of Lord Viṣṇu. They were desirous of having an audience with the Lord. When they arrived, they found the gate to the house was barred, and Jayā and Vijayā were standing beside the entrance protecting the privacy of the Lord.

"We have come to see the Lord," stated the four brothers.

"We are sorry," replied Jayā and Vijayā, "but the Lord is inside the inner apartments enjoying some private time with the Goddess Lakṣmī. No one may enter to disturb them."

The four brothers explained, "We are pure devotees of the Lord, and there is no time when the Lord will not make Himself accessible to Pure Devotion! Therefore, please inform the Lord that we have come, and that we request an immediate audience with Him."

Jayā and Vijayā again barred the way. "Our Lord is such a busy man, always fighting with aśuras, or attempting to satisfy devotees. He hardly ever enjoys an opportunity to relax alone with His wife. Why don't you come back tomorrow!"

The four brothers grew impatient. "We realize that you are only performing your duty and trying to serve the Lord. However, even with the best of intentions, no one has the authority to separate a pure devotee from the Lord. Therefore, we will certainly curse you. But because you have committed error in the performance of your service of the Lord, we will let you decide the nature of the curse. You can choose between seven births in the family of ṛṣis, or three births in the family of aśuras."

Jayā and Vijayā considered the decision. "Seven births in the world of mortal beings is too long to be away from heaven. It would be better to take three births in the form of aśuras, and get it over with quickly."

Then the four brothers took some water from the Gaṅgā and pronounced the curse, "Be born as aśuras for three births!" They threw the water upon Jayā and Vijayā, who were destined to manifest in the world.

## Madhu and Kaiṭabha

The first birth they took was in the form of the brothers Madhu and Kaiṭabha, otherwise known as Too Much and Too Little, who attempted to slay Brahmā as he sat in the lotus of Viṣṇu's navel. Too Much and Too Little have mandated action for all existence, and at no time will they allow an individual to be still. If one has Too Much, then he must get rid of some. If one has Too Little, then he must get some more.

Viṣṇu was deep in the mystic slumber of divine union at that time, so Brahmā sang a hymn of praise to the Divine Mother, Yoganidrā, Goddess of Mystic Sleep, in order to awaken him from his sleep and alert him to the attack. For five thousand years Lord Viṣṇu fought with the two aśuras. Realizing that they were invincible, he began to pray to the Divine Mother to show him how to defeat them. The Divine Mother promised that She would trap them by the excesses of their egotism.

Then Viṣṇu said to those two aśuras, "I am extremely pleased with your prowess in battle. I wish to offer you a boon. Choose from me a boon."

Those aśuras, Madhu and Kaiṭabha, replied, "Ha Viṣṇu! It is always the stronger that grants boons to the weaker. Seeing that we are stronger than you, and you have no way of defeating us, then it is you who should beg a boon from us. Go ahead and ask. Whatever you request, you shall not be denied."

Viṣṇu requested, "I want to know from both of you the means of your death."

Being tricked by the Divine Mother, the aśuras replied, "You can only slay us where there is no water. But you see, the whole world is flooded, so there is nowhere we can be slain."

Viṣṇu then took them upon his lap, and expanding his universal form, he killed them with his discus.

## Hiraṅyakṣa and Hiraṅyakaṣipu and the Story of Prahlād

The next incarnation of Jayā and Vijayā came in the form of the brothers Hiraṅyakṣa and Hiraṅyakaṣipu. Hiraṅyakṣa hid the earth underneath the sea of waters. All creation called out to Lord Viṣṇu to take birth in order to save the earth. Viṣṇu came as a boar, dove down beneath the waters of the sea, and lifted the earth upon his tusks. He placed the earth upon the waters, and killed the demon Hiraṅyakṣa in battle.

Then the brother Hiraṅyakaṣipu reigned in his place. Hiraṅyakaṣipu had won the boon that he could not be slain in the day, nor could he be slain at night. He could not be slain inside, nor could he be slain outside. He could not be slain by man, nor could he be slain by beast. He could not be slain by any weapons known to man. With the strength of that boon, Hiraṅyakaṣipu conquered the earth and the heavens. Then he made a law that no other should be worshipped but himself. He imprisoned all the ṛṣis, destroyed their temples, and made everyone worship him.

The King was blessed with a beautiful son named Prahlād. Prahlād was a divine child, and the first word to come out from his mouth was, "Viṣṇu."

The King became very angry with his wife. "Where did my son learn a word like that? You had better see to his proper education. I will not have such blasphemies uttered in my house. No one will say the name of my arch enemy!"

As the child grew up, he loved to sit for worship, and very much enjoyed singing devotional songs to the Lord. The King summoned the school master, "Teach my child the proper ways of aśura behavior. I don't know who put these faulty ideas in his head about worship, meditation and the respect for the Gods, but you had better teach him that I am the only one to be worshipped. You make him forget all this stuff about Viṣṇu!"

The teachers took him to the school. "Now class, we are born of the aśura race, and it is our duty to remember that these bodies that we wear are to be pleased at all times. The only worship that is ordained for aśuras is the worship of our King, and we have no responsibilities in life other than to enjoy through our senses as much as possible. This is the mark of a true aśura..."

At the recess, Prahlād went into the play-yard with the other children. "I've got a great game to play," he said. "Let us pretend we are ṛṣis meditating upon the Lord." He showed all the other children how to meditate. He even tied his hair into a top knot, and the children performed worship just like the ṛṣis.

"Oh King! Oh King!" cried the school master. "You had better get your son out of my school. He is corrupting all of the other students. He teaches them about the Gods, about pūjā and meditation. At recess he has them performing all of the things we instruct against. Please take that child out of my school before he infects all the other children!"

The King called his son, Prahlād. "My son, why can't you be like all the other children? Why is it you are always getting into trouble? When will you learn to be a good aśura and respect the laws and customs of our society?"

"Father," responded the young Prahlād. "I never did anything that was against dharma. I never performed any behavior that was disrespectful to the Lord. What is the complaint against me?"

"What Lord is it that you are seeking to please?" asked the King.

"Everyone knows that there is only One God of creation, Father."

"And what is the name by which you call this God?"

"He has so many names, but I call Him Viṣṇu," replied the son.

"Viṣṇu! My arch enemy! How dare you say that name in my house! Anyone who speaks that name in my kingdom shall be punished with death."

"Father, how can you be so antagonistic to the Lord? God will protect any devotee who surrenders to Him."

"And who is that God?" asked the father.

"Viṣṇu," replied Prahlād.

"Captain of the Guard!" called the King. "Take this sinner to the top of the mountain and throw him off from the highest peak. Make sure he will fall to his death. We will see what God can save you, when this living God standing before you has decreed your death."

The soldiers escorted Prahlād to the highest peak of the mountain. Before pushing him from the summit, the Captain requested, "Do you have any last words?"

Prahlād proclaimed, "Jai Viṣṇu!" and the soldiers pushed him from the top.

Just as Prahlād fell into the space below, Viṣṇu sent his eagle, Garuḍa, to catch the child in midair. They flew a couple of loops before the soldiers, and glided gently to the ground.

"We tried to throw him from the mountain, my Lord," stammered the Captain of the Guard. "But Viṣṇu's carrier, that eagle, came in the path and saved him.

"Then tie him up in chains and throw him into the sea!" yelled the royal father.

The Captain of the Guard escorted the prisoner to the side of the ocean, and made his soldiers tie heavy chains to Prahlād's body. The Captain requested, "Do you have any last words?"

Prahlād proclaimed, "Jai Viṣṇu!" and the soldiers pushed

him into the water. Prahlād sank to the bottom. Seeing His devotee in the depths of peril, Lord Viṣṇu became a fish, the Matsya Āvatār. The giant fish swam to where Prahlād lay, hooked the chain around His fin, and quickly swam to the surface, leaving the boy on the shore.

"Mahārāj," stammered the Captain of the Guard. "Even the sea won't take this child of yours. Now what shall be done with him?"

The King looked in amazement. Then he called his sister, Holikā. Holikā had won the boon from the divine fire that nothing could burn her. "Holikā, take Prahlād into your arms and hold him in a raging fire, so that he will be burned!"

The soldiers lit the fire, and Holikā hugged Prahlād to her bosom, and then jumped into the fire. Prahlād closed his eyes and recited the names of Viṣṇu. The flames rose up and completely engulfed them. Prahlād continued his japa. When he opened his eyes, he found that the fire had burned his aunt, but he did not even feel the heat. Even to this day we celebrate the salvation of Prahlād and the death of Holikā with the festival of Holi.

King Hiraṅyakaṣipu was enraged with anger. Was there nothing that could kill this child? "Where does this God Viṣṇu live, that you have the faith that He will protect you from every circumstance?" he asked of his son.

"Viṣṇu lives everywhere," replied the young devotee.

"Does he even live in the pillars of the palace?" The mighty King drew his sword.

"Yes, Father, he will be found even in the pillars of the palace," replied Prahlād.

The King struck the pillar with all his might. The stone and plaster cracked and crumbled with a tremendous roar, falling to the ground revealing a great being sitting upon a throne within. He was neither man, nor animal. He was half man, half lion, and he was terribly frightful. Hiraṅyakaṣipu ran for the door. When he reached the threshold, he could see that it was dusk, the sun was just settting. It was neither day or night. Then that great beast, Narasiṅgha, grabbed hold of the King and dragged him across the threshold, where he was neither inside, nor was he outside. And using the claws of his hands, the Āvatār of Viṣṇu tore open the stomach of Hiraṅyakaṣipu and drank the blood.

Prahlād sang hymns in praise of Lord Viṣṇu, and through - out the reign of King Prahlād, there was peace and prosperity in their land.

## Ekāvīrya and Ekāvālī

One day Lord Viṣṇu entered the inner apartments in Vaikuṇṭha, where He saw Lakṣmī peering out from the window. He called to her, but she didn't pay any attention. She merely stood gazing out the window. "Lakṣmī," called Viṣṇu. "What are you looking at?"

Lakṣmī was so attentive to what she was looking at, that she was not even aware that her Lord had entered.

"Lakṣmī," Viṣṇu called again. "Where are you?"

No response.

"Lakṣmī!" Viṣṇu called yet again. "What are you looking at with such rapt attention that you even ignore your own husband? You forget the presence of your Lord?" Viṣṇu came close to the window and looked out to see the Uchchaiśravā horse, the horse of Wisdom, which was produced from the churning of the milk ocean, flying across the sky.

"Oh Lakṣmī, if you are so enamored of horses, you go down to earth and become a horse!" Viṣṇu grew angry.

"Oh my Lord, what did you say?" inquired the amazed Lakṣmī.

"I said go down to earth and become a horse!" replied the angry Viṣṇu.

"Why would you have me do that? For such a small fault of mine, you are giving me such a grievous curse?"

"We have some karma to perform."

"How shall I become free of this curse?" inquired Lakṣmī.

"When the time is right, I will come as a stallion. We will have a child who is destined for greatness."

Lakṣmī went down to the earth in the form of a mare. Day and night she repeated the mantras of Lord Viṣṇu, and searched for the appearance of her Lord. In this way one hundred thousand years passed. She could not figure out where Viṣṇu was or what could possibly be keeping him so long. Finally she got an idea. She said, "Oṃ Namo Śivāya," and immediately Lord Śiva appeared.

"Hello, Lakṣmī," Śiva extended his greetings. "What are you doing down here in the form of a horse? Where is Lord Viṣṇu?"

"I have been waiting for Viṣṇu to show up for the last hundred thousand years," replied an impatient Lakṣmī.

"Then why did you call me?" inquired Śivā.

"Śiva, I must tell you the truth. One day Lord Viṣṇu was sitting in deep meditation. For a long time He did not move in the least. He merely sat there fully absorbed. When He awoke, I asked Him, 'Devadeva, Jaganāth, God of all Gods, Lord of the Universe, everyone looks to you for solace and protection, all existence meditates upon you. Upon whom were you meditating?'

"Then my Lord answered me, 'My beloved Lakṣmī, I was meditating upon Lord Śiva. Verily He is my inner Self.' That is why, Śiva, when after one hundred thousand years of chanting Viṣṇu's name and he didn't show up, I thought to call you."

"What can I do for you, Lakṣmī?" asked Śiva.

"Please remind my Lord that I am waiting for Him as per His command."

Śiva went to Vaikuṇṭha and said, "Hello Viṣṇu. What has happened to you? You look terrible, like there is no Lakṣmī in your house. It seems that you haven't washed your dishes in a long, long time. Where is your beloved wife?"

Viṣṇu was stunned into remembrance. "Śiva, you must excuse me. I have a very important function I must attend to on earth."

Viṣṇu excused himself, and went down to the earth where he became a stallion. Lakṣmī saw the stallion, and recognized him immediately. They gave birth to a beautiful son.

"Come, Lakṣmī," said Viṣṇu. "Let us return to Vaikuṇṭha."

"Have you no heart? How can we leave this poor defenseless baby alone?"

"Our karma here is complete. Let's go home," the Lord repeated.

"Lord, I can't leave my child like this," answered Lakṣmī.

"Okay," replied Viṣṇu, and he turned the baby horse into a human. "Let us go," he said.

With that he rose into the atmosphere and headed towards Vaikuṇṭha. Lakṣmī took one last look at her child, and fol - lowed her husband home.

Just then, the King Turvasu came, riding a chariot before his army. "Who has abandoned that child alone and in the wilderness?" wondered the King. "What a beautiful boy! I have been practicing ascetiscism for the last one hundred years in order to have a divine son. Certainly this is the son which God has promised. I shall take him home and raise him as my own."

The King lifted the child into his chariot and returned to his home. He raised that boy until he became a well-educated and well-mannered warrior of superior prowess. He was known as Ekāvīrya, the Warrior of Union, or He who has One-pointed attention. Turvasu performed all the rites of passage for his son, and saw to his education. When he was convinced that Ekāvīrya was fully qualified, he placed his son on the throne to become ruler of the land, and with his wife went to perform tapasya in the forest.

The King Rabhya had a beautiful daughter named Ekāvālī, the Spirit of Union. She was born from the divine fire at the time of sacrificial offering. The Princess Ekāvālī loved to play among the flowers, and every day she would move with her friends outside the city gates to play among the wild flowers by the bank of the river. The King informed his daughter that he worried for her safety, and built a beautiful garden within the palace for her to play, but Ekāvālī found the garden too tame, and once again wandered outside to play. Then the King sent an escort of soldiers to guard the girls as they played outside the city gates.

One day the wicked King Kālaketu, the Purveyor of Darkness, came to where the girls were playing. Seeing the beauty of the princess, he and his soldiers attacked the guards. Having caught the guards unaware, they were overwhelmed by his superior force, and Kālaketu stole the princess Ekāvālī. Kālaketu held her prisoner in his palace towers, along with her friend Yaśovatī. He ordered Ekāvālī to marry him, but the princess would not agree. She cried and cried. "What shall we do?" she asked Yaśovatī.

Yaśovatī replied, "I know the mantra Hrīṃ, the mantra of the Divine Mother Goddess. I shall make jāpā, and She will make my path clear so that I can summon help."

Yaśovatī began the repetition of the mantra. Suddenly the doors flew open, and Yaśovatī made her escape. She ran through the dark of night, and by morning she had reached the bank of a river. There she sat upon a rock crying, wondering which way she should turn for help.

Just then a handsome young prince came riding before a great army. "Oh, fair maiden, why are you crying? No one should be sad in this kingdom, especially while I am ready to serve you."

"My friend and I were stolen by the wicked King Kālaketu. He defeated our guards, took us prisoners, and locked us up in the palace tower. I was able to escape, but the Princess Ekāvālī is still held prisoner. The wicked King keeps saying that she must marry him, but she tells him that from her childhood the astrologers told her that she was destined to marry a man named Ekāvīrya," explained Yaśovatī.

"I am Ekāvīrya!" declared the prince. "Where is the palace of the wicked King? I am ready to engage him in war! I shall free my wife, and rid the earth of Darkness."

"No, my Prince. First you must become well armed. Seek initiation from the Guru Dattatreya in the Trilokī Tilakam, the mantra which is the highest expression of the three worlds. Then we shall go to fight."

Ekāvīrya bowed before Dattatreya. "Guruji, please initiate me in the mantra of the Trilokī Tilakam, by which I can slay the wicked King Kālaketu, the Purveyor of Darkness, and free my wife."

Dattatreya explained: "Hrīṃ, the totality of Māyā; Gaurī, She who is Rays of Light; Rudra, the Reliever of Sufferings; Dāyite, Giver of Compassion; Yogeśwārī, the Supreme Lord of Union; Huṃ, Cut the ego; Phaṭ, Purify; Svāhā, I am One with God! Go my son," Dattatreya said in blessing. "Defeat the evil King!"

Ekāvīrya marched into battle and defeated the wicked Purveyor of Darkness, King Kālaketu. He freed the captured princess, Ekāvālī, and when Yaśovatī explained to her friend all that had happened, she asked Ekāvīrya, "Please take me to my father. He will bless our marriage according to the customs of our family."

Then Ekāvīrya returned Ekāvālī to her family, and the King Rabhya and his family celebrated the divine marriage in accordance with all the traditions of their ancestors. Ekāvīrya and his divine consort, Ekāvālī, established the worship of the

Divine Mother in their kingdom, and set new ideals of respect during their reign. Their son's name was Kṛtavīrya, and his son was Kārtavīrya. Thus were the origins of the Haihaya dynasty of Kings.

## Viśvarāth Conquers India

There was once a great King named Ghade who had a tremendous dominion and was a very righteous and dharmic King. Ghade had a very noble son whose name was Viśvarāth. When Viśvarāth grew up to a suitable age, the King Ghade said, "Son, I have decided to retire to the forest to practice tapasya for the rest of my days. Please take over the responsibilities of maintaining and protecting this king - dom. I am going to devote the rest of my life to spiritual discipline."

Viśvarāth answered, "Father, the first duty of a son is to fullfill the desires of his father, and in every way possible assist the father in attaining emancipation. Therefore, if it be your wish that I take over the kingdom, I have nothing further to say. But please discuss this matter with our gurus and your ministers. Present this matter before the people, and let them determine whether or not they want me to be their King."

Ghade thought, "What a noble son I have."

Hecalled the gurus of the land, the Brahmiṇs and representatives of the people of his kingdom and said, "I wish to devote myself to the path of self-realization during my last years on earth. I have decided to retire to the forest and lead a life of asceticism, where I can practice meditation and contemplate a religious life free from the responsibilities of being a king. I have determind that my son, Viśvarāth, shall become the King in my place."

And all the people assembled, everyone, shouted, "Viśvarāth, Ki Jai! What a noble King we have! What a great example we have! What a wonderful son we will have as a ruler!" The people unanimously acknowledged Viśvarāth as the King of their country. Ghade retired to the forest with his queen and there began to practice tapasya.

After some time, Viśvarāth began to think, "A King of the warrior class is successful only insofar as he can expand the frontiers of his kingdom. It is not just sufficient that I have received this nation as an inheritance from my father, who built it for me. Shall I pass the same thing on to my children? I must add to the inheritance that I have received from my ancestors. Only then can I pass on my legacy to my own sons."

He called together all the learned and wise men of his kingdom and said, "I have decided to go to war and expand the borders of my kingdom."

All the gurus and sannyāsis, the Brahmiṇs and sādhus, unanimously said, "King, please don't do that! We are healthy, wealthy, and living at peace. We have abundance. Why will you go to war? If you take all the men from the fields to be soldiers in your army, who will harvest the crops?"

Viśvarāth didn't listen. He said, "My dharma as a kṣatriya King is to fight. I must fight and fulfill my dharma. What kind of fame and glory will I receive if I only take my father's inheritance and pass it down to my children? No one will remember that act. Only if I increase my family's wealth, valor and fame, will I be remembered. Take all the farmers and conscript them into the army. Be prepared to march off to war!"

By orders of the King, all the male citizens were conscripted into the army and trained for war. Viśvarāth marched off in conquest. In a short time he subjugated all the neighboring kingdoms and moved across the empire to conquer all of India. Victory after victory, he marched forward until no one knew the limits of his kingdom. Only after taking tribute from many Kings and taking the crowns from the heads of many princes, he was satisfied, and then he turned around and headed towards home.

## Vasiṣṭha's Cow

He had been marching towards his home for several days, and his troops had grown tired and hungry. When he came to the hermitage of Vasiṣṭha Muni, Vasiṣṭha was very pleased to hear that Viśvarāth, the King, had come to visit his aśrama. He sent sannyāsis and brahmācharis to meet the King and escort him to the hermitage with respect and honor.

Vasiṣṭha said, "My King, will you please be my guest for supper?"

Viśvarāth replied, "I have a tremendous army along with me. How is it possible that the King will feast while his soldiers go hungry?"

Vasiṣṭha said, "No, no! That is not possible! I invite you all. Please allow me the privilege of extending my hospitality to you all."

Viśvarāth was happy to accept Vasiṣṭha's invitation. Vasiṣṭha went to his cow, Nandi. He said, "Nandi, we have visitors today. The King has come along with his entire army. Let's offer them the hospitality of Brahmiṇs."

Nandi opened her mouth and out came sumptuous meals, pots full of food. Vasiṣṭha squeezed her udders, and the milk poured into buckets, from which came curd and ghee, which produced many dishes and sweets. Many things were made from Nandi's milk. All of the soldiers of the tremoundous army sat down to eat, and if a soldier wanted any particular dish to eat, the order was given to Nandi, and immediately that food came forth. They were the most sumptuous, luscious, epicurean delights that anyone could possibly imagine.

Viśvarāth was amazed. "What wonderful meals you have prepared, Vasiṣṭha! How could you feed so many people?"

Vasiṣṭha said, "It is my sacred cow, Nandi."

"What an amazing cow you have, Vasiṣṭha. I think that Nandi is the Kāmadhenu, the cow which gives satiation and fulfillment of all desires."

"Yes, in fact she is," agreed Vasiṣṭha.

Viśvarāth was very pleased, and he bowed down to the Guru Vasiṣṭha, and returned with his army to the kingdom. As he marched into his kingdom, he saw all the lands were barren. He looked at the long, drawn expressions on his citizens' faces and he saw that they had been living in abject poverty. He rode as a victorious King right through the main streets of the capital, yet no one had the energy to welcome him. When he arrived at the palace, his ministers came to greet him.

"What happened to my kingdom?" asked Viśvarāth. "There is no one here to greet us or shout for the homecoming of their victorious King? What kind of subjects are these? What has happened here?"

The ministers replied, "Your Highness, when you took all the men to fight in your wars, there was nobody here to harvest the crops. Who was here to tend the fields? Your subjects are starving. What will we do with all this gold that you brought? Can we eat it?"

The King thought, "What should be done now? How can we feed all the citizens?" Then he remembered the sumptuous meals he had received at Vasiṣṭha's aśrama. At once he made the decision to return to the aśrama and to bring the cow, Nandi, to his capitol.

Immediately he proceeded to Vasiṣṭha's aśrama and said, "Vasiṣṭha, please give me your cow."

Vasiṣṭha said, "King, I can't give you my cow. That is Nandi. I make all of my yajñas from her ghee. She is a member of my family."

Viśvarāth said, "Vasiṣṭha, I'll give you a hundred cows.

Give me that cow."

Vasiṣṭha said, "King, I am sorry. You keep your hundred cows. That is my Nandi. I can't give you my cow."

Viśvarāth said, "All right, Vasiṣṭha, I'll give you a thousand cows. Give me that cow."

Vasiṣṭha said, "Oh King, you keep your thousand cows. That is my Nandi. I make all of my yajñas from the ghee prepared from her milk. I am not going to give you this cow."

Viśvarāth said, "I need that cow, and if you don't give me that cow right now, I am going to take the cow by force."

Vasiṣṭha said, "You can try to take the cow by force, if you like to try to steal from a Brahmiṇ. But King, I am not going to give you the cow."

Viśvarāth said, "Captain of the Guard, put a rope around that cow's neck and bring her to my capitol!"

The Captain of the Guard called his soldiers, "Soldiers, put a rope around that cow's neck and take her to the capitol!"

The soldiers went as ordered and put a rope around Nandi's neck and began to pull on it. The cow said, "Vasiṣṭha, did you give me to that King?"

And Vasiṣṭha replied, "No."

"Then why are these soldiers putting a rope around my neck and trying to drag me away?"

"Nandi, I never told them they could do that. I never agreed to let you go, not by force and not by price."

"You didn't?"

"No!"

Suddenly Nandi bellowed, "Aaahhh!" And from her mouth came forth legions of soldiers, heavily armed, and they started to run to attack the King's army. The King's army began to fight, but all of his soldiers were defeated. The entire army was lost. Then Nandi's soldiers went after Viśvarāth. He ran! The soldiers ran after him with their weapons ready to strike. He ran all across the continent, with the soldiers running right behind. He ran and ran in flight, but the soldiers kept running behind. He ran in a circle and came back to the aśrama of Vasiṣṭha, where he fell at Vasiṣṭha's feet and cried, "SAVE ME! I take refuge in you. Please spare my life. I realize that the power of kṣatriya kings and warriors is nothing in comparison to the power of a Brahmiṇ. If you are gracious to me and spare my life, I will go to the forest to practice tapasya. I, too, shall become a Brahmā Ṛṣi!"

Vasiṣṭha said, "Okay, I spare you. Go perform your tapasya, and see what you realize within yourself."

Viśvarāth bowed to the Brahmiṇ Vasiṣṭha. He shed his armor and his weapons and put on the dress of a hermit, and went into the forest to begin the practice of austerities.

## Viśvarāth Becomes Viśvāmitra

So Viśvarāth began his tapasya. He sat absorbed in deep meditation for long periods of time. When he sat in the deepest meditation, he sent out such a strong vibration that three goddesses came: Mahākālī, Mahālakṣmī, and Mahāsaraswatī. Each put forth their essence, the essences of the wisdom which they embody. Those essences of wisdom united and manifested as Gaya - Wisdom; tri - three; Gayatri, the embodiment of the three forms of Wisdom: Creation, Preservation and Transformation, or Sattva guṇa, Tama guṇa, and Raja guṇa. This essence of wisdom became a Goddess known as Gayatri. She came to Viśvarāth in his meditation and blessed him, and She revealed to him the mantra of Gayatri:

"Oṃ Bhūr Bhuvaḥ Svaḥ Tat Savitur Vareṇyam Bhargo Devasya Dīmahi Dhiyo Yo Naḥ Pracodayāt."

Oṃ - The Infinite beyond conception

Bhūr - The gross body of sensory perception

Bhuvaḥ - The subtle body of internal mental conception

Svaḥ - The causal body of intuitive recognition
Tat - That
Savitur - Light of Wisdom
Vareṇyam - Highest
Bhargo - Wealth
Devasya - Of the Gods
Dīmahi - We meditate upon
Diyo Yo Naḥ - Give to us
Pracodayāt - Increase, literally, rising up.

Viśvarāth began to meditate upon this mantra and to recite the mantra again and again. Gayatri came to Viśvarāth in his meditation and said, "Viśvarāth, the chariot of the universe, I give you a new name according to your new character. Because you have brought this new realization to mankind, you have acted as a friend. Therefore, I give you the name 'Viśvāmitra,' Friend of the Universe."

So Viśvarāth became Viśvāmitra. He continued his tapasya and his meditation, and he became a Rāja Ṛṣi; a seer amongst kings. Through more purification he became a Deva Ṛṣi; a seer amongst the Gods. He continued to perform this tapasya for many, many years until his strength and will power were of unswerving condition. He could not be moved. He was completely absorbed in his sādhana and tapasya, and still he continued to meditate...

## The Origins of the Solar Dynasty

Brahmā gave his wisdom to the Seven Ṛṣis, which even today bless the heavens as the Big Dipper. Their names were: Marichi, Atri, Aṅgira, Pulastya, Pulaha, Kratu, and Vasiṣṭha. They were the original seven ṛṣis, or Seers of the Highest Divinity. In every Kalpa or age of time, seven other ṛṣis become seers of wisdom.

Marichi's eldest son was Kaśyapa. Dakṣa gave thirteen of his daughters to Kaśyapa in marriage. Amongst Kaśyapa's wives, two were most famous. One was Diti, of the earth, and the other was Aditi, of the heavens. From Aditi came forth the Devas, all the Gods, or Shining Ones. From Diti and his other wives came forth the aśuras, daityas, yakṣas, pannagas, the beasts of the earth and the birds of the air. These all sprang forth from Kaśyapa's generations.

Amongst the Gods there was one son who was extremely famous whose name was Sūrya, the Sun, the light of wisdom and warmth of devotion. His other name was Vaivaśvan, He Who Permeates the Universe. He had a son named Vaivaśvat Manu. Man means mind and U means Protector; thus Manu means the Protector of the Mind. He protects with Vaivaśvat, the universality of the light of wisdom and the warmth of devotion. He is the presiding Manu of the seventh Manvantara, which is this particular period of time in which we are living. Each period of time has one particular Universal Protector of the Mind, whose job is to establish respect for the rule of reason. The current Protector is the Universal Light.

Vaivaśvat Manu had a son named Ikṣvāku, who is the progenitor of the Solar Dynasty of Kings upon this earth. Ikṣvāku established his capitol city in Ayodhyā, and Brahmā sent Vasiṣṭha to become the family guru. Vasiṣṭha objected to this posting, but Brahmā assured him that the generations of Ikṣvāku would be famous supporters of Truth. "Even Rāma will take birth in this family," Brahmā said. "Can you imagine the honor of becoming the preceptor of the Lord?" Thereafter, Vasiṣṭha relented and accepted the position as the Guru to the Kings of Ayodhyā.

## Chyavana Muni and Sukanyā

Ikṣvāku had a son named Śaryāti, who was a gem amongst men. He was very generous, a virtuous King, who acted in every way as a father to the subjects of his kingdom. Śaryāti had one particular treasure of which he was extremely fond. He had a young daughter by the name of Sukanyā, whose very name means "the excellent virgin goddess."

Sukanyā used to go outside the palace to play with her friends. Accompanied by the King's guards, they would go to the forest and pick flowers and chase after the little animals, throw their ball and play and play. Sukanyā loved to play in the forest. One day the King went outside with his entire contingencies of soldiers to perform exercises. He took his daughter Sukanyā along with all her girl friends with him. He set aside an area in a very sacred grove in the forest for them to play. Stationing soldiers around the area, he left his daughter and her friends free to roam and play while he went off to supervise the maneuvers of his army.

As Sukanyā was frolicing about in that grove, she came across an immense anthill. It was a massive mound of earth that the ants had piled up. It looked very mysterious; a very strange sight to see. There were two balls of brilliant fire radiating out from the mound of dirt. Sukanyā became frightened and finding a stick, she poked it into the glowing embers.

Immediately she heard a groan, and becoming frightened at the sound, she ran off. She joined her friends and didn't say anything to anyone about the incident. After a few moments of play, she forgot all about it.

Suddenly all the soldiers of the King's army had their bowels stopped. The Captain of the Guard came to the King and said, "Oh King, all of our soldiers are in pain. Nobody can pass any stool or urine. All of their elimination is stopped. What shall we do? The soldiers are in great pain."

The King said, "I shall call the minister. Minister," he called. "The soldiers are in pain."

The minister replied, "Let's search for the cause of this pain. I have heard that Chyavana Muni - that great ṛṣi, has been performing tapasya in this neighborhood. Maybe, just maybe, this has something to do with some unwarranted interruption of his devotions. Let's go see."

The King's soldiers went off and began searching for the Muni. The soldiers were looking for any sign of the Muni, when one soldier walked by the ant hill from which emmanated a groaning sound. He saw a stick poking out from the hole in the dirt, and immediately began to brush away the dirt. He was so surprised to have uncovered Chyavana Muni, who had been sitting in Samādhi for such a length of time, that the ants had covered his body completely with dirt. No one could tell that the figure was a sitting sādhu through the two slits in the dirt, even though his eyes had been radiating like glowing embers from the light of his tapasya.

The soldier said, "Muni, who has done this terrible thing to you? Who put these sticks in your eyes. I shall bring the King here." Uncovering the Muni and making him comfortable, he ran off to get the King.

Śaryāti quickly came with his ministers. "Oh, Muni, my ancestors have always invited sādhus to come to perform tapasya here free from fear of any type of harm. Now some - one has injured you while you were sitting in meditation in this sacred grove, even while all my soldiers were here to protect you. I am the King of this nation, and I will not rest until I find the culprits who are responsible for putting you in such pain."

The Muni said, "Oh, King, you have not far to look, because the person who has done this to me is your daughter, Sukanyā."

"My daughter, Sukanyā, that angelic little girl? She only likes to frolic and play in the forest. She would never hurt any one."

"Call Sukanyā," ordered the muni.

Sukanyā was brought to her father. "Sukanyā," her father began, "this is Chyavana Muni, the aged and venerable sage whose reputation is known far and wide. Somebody has pierced his eyes with these sticks, and he has mentioned your name."

"Yes, Father, it is true. I did it by accident. I saw the fires shining out from the ant hill and I don't know why, but I poked it to see if it would move. Then I heard a groan and becoming frightened, I ran away."

"You see," said Chyavana Muni, "it was your daughter who made me blind."

Śaryāti, the King said, "Muni, how can I atone for this mis conduct? How can I give you recompense? I will give you villages for your support, hundreds of servants to take care of you. We will make good the loss. Grant forgiveness to my daughter. Oh Muni, release me from this debt."

The Muni said, "I am an aged man. I don't need wealth or villages. Who wants to be cared for by servants doing their duty to a master because of fear or obligation. Now I am blind and aged. Who will take care of me with love, tenderness and compassion? Certainly no servant would do that! A servant will only perform the requirements of duty, looking forward to release from servitude. No, King Śaryāti, if you want to put my heart at rest, then give me your daughter, Sukanyā, as my wife."

"Your wife? Sukanyā? She is the gem of the palace. A young, little girl. She will be a queen. How can I give my gem of the palace to an old, blind sādhu who lives naked in the forest? Oh, Muni, choose some other wish. I'll give you hundreds of girls, thousands of damsels, servants, wealth, gold, land. But please don't take my Sukanyā away from me."

"No!" said the Muni. "Your daughter has done this to me, and it is only she who can serve me with care and devotion."

"But," said Śaryāti, "a father's duty, as well as his delight, is to arrange a suitable match for his daughter. My young, beautiful daughter married to an old blind ascetic from the forest? How can I think of such a match? She is a noble girl. You are a sādhu. Sukanyā was raised with all the comforts of life, and you have nothing to offer her. She is young and soon her body will develop into maturity, and she will have desire for a passionate husband.You will have no capacity to satisfy that desire. She will have desires to have children and your age for having children has gone. In every way this is an unsuitable match. A father's primary duty is to give his daughter in marriage with honor and dignity in a suitable relationship. I cannot give you my daughter!"

"Well," said Chyavana Muni, "you may think over the matter."

Śaryāti returned to his kingdom.

The Captain of the Guard came to the King. "Sire, the soldiers are groaning in pain. No one can urinate. No one can defecate. No one has had any elimination of any kind. Everyone is suffering in pain. You are the King of the nation. Please remove the suffering of your subjects."

"I will not give my daughter to that old sādhu! This is not in accordance with my dharma. I would roast in hell for centuries if I committed such a dastardly act."

Some time went by and the citizens were in agony. Sukanyā came to her father and she said, "Father, I have decided that I want to live a dharmic life. Just as Sāvitrī was to Satyakāma, who walked into the very house of death itself to save her husband's life; just as Ahālya was to Gautam; just as Arundhatī was to Vasiṣṭha; just as Śakti is to Śiva: all of these women are emblems of purity, steadfastness and devotion in their marital affairs. In the same way, Father, please give me in marriage to Chyavana Muni. I will be his Śakti. He will be my Śiva. Together we will realize the four - fold aims of life. Dharma, Artha, Kāma and Mokṣa. What greater honor for a daughter of a King than to marry a ṛṣi and become a great seer, a Tapasvinī, someone who lives in the forest in divine contemplation, free from the cares of worldly life. Father, please give me in marriage to the Muni."

"My daughter, I can't give you in marriage to that old, blind sādhu!"

"Father, you must. You must relieve the sufferings of your subjects. You must save your army from pain. You must allow the citizens to go about their business of life, and allow me to pursue the path of self-realization by uniting with Chyavana Muni, serving him, and taking his wisdom. What finer, more nobler union, could you seek for your daughter?"

Hearing these words of wisdom and renunciation from Sukanyā, Śaryāti was very pleased and taking his young daughter into the forest, he found Chyavana Muni. The entire kingdom followed him. All the army and the citizens came to see the betrothal of Chyavana Muni and Sukanyā.

As the priests pronounced the mantras and united the two in holy matrimony, all the soldiers and citizens defecated right there. What a relief!

Sukanyā took off the clothing of a royal princess and she adorned herself in garments made from the bark of a tree. In every way she adapted herself to the forest life just as the Munis and ṛṣis live.

Sukanyā cared for her husband with the greatest devotion. Before he awoke in the morning, she had already been down to the river and had brought and heated the water for her husband's bath. Just as dawn would break she would wake her husband, take him for the calls of nature, dress him, and pick flowers and fruits for his worship. She would have everything ready for his pūjā beside his seat for worship. She would cook his food so that when he was done with meditation and worship, she could feed him. After laying him down to rest, she would wash the dishes and utensils and then return to massage his feet. At night she would make a fire and he would tell her stories, the teachings and traditions of the great noble souls which instruct and inspire. In this way she passed her life in the forest, and she was very happy.

Years passed in this way. The young girl Sukanyā grew and grew into the most radiant gem of the forest. Her aura of light pervaded the atmosphere wherever she walked. All the beasts of the forest would protect her from any harm. All the little animals would eat from her hand. Never was there a woman who radiated such inner beauty as Sukanyā. Her soul was a light in the dense darkness of the forest.

One day Sukanyā went to pick fruits and berries. She came to where the stream flowed into the lake. Much to her surprise, the twin Aśvins, the physicians of the Gods, stood there. Seeing Sukanyā, the two Gods exclaimed, "Oh my, what a beautiful lady. Are you a married lady or are you single? And if you are single who is your father? And if you are married who is your husband? What is a gem like you doing in this forest? You look like you should live in a heavenly palace."

Sukanyā said, "I am Sukanyā, the daughter of Śaryāti, the King of Oud. My father gave me in marriage to Chyavana Muni. My husband is blind and I came here to get fruits and nuts for our meal."

"You, a princess, married to that old, blind sādhu, Chyavana Muni? What nonsense is this? We had learned that fathers like to give their daughters in marriage to a suitable match. What is a beautiful princess like you doing married to an old, blind Muni living in the forest, wearing the bark of trees, and picking fruits and roots to eat? This does not sound like a suitable match. You leave that old blind man. Come with us. You are like a goddess. Come and travel around the three worlds and enjoy with us just like the Gods."

Sukanyā said, "Please don't speak that way to me. I am the wife of Chyavana Muni. He is my husband, and I serve him with honesty. I am not going to run off with you or anyone else. If you want to talk that way, go tell the Muni all of this. Don't talk to me like that!"

The Aśvins laughed and said, "We are very pleased with your devotion. Go ask your husband if he would like to have his eyesight back."

Sukanyā immediately ran off to ask her husband. "Husband, I am sorry to disturb you, but two Gods named Aśvins have sent me to ask if you would like to have your eyesight restored."

Chyavana Muni said, "Do whatever they say. I will give you Chaṇḍī Devi's mantra. Oṃ Hrīṃ Chaṇḍikāyai Namaḥ. Perform whatever they say without question. But before you act, remember the goddess. Say the mantra. She will guide and protect you."

Hearing this answer from her husband, Sukanyā returned to where the Aśvins were staying. She said, "Oh Gods, I consulted with my husband and he instructed me to do as you say."

"Fine, Sukanyā. Bring your husband down here to the river."

She brought her husband, slowly leading him down to the bank of the river. The two Aśvins, the twin Gods, then got on either side of Chyavana Muni, and led him into the water. When they were out from the shore just far enough, they all ducked down underneath the water. After some time they stood up again, and all three looked exactly the same in every way. Even the clothing they wore was the same. They were radiant princes, strong and heroic, decked with jewels and gems, handsome in every detail, and in one voice the three of them said together, "Alright, Sukanyā. Which one of us is your husband?"

Sukanyā's heart dropped. "Which one is my husband? If I choose the wrong one I will be guilty of breaking my vow of chastity. Which one shall I choose? They all look alike. They all sound alike. What shall I do?"

She was looking to see which one he could be. Which one? If she should choose incorrectly, she would be guilty of the hideous crime of associating with a man other than her husband. For that she would lose all the merits of her spiritual discipline. Which one should she choose?

Then, somewhere inside, she remembered her husband's instructions.

"Remember the Goddess. Remember the Divine Mother. Oṃ Hrīṃ Chaṇḍikāyai Namaḥ."

She began to recite the mantra.

"Which one of us, Sukanyā? Which one of us?"

Suddenly there was a knowing of the subtle body of her husband. She wasn't fooled by the gross body. She saw very clearly inside and she chose. "You are my husband. Please come to me!"

Chyavana Muni, in his new body as a young man, a strong handsome prince with eyes! He was covered with jewels, silks and wealth. The Muni came and embraced his wife. Then he ran over to the two Aśvin Gods, and he bowed down to them. "Oh, Gods, you have done such a beautiful service for me. You have given me this new body with my eyesight restored, along with health and wealth. Now I can enjoy a married life with my beautiful wife. How can I ever repay you?"

The Aśvins said, "At every sacrifice Soma is offered and Indra never lets us have a share. He passes the Soma around to all the other Gods, but we never get to drink. We are really curious what it is like to taste Soma. Everybody else in heaven gets some. All the Gods get to drink. But Indra says, "You are physicians. You are not supposed to drink. You are lower class people, not full Gods. You are not full Gods, so you can't drink Soma."

Chyavana Muni said, "It shall be done. I shall force Indra to give you a taste of Soma."

The Aśvins were very happy. Chyavana Muni also was very happy. He went back to his hermitage and started to enjoy the company of his wife. Oh how they loved and enjoyed each other's company!

Some time passed. One day the King Śaryāti thought, "It has been so many years now. I wonder how my Sukanyā is getting along? How is she? What happened to her? I have not heard any news about her in such a long time. Was the forest life too much for her? How did she live with that old man? Was she able to serve him?" In this way his thoughts kept turning towards his daughter, and this day he resolved, "I must go to find her and see what has become of her."

The King took his guards and marched off to the sacred grove where Chyavana Muni was living. King Śaryāti was so surprised when he entered the grove and saw the radiant Sukanyā in the arms of her young lover. The King said, "What a dastardly deed I have committed in giving my beautiful young daughter to that old blind Muni! Surely she took this young lover and they killed the old sādhu, and now this sin is my responsibility."

The King called out to his daughter, "Sukanyā, you are a disgrace to our nation! You have brought doom upon the kingdom! You have destroyed the lineage of our kingdom! Our family is ruined by your sinful conduct!"

"Daddy, what are you talking about?"

"Where did you find this young prince you are so joyously associating with? Surely the two of you conspired to kill that old Muni, that great wise Brahmiṇ, knower of the Supreme Truth. What a sin, what a heinous crime!"

"Father, this is my husband, Chyavana Muni."

"How did that old blind sage turn himself into a young, handsome prince?"

"Father, we won the boon from the Aśvins. Now we need your help. We have promised to make a great fire sacrifice to offer thanks to all the Gods for giving my husband a new body and a new life. Father, gather all the ingredients for a sacrifice. Call all the Munis. We shall make a sacrificial fire of all sacrifices."

Śaryāti was excited and pleased. He invited all the sages and Munis, and gathered the ingredients. Chyavana Muni, himself, presided over the sacrifice. As the yajña was progressing, it came time to offer the libation of Soma juice. Chyavana Muni made the Soma juice. He presented Indra with his portion and he gave Agni his portion; and Aryamān and Yama and Sūrya. All the Gods in their turn took their portions of Soma.

Then Chyavana Muni said, "And now, this portion of Soma is for the Aśvins!"

"Stop!" said Indra. "The Aśvins can't drink Soma."

Chyavana Muni said, "I am the host of this sacrifice, and I have offered them Soma."

Indra said, "I am the King of heaven. The Aśvins do not drink Soma."

Chyavana Muni said, "They can drink."

Indra said, "They can not drink!"

Chyavana Muni got mad. He went back to the fire and began to pronounce the secret mantras. A black billowing cloud came out of the fire, and took the form of the terrible aśura, Maud. It came and bowed down before Chyavana Muni and said, "Master, you called? What shall I do for you?"

Chyavana Muni said, "Get Indra!"

Maud immediately began to pursue Indra, and Indra ran for his life. Wherever he went, Maud was right behind him.

"Stop! Stop! Save me!" yelled Indra.

Chyavana Muni said, "Allow the Aśvins their drink of Soma."

Indra said, "Alright. But take away the force of this demon. Get this aśura away from me."

Chyavana Muni called the aśura. "Thank you for your good work, Maud. But now I must cut you in half. I shall cut those parts in half again, because as a whole you are much too powerful. I am cutting you into four pieces, and I shall give one piece to greed, one piece to lust, one piece to intoxication, and one piece to gambling."

Speaking thus, he cut apart the demon and distributed its force. "Now let the Aśvins drink their Soma libations," he declared triumphantly.

The Aśvins were pleased to get their drink of Soma; Chyavana Muni, in a new body with beautiful eyes, got to enjoy with his wife; Śaryāti, the King, fulfilled his dharma; and the citizens were able to evacuate their bowels.

## The Story of Sudarśana

There was once a King of Ayodhyā named Puṣpa. He had a dharmic son named Dhruvasandhi, who upheld the traditions of the solar dynasty. Dhruvasandhi was an ideal King in every way. He was truthful, religious, and constantly engaged in seeking the welfare of his community. Under his leadership, the kingdom of Ayodhyā flourished.

Dhruvasandhi had two wives, whom he loved very greatly. The first was Manoramā, the daughter of Vīrasena, the King of the Country of Kaliṅga. The second was Līlavatī, the daughter of Yudhājit, the King of the Country of Ujjain. Both of the wives were very beautiful, and both were much beloved by the King Dhruvasandhi. Both wives conceived nearly the same time, but Manoramā was the first to give birth to a handsome son named Sudarśana, Excellent Intuitive Vision. Less than a month later, Līlavatī gave birth to her son, whom they named Satrujit, the Victor over Enemies. Dhruvasandhi was the happiest monarch alive, and he united his family with so much love and joy! He loved his two wives immensely, and he loved his two sons equally.

One day while the children were still young, the King went hunting in the forest. He killed many wild animals fit for sacrifice: deer, elephant, boar, rabbits and rhinoceros, and in every way thoroughly enjoyed himself according to the customs of the kings of that era. While he was hunting, an enraged lion suddenly attacked him. He fought valiantly with his sword, but the lion tore at his flesh with his sharp claws. The soldiers shot arrows at the lion, but by the time the lion stopped, the King had been mangled to death. The soldiers shot more arrows at the lion, who was killed on the spot.

Thereafter, the soldiers sent a message to the ministers, and the ministers counselled with Guru Vasiṣṭha to install Sudarśana, the oldest son, on the throne. Immediately both of the grandfathers, the Kings Vīrasena and Yudhājit, came to Ayodhyā along with their armies to lobby for the succession of their daughter's sons. Yudhājit accused Guru Vasiṣṭha of conspiring with Vīrasena to get the throne for Sudarśana out of greed for wealth. Becoming angry at the prospect of Satrujit's being denied the kingdom, he challenged Vīrasena to battle. Tributary princes came along with their armies, and the stage was set for a battle of the proportions of the Mahābhārat.

The nation went to war in a terrible battle of succession, and there were as many soldiers as stars in the sky. The blood of the wounded and dead ran like a river, and there were uncountable casualties in the war. Ultimately, King Yudhājit shot an arrow which severed the head of Vīrasena from his body, and Satrujit was declared the King.

Hearing the news of her father's death, Manoramā was filled with fright for the safety of her son. Quickly she bundled Sudarśana in ragged clothing and fled from the kingdom. They wandered in the forests for many days, until they came to Chitrakūṭa, where they took refuge in the hermitage of the Ṛṣi Bhāradvāja. The sage Bhāradvāja said, "To give protection to one in distress is to gain merits even greater than those acquired by performing sacrifice. Then to protect one who is very much afflicted by fear for their personal safety, one who is helpless and has no other place to go, should produce even greater merits. You stay here in this aśrama and raise your son. I shall assume the responsibility of your protection."

Then Manoramā was freed from her anxiety, and dressing in the apparel of a tapasvinī, she began to raise and educate her son in the muni's aśrama. Meanwhile, Yudhājit installed his daughter's son upon the throne of Ayodhyā, and appointed loyal ministers to administrate the kingdom on behalf of the young child. He then returned to his own land in Ujjain.

Some time had passed when Yudhājit learned through his spies that Manoramā had been raising her son, Sudarśana, in Bhāradvāja's aśrama. He immediately set out with a great army, determined to once and for all settle the matter of the ascendancy to the throne of Ayodhyā by his grandson. Yudhājit determined to kill the minor son of Manoramā so that there could be no further question of a claim to the throne. With that objective in mind, he proceeded to Bhāradvāja's aśrama.

His army encircled the hermitage with a great force, and then the King pounded on the aśrama gate. "Oh Muni! Open your gate and give me Manoramā and her son!" bellowed the King.

Then the Ṛṣi Bhāradvāja replied to Yudhājit, "Oh King, Manoramā and her son, Sudarśana, have taken refuge in this aśrama. He is a minor child, and she has been overcome by fear. Please return to your homes, and leave us to live in peace. They are no threat to you now."

"I will never let them live!" called Yudhājit. "If you do not give them to me willingly, then I will take them by force!"

"If you desire to take them by force, then there is nothing that I can do. But the result will be the same as when the King Viśvāmitra tried to take the cow from Vasiṣṭha's aśrama," answered the ṛṣi.

Seeing Bhāradvāja's resolve, Yudhājit summoned his Prime Minister. "What happened to the King Viśvāmitra?" he asked.

"My King," replied the minister. "Please do not argue with the ṛṣis. King Viśvāmitra was totally destroyed when he tried to take Vasiṣṭha's cow. My King, let us return to our homes. There is no difficulty they can create now. Wait until the time is right, and then we will strike."

Hearing the minister's advice, the King Yudhājit bowed down to the Guru Bhāradvāja and returned to his native land. Manoramā was freed from fear, and Sudarśana took his education and initiation, and performed tapasya under the direction of the sages. Sudarśana became an expert in many branches of learning and received the darśana of the Divine Mother. He served his mother with great devotion, and meditated along the banks of the Gaṅgā near Chitrakūṭa.

## Sudarśana and Śaśikalā

The King of Benares, Subāhu, had a very beautiful daughter named Śaśikalā, the Particle of the Moon. One day Śaśikalā heard of a wonderful prince, endowed with all auspicious qualities, as beautiful as the God of Love, full of heroism and charm, living in the forest with the name of Sudarśana. Śaśikalā began to dream of this Prince of Peace, began to love him, and began to desire him as her husband. One day she had a dream that the Divine Mother appeared to her and said, "Ask the boon from me. Sudarśana is my devotee and he will fulfill your desires."

Śaśikalā awoke and her face was covered with bliss. Everyone noticed the special radiance. Her mother and friends asked her about it, but she was too modest to speak.

One day, when Śaśikalā was sitting in a garden, she saw a Sannyāsī coming into the city. She went to that sādhu and requested, "Oh noble Sir, where are you coming from?"

The Sannyāsī replied, "I am coming from the forest area of Chitrakūṭa, where I dwell in the aśrama of the Ṛṣi Bhāradvāja. I have one errand to perform in the city."

"What is in the forest area of Chitrakūṭa, which has extraordinary beauty, that is worth describing?" she inquired.

"The most wonderful thing in that forest," he replied, "is the Prince Sudarśana, the son of Manoramā and King Dhruvasandhi. He is endowed with all the auspicious qualities and in every way is the most fitting husband for a princess like you."

Subāhu's daughter, Śaśikalā, became submerged in a sea of love. She could think of nothing else. She began to recite the mantra of the Goddess Sarasvatī, Oṃ Saṃ Sarasvatyai Namaḥ, and began to feel the blessings of the Goddess.

Sudarśana continued his tapasya and became extremely accomplished and blessed. Wherever he went in the forest, because of the power of his spiritual discipline, it seemed as though he was accompanied by a full contingent of soldiers. He became pure and peaceful, yet he projected strength and power. Still, he only used his powers for good. By living in the forest and by constantly meditating on the Goddess, Sudarśana realized a greater happiness than those who obtain the sovereignty of a kingdom.

Finding that his daughter Śaśikalā was being perplexed by love, Subāhu called for the festival of her Svayambara, the ceremony of choosing her husband. When Śaśikalā saw the preparations being made for the ceremony, she went to her father and said, "Father, I have already seen in a dream that the Divine Mother has instructed me to marry Sudarśana, the son of Manoramā and the King Dhruvasandhi. Therefore, please do not make this public display."

Her father became very angry and said, "Sudarśana is an unprotected minor, exiled in the forest! He has no kingdom, no army, no wealth; he lives eating roots and fruits with his mother and the munis of the forest! Not only that! His grandfather Vīrasena, was slain by Yudhājit, the King of Ujjain, and Yudhājit has vowed to kill Sudarśana at his first opportunity to prevent any controversy regarding the throne of Ayodhyā. I will not permit such a marriage for my daughter!"

Śaśikalā again told her mother, "The King Śaryāti gave his daughter, Sukanyā, to the blind Chyavana Muni as his wife. The Goddess Bhagavatī has already told me in a dream that Sudarśana shall be my husband. A woman can attain liberation if she surrenders herself completely to her husband. Therefore, I shall live in whatever way my husband lives. Do not deny me my dharma. Sudarśana will be my husband."

Before the event of her Svayambara, Śaśikalā became very anxious. She summoned one Brahmiṇ and requested him to deliver her message to Sudarśana. "Please come quickly! My father has called for my marriage betrothal, but the

Divine Mother has told me clearly in a dream that I am only to marry you. By mind and word and deed I have already surrendered to you as my husband, and with the blessings of the Divine Mother, our ultimate fulfillment is assured. Please have faith in Her, at whose command exists this entire universe with all that moves and moves not, and present yourself without fail."

When Sudarśana received that message from Śaśikalā, he asked the Ṛṣi Bhāradvāja what he should do. Bhāradvāja gave his blessings for Sudarśana to attend the festival, and Mother Manoramā grieved with despair. "You are my only son. Please don't leave me. Yudhājit has already slain my father, Vīrasena, in order to protect that kingdom, and he has vowed to slay you. You are a minor son, and my only future. Please don't leave me."

"Whatever the Divine Mother has ordained is destined to happen," answered Sudarśana. "I am the child of the Divine Mother, and I have no fear. Mother, please banish all fear from your heart."

Manoramā again spoke, "My son, I cannot live without you. I will accompany you to the Svayambara."

Manoramā and Sudarśana received the blessings of saints and sages, and set out to Benares. The King Subāhu welcomed them with respect, and provided them with a residence as he did the other royal families. The Kings were filled with wonder that Sudarśana had come alone and without fear. Yudhājit said that he would accept the princess's marriage to any other family; but if Śaśikalā would choose Sudarśana, "She will become a widow on her very wedding day!"

All the Kings assembled in the Svayambara hall, and Subāhu called for his daughter to come. Then Śaśikalā sent a message to her father, "Father, I have no desire to judge the merits and demerits of many men. I have a yearning to protect my chastity, and surrender myself purely to my husband. I have already understood that the Divine Mother wants me to marry Sudarśana, and I have accepted Her will. Please do not make me present myself in the public hall to make a mockery of my faith by standing before all those lustful men to judge them by their appearance alone. Please call off this event and give me in marriage to Sudarśana."

Then Subāhu was plunged into dejection. He became filled with anxiety, thinking, "All of these Kings have come here with their mighty armies, looking for an excuse to start a fight. I haven't the strength to counter an offensive; their collective numbers are much too great for my forces. Sudarśana, too, is alone, a child without wealth or army. How can I fulfill my daughter's request? How can a father, who longs for the happiness of his daughter, deny her request which is in accordance with dharma?"

Then Subāhu said to the assembly of Kings, "Oh Kings, my daughter has refused my request to come into the Svayambara hall, even though both her mother and I have tried every method of persuasion. I am afraid she is being troublesome to me, and she will become troublesome to yourselves as well. Nobody wants to be burdened with a quarrel - some wife. Therefore, please excuse me. I cannot force her to attend, nor can I force her to choose. I am your servant. I offer you all a portion of my wealth. Please take this as a sign of my respect, and return to your homes."

There was silence amidst the assembly of Kings. Then arose Yudhājit who said, "Oh King Subāhu, you have invited all these Kings to attend the marriage ceremony, and now you are going to give your daughter to that poor, homeless Sudarśana? What kind of a fool are you to make such a decision? What an insult to all the royal families assembled here, that you should choose an alliance with this minor child who has no army, who is alone, with no wealth or strength, over the extended hand of friendship of more powerful monarchs. Do not be a fool. Give your daughter to my grand - son, Satrujit, and we will have dominion across the entire North of India. I have already vowed to kill Sudarśana, and if you persist in this ridiculous desire to make your daughter an early widow, then I will kill you as well!"

Subāhu went with his wife and together they tried to explain the situation to Śaśikalā. "Daughter, the Kings are enraged at what they perceive to be a grave insult. They are heavily armed and are looking for some pretext to come to battle. We are in great difficulty. We do not have sufficient force to subdue their armies. Often members of the royal families have been given in marriage to assist in political alliances. Could you help out by choosing someone else? Otherwise, there is going to be bloodshed. Or let me make a contest of strength or valor, so that the victor may marry you. In that case the best man will win, and we will certainly avert calamity."

The determined Śaśikalā replied, "Father, what you propose is immoral. In my heart my marriage has already been consummated. What you ask is that I commit adultery. Please do not make me think of such a thing. Our dharma instructs that chastity and marital fidelity are values to be respected; adultery is not condoned for anyone. Then why again and again are you counselling me to abandon my path of dharma? Please Father, put the Kings off on some pretext until tomorrow, and then perform my marriage tonight with Sudarśana. Whatever the Divine Mother has planned for us, I will accept. If I am meant to live as a hermit in the forest, then I shall do so. If the Goddess wants my husband be slain in battle with his relatives, then I shall sacrifice my life as well. If it is meant that we become a royal family, then whatever the Goddess will decree, that I shall accept!"

Hearing his daughter's obstinate resolve, Subāhu was filled with wonder at her faith, and trusting his daughter in his heart, he determined to fulfill her desire. He returned to the Kings in the assembly hall and said, "Kings, my daughter will not come today to be present in this assembly. Please, all of you take your food and enjoy our hospitality. Please return tomorrow, and together we shall decide on a contest that will allow the worthiest man to win the bride."

All of the Kings agreed and returned to their respective accommodations. Meanwhile, the King Subāhu began to celebrate the marriage of his daughter. Throughout the night he made the offerings of pūjā, accompanied by the recitation of Saṃskṛt texts by learned Brahmiṇs, and gave his daughter, the beautiful Śaśikalā, to Sudarśana. The bride was radiant like a second Lakṣmī, and all were filled with joy and delight.

When the marriage was completed, Subāhu addressed Manoramā, "Oh royal daughter, I now have become your servant. Please accept the half of my kingdom, and live here with your son and daughter-in-law. By performing this marriage according to the will of God, the other Kings have become our enemies. Please, stay here in Benares and let me protect you."

Manoramā replied, "Oh King, no words can express the joy of my heart at your generosity. No other King would have been so subservient to the will of God as to give his beautiful daughter to my impoverished son. But the ṛṣis of the forest have proclaimed that my son will become the King of Ayodhyā. Therefore, let us have faith in the Divine Mother, and allow events to unfold according to Her will."

In the morning the other Kings learned that the marriage had been consummated, and in great anger they went out from the city to take counsel with one another. Yudājit told the Kings, "No one can blame me now! Subāhu lied to us, he cheated and disgraced us. Now I will certainly kill Sudarśana and Subāhu. I will take that Śaśikalā to give to my grandson for a wife, and all of you can plunder the kingdom!"

The Kings determined to block Sudarśana's route when he would try to leave the city, to kill him, and steal away his wife. Subāhu learned of the plot to attack, and tried his best to keep Sudarśana in Benares. Then Sudarśana told his father-in-law, "Please grant us leave to fulfill the Divine Mother's will."

Sudarśana took his mother and his new bride Śaśikalā upon his chariot, and embarked upon the journey. He had decided to return to the aśrama of the Ṛṣi Bhāradvāja, take his blessings, and then proceed as he was instructed. Subāhu, fearing for his daughter's life, followed behind with his army. Knowing no fear, Sudarśana began to approach the place of ambush. He was reciting the mantra of the Goddess.

Yudājit and Śatrujit surrounded the advancing chariot with their great armies, and began firing arrows and weapons. Just then the Devi Bhagavatī Chaṅḍī appeared. She was sitting upon Her lion holding various weapons in Her hands. The Kings were struck with awe. They had never seen such a sight before as this wonderfully beautiful Lady riding on a lion. The lion roared, and the elephants of the armies became stricken with fear.

Sudarśana drove his chariot right through the ranks of soldiers. "Stop them!" commanded Yudājit. "Are you going to let them go because you're afraid of one Lady mounted upon a lion? They have insulted all the Kings, and I have vowed to kill them!"

Yudājit and Śatrujit pursued Sudarśana's chariot firing their weapons, while the other Kings and soldiers looked on in amazement. Sudarśana fired his arrows in return which cut the enemies' arrows to pieces. When the fighting grew intense, the Divine Mother became angry. She began to fight with all of Her weapons. She shot Her arrows at Yudājit and

Śatrujit, and both fell from their chariots to their death.

Then Subāhu, along with the assembled Kings, began to sing a hymn of praise to the Divine Mother. He praised Her with most fervent devotion. The Mother of the Universe was pleased with him and gave Her blessings: "Oh King, as long as the earth remains, the City of Benares shall remain, and as long as the City of Benares stands, I shall never leave that place."

Sudarśana asked the Mother, "How shall I serve you?"

The Goddess ordered him, "Become the King of Ayodhyā, and govern the country of your ancestors. Conduct my worship with full devotion, and I will never forsake you."

Then Sudarśana was crowned King of Ayodhyā, and he, along with his wife Śaśikalā and his mother Manoramā, returned to govern the country of his ancestors. He established the worship of the Divine Mother, and performed Her discipline regularly with full devotion. Once again Ayodhyā became the Place without War.

Subāhu returned to Benares, and began to worship the Divine Mother with his greatest devotion, so that the Goddess would always remain in Benares.

## The Story of Satya Vrat

There was once a King named Aruna, born in the lineage of the decendants of Ikṣvāku. Aruna means love. Aruna's love is different from the love of passion and attachment. It is the love which makes men divine. Aruna was such a wonderful King and had so much Love, that ultimately he became the charioteer of Sūrya, the Sun. His kind of Love can be the driver of the conveyance of the Light Wisdom, so his is the universal love based in wisdom.

Aruna came to the earth several generations after Ikṣvāku had lived, and was born in the house of the Solar Dynasty.

Aruna was a very righteous King. He treated his subjects like his own family, and always made decisions on the basis of equity, fairness, and justice. He was a valiant and noble King, who constantly acted with compassion and universal love and was never selfish.

He had a son by the name of Satya Vrat, One who is True to his Vow. Satya Vrat grew up in the palace, but even though his name was the One who is True to his Vow, he was always in trouble. He would run around with his friends and create havoc. Wherever he went, he would create another problem. In this way the child grew up always being scolded, but he was very true to his vows.

One day when Satya Vrat was just a teenager, he came by a village of Brahmiṇs as they were conducting a marriage ceremony. Satya Vrat rode in his own chariot, picked up the bride, put her in the chariot, and rode off with her.

The Brahmiṇs cried aghast, "Oh, my God, we are doomed!"

The whole village went to the King, including all the puṅḍits and Brahmiṇ priests, and said, "Aruna, Oh King, you are such a gracious and loving, generous and wise father to your children. What are we to do? The duty of the King is to protect the citizens. Yet here is your son, the heir to the throne, stealing away a Brahmiṇ girl on the day of her wedding. We want justice! Who is going to protect us if the King doesn't? Your son is the culprit! What a horrible fate to have our girl stolen away on the day of her wedding!"

The King called Satya Vrat. "Satya Vrat, what have you to say for yourself?"

Satya Vrat replied, "Father, it wasn't all that bad."

"Why not?"

"Well, according to Hindu law, the marriage is not complete until the bride and groom have taken seven steps around the fire. Seeing as they hadn't take the seven steps yet,

I am not guilty of stealing the bride. According to our Hindu law, she wasn't married."

"King, this will not do," the Brahmiṇs complained.

The King turned to his Guru, Vasiṣṭha, and asked, "Oh Respected Guru, what should be done for the peace and harmony of my kingdom?"

Vasiṣṭha thought for a moment and said, "King, having a son who causes difficulties to your subjects is worse than having no son at all. Exile the son to the forest!"

Under orders from the King, Satya Vrat was exiled to the forest. Satya Vrat sat alone in the forest under a tree and thought, "Am I really so unworthy that my father would throw me out of the kingdom? I can't even go home. Now I have no father. I have no mother. I have no friends. I have nothing to eat. What am I going to do out here by myself? I don't know how to do pūjā. I don't know how to do jāpa. I don't know any mantras. I don't know anything about all that tapasya stuff. But right now I am making one vow: I am going to really be Satya Vrat. I will speak the truth and I will do what I say."

Satya Vrat began to live in the forest. He made a bow and some arrows and used them to hunt in the woods. In this way he forgot all about the kingdom. And he never told a lie. He lived very simply in the forest amidst nature, just taking the minimum necessities of life.

Some years passed. Then came a great famine. There was drought in the entire land. Viśvāmitra's wife was alone in the hermitage with all their children, while her husband was away in another land deep in meditation. As the days of drought and famine went on, she saw her children crying out because of hunger. She thought, "What am I to do? First, I was living peacefully in this aśrama with my children. My husband was off meditating, and I could pick fruits and herbs from the forest. With that I could feed my family. But now there are no more fruits and herbs in the forest. My children are crying out in hunger. What shall I do? I have no choice but to sell one of my sons. If I get some money, I'll take that money and feed the other children."

Resolving thusly, she took a rope and put it around her son's neck and started to lead him to the market place. The child was crying, and the mother also was sad. Just as they were approaching the edge of the forest, Satya Vrat saw this pitiful sight and said, "Lady, what are you doing? Why is your son crying like that?"

The muni's wife replied, "Oh Prince, we have nothing to eat, and we have no money. My children are crying out for want of food, so I have determined to sell this one son so I can feed the other children."

Satya Vrat said, "Oh Lady, that is a terrible thing to do. Please don't do this! Go back to your aśrama. I am a hunter, and every day I'll put some meat on the tree outside your aśrama. You can cook the meat and feed your family. Every day I will provide you something. This is my vow. I am Satya Vrat, one who is truthful to his vows."

Viśvāmitra's wife was ecstatic with joy. She took the rope off her son's neck and led him back to the aśrama. Every day Satya Vrat would hunt in the forest, and he would find a rabbit or a bird or some kind of animal. He would shoot the animal with his arrows and cut off a piece of meat for himself, and the rest he would hang from the tree outside the muni's aśrama. And every day Viśvāmitra's wife would come to the tree, where she would find a piece of meat. She would take it down and prepare it and cook it to feed to her children. In this way, a long period passed. But still it didn't rain.

One day, Satya Vrat didn't find any game in the forest. He searched the entire forest, but he couldn't find anything. He thought, "What should I do? Should I give her a piece of my own flesh to eat? I have a vow to provide her with something to eat. How can I forsake my vow?"

Just as he was thinking about this, he looked over in a thicket and saw there was a cow. Not only was it a cow, but the cow belonged to Vasiṣṭha Muni. He thought, "That cow belongs to the same Vasiṣṭha who advised my father to exile me from the kingdom! I am angry with him anyway. There's a cow and I need to give some meat to the muni's wife!"

He took his arrow and without further thought, he shot the cow. He cut up the meat and hung it from the tree. Viśvāmitra's wife, without thinking that it might be cow's meat, came and took the meat down from the tree. She prepared it, served it to her children, and also ate of it herself. Unknowingly, they all ate the cow's meat.

Vasiṣṭha started to look for his cow, but he didn't find her anywhere. He called and searched and looked everywhere for the cow, but he didn't find the cow at all. Then he sat down in meditation and saw that Satya Vrat had killed the cow. "That no-good exiled prince! That brat of a prince who is always in trouble! He killed my cow!" Vasiṣṭha got very angry with the prince, and he took some water in the palm of his hand and said, "Satya Vrat, I pronounce a curse on you! You become Triśaṅku."

Tri means the number three, and śaṅku means a mark of leprosy; Triśaṅku bears three marks of leprosy. Vasiṣṭha threw the water, which bound the curse, and immediately Triśaṅku broke out with three marks of leprosy on his fore - head. He had a horrible appearance, and he was extremely pained.

"What a horrible curse of leprosy I have received," exclaimed Satya Vrat. "It was really no fault of my own. I had to protect my vow by providing some meat to the muni's wife."

Triśaṅku remained in the forest. One day, as he was chasing a wild pig, he heared the pig groan, "Aiṃ." And Triśaṅku thought, "What kind of noise is this, Aiṃ?" For some reason he started to repeat the same syllable Aiṃ. Triśaṅku started to say, "Aiṃ, Aiṃ, Aiṃ!" Without understanding what he was saying, or what it meant, he continued to recite the strange sound he learned from the pig.

Then one day the Goddess Sarasvatī came to bless him. She said, "Triśaṅku, you have been faithful to your vow, and you have not transgressed the truth. What would you like from me?"

Triśaṅku said, "I want to have my beautiful body back and get rid of this leprosy. I want my father to give me my kingdom back, and I don't want to be an outcast living alone in the forest anymore."

Sarasvatī said, "Tatā-stu, I grant you that boon. Even now your father's ministers are on the way to come to find you."

Sarasvatī dissolved inside and Triśaṅku began to shine with his beautiful appearance again. Just then the King's ministers found the prince in the forest. They said, "Oh Prince, your father has been so anxious for you. Please come home."

The prince was pleased to return with them.

When Triśaṅku/Satya Vrat came to the edge of the kingdom, his father rode out of the city to greet him. He said, "My son, I have been so concerned about you. My time has come to go to the forest to perform tapasya. Now you take charge of the kingdom. I am going to perform the spiritual discipline by which I can ascend to my heavenly abode."

So Satya Vrat was crowned the King, and he began to reign over his kingdom.

One day, Satya Vrat went to the Guru Vasiṣṭha, and said, "Guruji, Vasiṣṭha Muni, please perform the sacrfice by which I, too, can ascend to heaven."

Vasiṣṭha said, "That is not possible. You were a brat as a child. You were always in trouble; you disobeyed; you stole the Brahmiṇ's wife; you killed my cow; you are a sinner, and you can't go to heaven. Especially not right now."

"Why can't I go to heaven now?"

"No one can go to heaven with an earthly body. So if you behave yourself for the rest of your life and don't sin anymore, then we can perform a sacrifice for you, so that after you leave this earthly body, you can go to heaven. But the body will stay here. No one can take their body to heaven."

Satya Vrat again requested, "Mahā Ṛṣi, Guruji, Great Wise One: you know all of the sacrifices. Why don't you perform the sacrifice so I can go to heaven right now?"

Vasiṣṭha again replied, "I already told you that is impossible! Nobody can go to heaven with their body right now. Wait until you leave this body and then maybe you can go to heaven if your karma is perfect."

Satya Vrat said, "Guruji, you're just picking on me! You didn't like me from my childhood. It was you who advised my father to exile me from the kingdom! It was you who cursed me to become afflicted with leprosy! If you don't do this sacrifice for me right now, then I'll have to find another guru to do it for me. But I want to go to heaven with my body!"

Vasiṣṭha said, "You were a foolish child and nothing has changed at all. Now you are behaving like a cāṇḍālā, an out - cast, and I curse you! You shall become a cāṇḍālā!" Vasiṣṭha took some water in his hand, and threw it at Satya Vrat.

Immediately, the crown fell from his head. Satya Vrat's golden ornaments fell off, his silken robes became tattered rags, and he became most wretched and decrepit. He said, "Oh my gosh, I am doomed! I can't let my subjects to see me like this. What a disgrace!"

Satya Vrat had one son named Hariścandra. He called his young son, Hariścandra, and said, "Son, see the terrible condition that has afflicted me. You take over the leadership of the affairs of state. I am going to the forest to perform Prayaścitta, the tapasya of repentence. I will try to find some way to relieve this terrible condition."

## Satya Vrat Goes to Heaven

Hariścandra was crowned as the King. Satya Vrat, Triśaṅku, now suffering in a deplorable condition, went to the forest in great sorrow and pain.

Some years passed. Viśvāmitra returned to his hermitage after practicing tapasya. When he saw his wife, his heart melted. He said, "My wife, tell me how you passed the days of the drought and famine? How did you survive? I, myself, was striken with a terrible condition. At one time I found myself so hungry, I broke into the house of a cāṇḍālā. I went directly into his kitchen, where I saw a little bit of leftovers of some dog meat he had cooked some days before. I reached into the pot to eat it. Just then the cāṇḍālā came home. He said, 'Oh Brahmiṇ, what are you about to do?'

"And I replied, 'I am in great pain from my hunger, so I am going to steal this dog meat from a cāṇḍālā, and eat it, so that I can save my body!'

"The cāṇḍālā said, 'Oh Brahmiṇ, learned that you are, please stop! Don't do that. My life is defiled. I am unclean. I am unworthy to provide food for a Brahmiṇ. The pots and utensils are unclean, the meat itself is unclean. It is not befitting a Brahmiṇ. Please, don't eat defiled food, because it is written, 'He who eats defiled food, becomes defiled him - self'. Don't sacrifice your noble birth as a Brahmiṇ to become a cāṇḍālā in your next life!'

"Again I replied, 'My first obligation is to preserve my life. Because this human life gives me the opportunity to perform the sādhana, the spiritual discipline, by which God-Realization is obtained, I am required to protect my life. If I commit any offense in doing so, then I can always perform some tapasya of repentence. But if I allow this human life to slip through my fingers, before my goal of Perfection of Realization is reached, then I will be guilty of a greater crime.'

"The cāṇḍālā said, 'Oh Noble Brahmiṇ, be that as it may. I am requesting you, please don't commit this sin of stealing defiled meat from a defiled being and eating the dog meat of a cāṇḍālā. Surely the Gods will help you in your plight.'

"Again I replied, 'I cannot wait any longer for the Gods to help me. I am very disturbed by these pangs of hunger. Now, I must take some nourishment for this body! I will eat the meat!'

"Just then a bolt of lightening flew across the heavens. The clouds began to thunder and the rain fell! I put down the meat and ran outside and raised my arms up to the heavens and rejoiced! The Gods had sent rain! The drought was over! The famine was finished!

"And therefore, my dear wife, I came home to see how you and the children got along during the period of drought."

The muni's wife said, "Husband, I, too, was very perplexed by hunger. It was most pitiful to hear the cries of my children who were hungry. They kept saying, 'Mother, give us some - thing to eat!'

"At first I gathered wild rice and grains from the forest, but then there was none. Then I gathered berries and fruits, but then they too were finished. Then I gathered roots, but they became exhausted as well. When my children were crying so pitifully for food, I was in such a detestable state that I didn't know what to do. Then I decided to sell one of our sons. Perhaps a rich man would purchase him, and with the proceeds of the sale, I could buy some food to keep the others alive. Just as I was in route to the market place, Satya Vrat came and said, 'Oh Dear One, don't commit this horrible act. I will provide meat for your family every day so long as the famine lasts.'

"Every day I went outside the aśrama and found a piece of meat tied to the tree. But then one day, quite unknowingly, that prince, Satya Vrat, killed Vasiṣṭha's cow. For this,

Vasiṣṭha cursed him to be a cāṇḍālā, and again he was exiled from the kingdom. Now, my husband, we must do something to repay the kindness of Satya Vrat."

Viśvāmitra immediately went to where Satya Vrat was staying in the forest. He said, "Satya Vrat, you appear to be in a detestible condition. How did you get to be like this?"

"I went to my guru and said, 'Vasiṣṭha, please perform the sacrifice by which I can ascend to heaven in this body.' And when Vasiṣṭha refused, I said, 'Vasiṣṭha, if you don't do this sacrifice for me, then I will have it performed by some other guru.' Whereupon Vasiṣṭha cursed me to become a cāṇḍālā. Now you see my pitiful condition. I can never go to heaven with this despicable body."

Viśvāmitra said, "I personally will send you to heaven, right now with this very body. You have done such a great service to my family, and thereby you have become my great benefactor. I will see that you get to heaven. Bring me the articles needed for the sacrifice."

Satya Vrat began to collect all the required articles and he brought them to the sacrificial altar. Viśvāmitra invited all the other munis, "Come to the Sacrifice!"

But Vasiṣṭha ordered them, "Don't anybody go!"

And no munis would disobey Vasiṣṭha's order.

Then Viśvāmitra said, "Satya Vrat, sit by the sacrificial dais. We will make this sacrifice by ourselves!"

Satya Vrat sat down, while Viśvāmitra enkindled the sacred fire. He began to recite the mantras and he said, "Go up, Satya Vrat. Go to heaven!"

Immediately, Satya Vrat lifted off the earth and began to ascend to the heavens. He moved up, up, up through the clouds, through the atmosphere, and he moved towards the heavens. Some of the Gods were sitting near the door of heaven and said, "Indra! Look at that cāṇḍālā, that outcast. That defiled being is coming up to heaven!"

Indra came running to the gate and said, "Satya Vrat! Triśaṅku in a cāṇḍālā form! What are you doing here? Go back to earth! No cāṇḍālā can come through the gate of heaven!"

And Satya Vrat started to fall. He fell through the clouds, and as he approached the earth, he started screaming, "Viśvāmitra! Viśvāmitra! Save me! Save me! I'm falling!"

And Viśvāmitra called out, "Stop! I sent you to heaven! No one has the authority to disallow you! Go back to heaven!"

Immediately Triśaṅku began to rise into the air. As he pushed through the clouds, he came near to the gate of heaven, and Indra said, "What are you doing back here? I sent you to earth. Go back!"

Again Satya Vrat started to fall. Then Viśvāmitra said, "Stop!"

And Indra said, "Stop!"

There was Satya Vrat, stuck in the atmosphere halfway between heaven and earth. He could neither go up, nor could he go down. He was stuck in the middle.

Viśvāmitra said, "Indra! You take this man to heaven."

Indra said, "He is a cāṇḍālā, an outcast, in a despicable body. There is no way he is coming to heaven! You take him back to earth."

In great anger Viśvāmitra replied, "All right, we'll see about this!"

He began to recite the Gayatri mantra, and made offerings to the sacred fire and said, "All the merits which I have obtained from all the tapasya that I have performed, I give to Triśaṅku! Now Triśaṅku, go to heaven."

Indra said, "He can't come in!"

Viśvāmitra began to chant the Gayatri mantra once again. "What are you doing?" asked Indra.

Viśvāmitra replied, "I am making a new creation, with a new heaven and a new Indra! If Satya Vrat is not welcome in your heaven, then I will send him to that heaven."

Indra said, "Stop! We don't need a new creation. I don't want another heaven with another Indra. I'll allow Satya Vrat into this heaven. But not with that body. Let him have a divine body, and then he can enter."

There in the middle of the atmosphere where Satya Vrat was suspended, he suddenly became endowed with a beautiful, healthy divine body. He was dressed in silken garments and golden ornaments. Indra sent the Devas with a chariot that flies through the air, and Satya Vrat sat down as they escorted him up to Indra's heaven. Indra gave him a place in heaven, because of the strength of Viśvāmitra's tapasya.

## Varuṇa Grants Hariścandra a Son

After Satya Vrat ascended into heaven, Hariścandra, his son, began to rule in his place as the King of Ayodhyā, King of the Solar Dynasty. Hariścandra was the most truthful, the most just, the most generous King that Ayodhyā had ever seen. Of all the Kings of the Solar Dynasty, Hariścandra was a gem. His community was very prosperous, and the citizens lived in peace and contentment in every way.

But Hariścandra didn't have a child. He thought to himself, "It says in our scriptures that if you don't have a son who can perform the funeral rites when you leave this earth, then you can't go to heaven. Who will offer piṅdas, funeral cakes, at the annual memorial ceremonies? How can I go to heaven if I don't have a son? There won't be anyone to care for me. Who will be the heir to my throne? My people will be without a leader, without a protector. Without a defender my whole kingdom may be over-run by thieves or enemies. There will be no one to guard the peace, no one to maintain the prosperity. I personally will not attain salvation. I had better go to my guru, Vasiṣṭha, and ask him what to do."

Thus reasoning, Hariścandra went to Vasiṣṭha and said, "Vasiṣṭha, with your blessings I have become very successful as a King, but as a human being I am doomed to damnation. I don't have a son to succeed me. What shall I do?"

Vasiṣṭha said, "Worship Varuṇa, the Lord of the Waters. Varuṇa, being pleased, will grant you a son."

Hariścandra went off to perform tapasya. He started to meditate and to perform various forms of Yoga. In many ways he worked to propitiate the Lord Varuṇa. After some time, Varuṇa came to him and said, "What would you like?"

Hariścandra replied, "Lord, there is nothing so painful as to not have a son. Please, Lord, bless me with a son."

And Varuṇa said, "What will you do for me if I give you a son?"

Hariścandra replied, "Anything you want."

Then Varuṇa said, "If I give you a son, I want you to give the son back to me. I want you to sacrifice the son."

Hariścandra assented, "There is nothing worse than not having a son. Certainly I will do whatever you ask. Give me a son and I will sacrifice him to you just as you request. I am Hariścandra, the King who always keeps his word. This is my vow, this is my promise."

Varuṇa said, "Tatā-stu, I grant you the boon. I grant you a son."

Hariścandra went home and soon his wife was pregnant with a child. The King's joy knew no bounds! Unlimited joy! He summoned the Brahmiṇs and performed the prenatal ceremonies. In the fifth month of his wife's pregnancy, he performed the Simantaṇāyaṇa, the parting of the hairs of his wife. He placed sindhūr in her hair, a bright red vermillion powder, and offered madhu parka for her to drink, a cold drink made of yogurt, ghee, honey and sugar, and he blessed her. In the seventh month he performed more ceremonies. And when the child came out of the womb, Hariścandra's pleasure knew no limits.

Just then Varuṇa came and said, "Now you have a son. Oh King, you who are truthful to your vow, sacrifice the son. Give him back to me."

The King thought for a moment and then said, "Lord, this child has just come into the world. He hasn't even had the blessing of a birth celebration. How can you sacrifice a child who hasn't had a birth celebration? This is unheard of in the scriptures. Lord, let me please just perform the Jāta Karma, birth ceremony, and then I'll perform your sacrifice, just as I promised."

Varuṇa said, "That sounds like a wise idea. Go ahead. Perform the Jāta Karma."

Then the King Hariścandra invited many Brahmiṇs to assemble and they chanted the sacred mantras and blessed the child. Hariścandra gave great gifts to many people. He was so happy!

When the celebration was completed, Varuṇa came and said, "All right King, perform the sacrifice."

Immediately the joy fled from the King's mind, and he was oppressed by sorrow and beset by thought, "Oh, what shall I tell him now? There is nothing more painful than not having a son. How can I sacrifice the son who has come to me through the blessing of God? I only have one son." He said, "Varuṇa, you are the knower of Dharma. I have just a small intellect in comparison to the magnitude of all your vast knowledge. You know the right way to perform Dharma. But let me just ask you this one question: when we perform any Vedic sacrifice, both the wife and the husband should be participants. It is not according to rule for just the husband to perform any sacrifice alone. The wife is known as the Bhagidār, the equal co-sharer. So how can we perform a sacrifice where the wife can't come? Now it says in the scriptures that ten days after a child has taken birth, the father becomes pure. In the case of a woman, the time limit stipulated is thirty days. So, Varuṇa, if it meets your approval, just wait until the end of the month when my wife will become pure, and then together we can perform the sacrifice."

Varuṇa said, "Well, that sounds like a very amicable arrangement. I have no difficulty, but just make sure you keep your word."

Hariścandra's heart lept for joy! He was so happy!

In a flash the thirty days went by. Hariścandra said, "Hmm. The day has come to give my child a name."

He went to his guru, Vasiṣṭha, and they examined the astrological charts prepared for the birth of the new child. They gave him the name Rohitaśva, the Red Horse. Rohi has another meaning - the rising sun; the Horse who Shines like the Rising Sun. When the Gods and demons churned the kṣīrasamudra, the ocean of milk, many beings came out from that ocean. After Mahālakṣmī came Ucchaiśravas, the aśva, or horse which embodies all wisdom. So here is Rohitaśva, the Horse, Embodiment of the Wisdom Which Radiates like the Rising Sun. This was the meaning of the name given to the child.

Hariścandra celebrated the rite of passage for the naming of his child, and made a feast for his entire kingdom, giving great dakṣiṇas as gifts to the Brahmiṇs. They had performed all the ceremonies and the fire sacrifice, singing songs of joy and gladness, when Varuṇa came and said, "Oh King, fulfill your vow. Sacrifice the child!"

Hariścandra said, "Lord, I am ready right at this very moment to do exactly as you say. But first I want your opinion on one question of the law of our dharma. It is said that in order for a victim to be fit for a sacrifice, he must have some teeth. How can you sacrifice an animal that doesn't have any teeth? Now I see that is written right here in the scriptures. Lord, if you think this is wrong, tell me and I'll perform the sacrifice right now. But if you are in agreement with the scriptures, just wait six months until we perform his Annaprașan, the eating of his first food, after his teeth have come. Then we will perform the sacrifice without any hesitation. But I don't want to give you an improper victim for your sacrifice."

Varuṇa said, "King, I think you are putting me off. Be sure you don't get too much attached to this child of yours! I grant your wish. Go ahead and perform the child's Annaprașan, the first eating of solid food. Then we'll have the sacrifice."

Varuṇa disappeared, and Hariścandra was full of joy! He began to play with his child, and to watch the child grow.

Six months passed by. The Brahmiṇs convened to perform the sacrifice and chant the mantras that accompany the feeding of the first rice. The child was eating his first meal, when Varuṇa came. "Okay King, perform the sacrifice now!"

And the King replied, "Lord Varuṇa, you know the child still has the hair on his head that he had when he was born. How can I sacrifice to you an impure victim like that? Let me first perform his Curākaraṇ ceremony and take off all the hair from his head. Then he will be a fit victim for sacrifice. This I promise you."

And Varuṇa replied, "See that your words do not become untrue. Don't tell lies to me. I grant you the boon. Shave the child's head, and then we will perform the sacrifice."

The time went by and they shaved the child's head and Varuṇa came and said, "All right King, give me the child."

Hariścandra said, "Varuṇa, I'm sure you know that in a sacrifice of this nature, only one who is twice-born is fit to be the victim offered to God. Let me first perform his Upaṇāyaṇ ceremony, which confers upon him the sacred thread, and make him twice-born. Then I will perform your sacrifice without hesitation."

Varuṇa said, "King, I think you are getting very much attached to this child. You seem to be leading me on, and stalling me with one excuse after the other. But I allow this delay. Go ahead and perform the Yajñopavitam ceremony, and make him twice-born. Give him the sacred thread, and initiate him into the Gayatri mantra. It is written that for a Brahmiṇ child the appropriate age is eight years; for Kṣatriya children the age is eleven; for Vaiśya children the age is twelve; and for Śudra children the age is fifteen. Therefore, go ahead and perform the Upaṇāyaṇ ceremony."

Hariścandra was very happy.

Time went by very quickly. When Hariścandra performed the Upaṇāyaṇ ceremony for his son, Varuṇa came and said, "Make the sacrifice."

And Hariścandra replied, "Lord, the only really fitting victim for your sacrifice will be one who is knowledgeable. Why would you allow the sacrifice of an ignorant child? Only the child who is knowledgeable may be a fit offering. Certainly that should be the criteria. First let the child study with his guru. After his Samavārtan ceremony, after he returns from the guru's home having studied the Vedas, then let him come into the sacrifice and I will offer him for sure."

Varuṇa said, "Make no mistake, King! If you don't follow every letter of what you have promised me to do, I am going to curse you!"

Hariścandra replied, "I have never spoken a lie, and I promise you I will do just as you command me to do! As soon as the child returns from his guru's aśrama, we will perform the sacrifice."

Varuṇa said, "Okay, send the child to be educated. But make no mistake: you will have to perform exactly as you have promised."

The child was sent to the guru's aśrama. The years passed quickly, while the child Rohitaśva studied all the Vedas and the treatises on politics and economics and how to be a good father to his nation. When he had committed all of this knowledge to memory, he gave the appropriate dakṣiṇa to his Guru, and started on his way home. Just as he was on the way, Indra came and said, "Son, don't go there! Don't you know that if you go there, your father is going to offer you as a victim in a sacrifice? Save your life! Run to the hills! Hide out in a cave, and when your father dies, then we'll call you. Then you will come and inherit your kingdom. Don't give up your life right now by going to your father."

When Rohitaśva heard this, he became frightened, and not knowing what to do, he ran for the hills and hid out in a cave.

Varuṇa came to the King, and said, "Okay King, it's time for your son's Samavārtan ceremony. Your son should have returned by now, and the ceremony should have been completed. Perform the sacrifice as you have promised!"

The King answered, "Oh Lord, my son has not come home yet. How can I perform the sacrifice?"

Varuṇa said, "Time after time you have put me off for one reason or the other, and now this is just another lame excuse! You have no intention of fulfilling your dharma! You have just been putting me off and lying to me time after time. Now you perform the sacrifice or I am going to curse you!"

The King said, "Oh Lord Varuṇa, I am not trying to put you off. I am telling you the truth! I have no son to sacrifice to you. Please take pity on me!"

Varuṇa said, "You are responsible for this. How can I take pity on you? I curse you! You will be afflicted with disease!" And he threw some drops of water at the King Hariścandra.

The King immediately became afflicted with a terrible disease which caused great pain. Some time passed while he was suffering the terrible pains and discomfort of disease. News of this came to Rohitaśva in the cave where he was living in the forest. He thought, "I must go to see my father who is suffering. What good is it to be a son who does not redeem the pain of his father?"

He started on his journey to see his father the King, but Indra came to him and said, "Stop, oh Prince! Don't go there! The only way your father can be freed from his pain is by killing you! Don't invite your own destruction. Go back to your mountain cave where you will be safe. When it is safe for you to come, then we will call you."

Rohitaśva became afraid and fled back to the mountain cave where he had been staying. Hariścandra remained afflicted with disease. Thereafter the King called his guru and said, "Vasiṣṭha, what shall I do? Here I am afflicted by disease and pain, and the only way out of this is to offer my own son in sacrifice. Even so, my son is not here. Now I have no way to offer the sacrifice. But I can't stand this pain any longer. What shall I do?"

Vasiṣṭha replied, "King, there are many different types of sons. There is a son that is born from the union between the husband and wife; there is a son that is born from knowledge, by means of initiation; there is a son that is won from the spoils of war, who has been stolen by force of arms; there is a son who has been given shelter as an orphan, who seeks refuge with a father; and there is a son who has been purchased by paying a fitting price. Therefore, oh King, find another son!"

The King was ecstatic with joy! He called all the ministers and said, "Ministers, go throughout the kingdom, and see if anyone will sell me their son!"

The ministers went through the kingdom, and called out: "Will anyone sell their son? The King is in need of a son! Will anyone sell their son?"

Now there was a poor Brahmiṇ whose name was Ajigartha. Ajigartha had three sons. Their names were Śunaḥpuccha, Śunaḥśepha and Śunolaṅgula. Because he was very poor, he was having difficulty providing food for all three of them. When he heard of the King's desire to purchase a son, he thought, "I could sell one of my sons, and with the money I receive, I can feed the other two." Now his oldest son was needed to perform the funeral rites when he left his body. His youngest son was too young to understand what was going on. He chose his middle son, Śunaḥśepha, and decided to sell that son.

The King asked, "What will you take for your son?"

The Brahmiṇ replied, "One hundred cows laden with gold."

The King said, "Sold! I give you your price. Give me the son!"

Śunaḥśepha was crying in terror as they bound him to the sacrificial post. The Brahmiṇs were reciting the mantras of the yajña, chanting the formulas of the human sacrifice. All the ṛṣis were present, while the King was lying in the sacrificial arena suffering in great pain. The executioner raised his sword to decapitate the victim, and the victim, Śunaḥśepha, cried out in fear.

Suddenly, the executioner put down his sword and said, "Oh King, I cannot decapitate this victim. This young boy is crying so pitifully. Please, show him mercy!"

The King said, "Why doesn't Varuṇa show me mercy? I have so much pain! What will we do? Is there anyone here who will decapitate this victim and free me from my pain?"

Then the Brahmiṇ, Ajigartha said, "Oh King, double your price, and I'll do it myself."

Everyone began to shout, "Boooo! What kind of father are you? You would slay your own son, even when the executioner couldn't do it?"

And Ajigartha answered, "No one knows the difficulties of poverty. Each of you is so pious because you have plenty, but to be freed of the curse of poverty, even a Brahmiṇ can slay his own son. Give me my price, and I'll perform the sacrifice."

The King said, "I grant you the price! Give him another

hundred cows laden with gold."

Ajigartha became the executioner who raised the sword over the victim, his own son. The victim was crying so pitifully! Just as he was about to strike, Viśvāmitra stood up and called, "Stop! Oh King. The King is the father of his people. The greatest virtue of a kṣatriya King is compassion. The sacred duty of a King is to protect his subjects. And here you are about to commit this terrible deed of causing a father to kill his own son."

The King said, "I have so much pain! This is the only way to free myself from disease."

"You must forgive this child!" called Viśvāmitra.

"Why doesn't Varuṇa forgive me?" replied the King. "None of this was due to any fault of mine. I am the victim of circumstances."

Viśvāmitra ran up to where the child, Śunaḥśepha, was bound, and gave him initiation in the Varuṇa mantra by whispering the bīja mantra "Vaṃ" in his ear. Śunaḥśepha began to loudly chant the Bandan Mukta Śukta, which became the 28th Hymn of the First Mandala of Rig Veda:

नमो महद्भ्यो नमो अर्भकेभ्यो

नमो युवभ्यो नम आशिनेभ्यः ।

यजाम देवान् यदि शक्नवाम

मा ज्यायसः शंसमा वृक्षि देवाः ॥

namo mahadbhyo namo arbhakebhyo
namo yuvabhyo nama āśinebhyaḥ I
yajāma devān yadi śaknavāma
mā jyāyasaḥ śaṃ
samā vṛkṣi devāḥ II

I bow to the Great Wise Beings of the past. I bow to the Great Wise Beings of the present. I bow to the Great Wise Beings of the future. If there are any unknown Great Wise Beings of any time, I bow to them as well. With one-pointed attention, I bow to them all. Bless me all of you.

Just then Varuṇa came to the sacrifice and ordered, "Release the child!"

The King replied, "Oh Lord Varuṇa, if you release me from my pain and disease, I will certainly release this child."

Then Varuṇa proclaimed, "Okay King, be free from pain!"

Suddenly all of the King's disease and pain was healed. The child, Śunaḥśepha, was freed, and all the Brahmiṇs in the assembly shouted with joy for triumph!

Śunaḥśepha said, "Oh learned Brahmiṇs, now that I am free, please tell me to whose house shall I go? Who is my father now?"

Some of the Brahmiṇs said, "Ajigartha is your father."

Others said, "Hariścandra, the King, paid the appropriate price for you. Go to the King's house."

Vasiṣṭha stood up amidst the assembly and said, "No. Viśvāmitra gave him the initiation in the māntrā which saved his life. Now he is your true Spiritual Father. You go home with Viśvāmitra."

Then Viśvāmitra embraced Śunaḥśepha with fatherly love, and together they returned to his house. Hariścandra completed the yajña along with all the sacrificial rites, and gave great dakṣiṇas to the Brahmiṇs and Ṛṣis, and especially to his own Guru Vasiṣṭha, the likes of which had never been seen before. There was a great celebration throughout the kingdom.

## The Enmity Between Vasiṣṭha and Viśvāmitra

After Hariścandra was freed from the dreadful curse of disease and reunited with his son, Rohitaśva, he lived and ruled in Ayodhyā along with his wife Śaivyā, literally She who manifests Śiva, and their son. Yudh means war and A means without; Ayodhyā is the place without war, the land of eternal peace. Hariścandra along with Śaivyā and their son Rohitaśva saw the kingdom of Ayodhyā grow in fame and prosperity. Health and wealth and welfare were enjoyed by all the citizens, and in every way it was the ideal community governed by an ideal King.

Did you ever notice that even amongst spiritual seekers, there is a hierarchy of attainment? Just as in a church there is a deacon and a pastor or minister, and above them a bishop and a cardinal and the Pope; so also amongst the seers of the Sanātan Dharma, there is a designation of Sādhus, Sānts, Svāmis, Mahātmas and Ṛṣis. These meanings have become blurred over time, because people have taken titles of their own accord, but even the title of Ṛṣi included many degrees. Now iṣ means to desire, iṣa, the object of desire. Ra means again. Ra plus iṣa equals Ṛṣi, and Ṛṣi means he who again is the object of desire, the knowledgeable one, who knows how to control desire. Iṣa also means to perceive and to rule: Perceiver of all, Ruler of all. He who again rules over all, he who again sees all. Ṛṣi.

There are Ṛṣis and Mahāṛṣis, Rājaṛṣis, Devaṛṣis and Brahmāṛṣis. A Ṛṣi is a seer, a wise being, and a Mahāṛṣi is a great seer among seers. A Rājaṛṣi is a great seer amongst kings, and a Devaṛṣi, like Nārada Muni, is a great seer among Gods. He can transfer his physical body, or transcend the physical plane, and move between the Devaloka, the realms of the Gods, and human consciousness, at will. And the

Brahmāṛṣi is a knower in the fullest essence of the wisdom of Brahmāṇ, the wisdom of nonduality, that "I am the Supreme Divinity."

One day Viśvāmitra went to visit Vasiṣṭha, and he saw that Vasiṣṭha was adorned with great honor and respect. Viśvāmitra asked him, "Vasiṣṭha, from where did you receive such a tribute of honor? Where did you get all this wealth and all of these tokens of esteem?"

Vasiṣṭha replied, "From my disciple, Hariścandra."

Viśvāmitra asked incredulously, "Your disciple Hariścandra has provided his guru with such wealth?"

Vasiṣṭha replied, "Yes, that is the honor that he has shown to a Brahmāṛṣi, a knower of the oneness of Brahmāṇ."

Viśvāmitra said, "Vasiṣṭha, have I not also attained to the status of a Brahmāṛṣi? By the tapasya of my will-power I brought the Gayatri mantra for the upliftment of all humanity. Through the force of my tapasya I sent Satya Vrata to the heavens. Through the application of my wisdom, I initiated Śunaḥśepha in the Varuṇa mantra, and thereby saved his life. I also freed Hariścandra from the curse of Varuṇa. Certainly I, too, am a Brahmāṛṣi."

Vasiṣṭha said, "No, Viśvāmitra, you are not yet a Brahmāṛṣi. There is much left for you to understand. It's not quite so simple. You may have become a Rājaṛṣi by now, but just because you have attained a few siddhis, spiritual powers, that you can flaunt in the public eye, that doesn't make you a Brahmāṛṣi."

Viśvāmitra was insulted. Ever since he tried to steal Vasiṣṭha's cow, he had been striving for equality with Vasiṣṭha. He became angry at this insult and said, "I'll show you!"

Viśvāmitra went off to practice even more tapasya. He sat in the stillness of meditation and became completely absorbed in the practice of austerities. And some time passed.

## The Examination of Hariścandra

One day Indra presided over a great conference in heaven. He summoned all the Gods, along with all the Ṛṣis and Mahāṛṣis, the Rājaṛṣis, Devaṛṣis and Brahmāṛṣis. Everyone was invited to assemble. When the participants were comfortably seated, Indra said, "I have one major question of philosophical import, and I request all of you to give your opinions."

Vasiṣṭha rose amidst the assembly and said, "Excuse me Indra, I don't see Viśvāmitra present at this assembly."

Indra replied, "Viśvāmitra? That King who is still stuck in showing off his egotism? He is filled with the pride of his attainments. Why should there be a place here for him?"

Vasiṣṭha said, "Yes, but even so, he is striving hard in the path of realization. He is trying to become a Brahmāṛṣi. Therefore, he too, should be consulted in this matter of philosophical importance."

Indra agreed, "All right, as you suggest. Send a messenger to Viśvāmitra and tell him that his presence is requested in Indra's heaven."

Nārada Muni was dispatched as the messenger, and proceeded to where Viśvāmitra was sitting in Samādhi, in the full and complete absorption of his tapasya. Nārada said, "Viśvāmitra, the Gods have assembled at Indra's heaven for a great conference on matters of Philosophy. All the Ṛṣis, Mahāṛṣis, Rājaṛṣis, Devaṛṣis and Brahmāṛṣis have assembled along with them. Vasiṣṭha suggests that you, too, should be in attendance."

"You mean that Vasiṣṭha has recognized me as a Brahmāṛṣi, too?" asked Viśvāmitra.

"Oh no, that was not his proclamation! He said that you are striving hard to become a Brahmāṛṣi, and therefore, your opinion should be heard as well."

Viśvāmitra was somewhat disappointed when he replied, "Oh, all right, I will go with you."

They mounted on an aerial car and ascended to the heavens of Indra. Arriving in heaven, they exchanged greetings with all assembled, and then Viśvāmitra took his seat next to the Guru Vasiṣṭha. When he was comfortably seated, Indra said, "Now, I shall put forth my question. What is the strongest power on earth?"

Vayu immediately stood up and responded, "The wind! The wind blows anything away."

Agni stood up and said, "Fire! It can burn anything!"

Yama stood up and said, "Death, no one can escape from Death!"

And so each of the Gods took his turn and proclaimed himself to be the most powerful being on earth. Finally Vasiṣṭha stepped forward into the assembly and said, "Fellow divinities, I shall proclaim in truth what is the strongest power on earth. The strongest power on earth is Truth!"

Viśvāmitra stood up and said, "What do you mean the strongest power is Truth? Look at the earth. Everyone there is a liar, a cheater, and a thief. They will steal for money and lie for money and there is no one who is devoted to Truth!"

And Vasiṣṭha replied, "What if there was one man who would sacrifice everything for Truth, who would give up his own Self, all his attachments, all his egotism and possessions, then would you agree that Truth is the strongest power on earth?"

Viśvāmitra asked, "Where is there a man like that?"

Vasiṣṭha answered, "The King of Ayodhyā, Rāja Hariścandra."

"Ha!" responded Viśvāmitra. "Hariścandra? He cheated Varuṇa out of the sacrifice that he had promised. He put him off time and time again with this excuse and that excuse. He made up one story after another story in order to avoid fulfilling his vow! You are only saying that because he gave you so much wealth and honor. Now, even the great Vasiṣṭha has sacrificed Truth to become a servant of wealth."

Vasiṣṭha said, "You'll see, Viśvāmitra! Hariścandra is endowed with nobility and steadfastness in Truth."

And Viśvāmitra replied, "Oh Vasiṣṭha, you must be joking. That King is a liar and will forsake the Truth as soon as it becomes convenient. I am willing to bet you all the spiritual merits I have attained from all the pūjās that I have performed that you are wrong!"

Vasiṣṭha looked at Viśvāmitra, "As you like, Viśvāmitra. I have firmness of faith. If you would like to rid yourself of all your spiritual merits, you may do so. I accept your challenge. You may test him any way you like." The assembly concluded with this wager being made, and all the Gods went to see what would happen.

Viśvāmitra came down to the earth, sat in the forest and began to perform tapasya. One day Hariścandra went into that forest to hunt. Through his power of mantra, Viśvāmitra called Māyā and caused it to rain. A tremendous storm ensued, and Hariścandra somehow became separated from his friends and the rest of his hunting party, and he became thoroughly lost. Viśvāmitra again called Māyā and made the sun come out. It became very very hot. Hariścandra began to get thirsty. He became hungry. His clothes were wet and gummy. He was tired and thirsty and hungry and lost in the most dense part of the forest. It was a deplorable situation.

He wandered in this circumstance until he came to a little clearing and found the hermitage of Viśvāmitra.

"What a great relief," thought Hariścandra as he dismounted from his horse and went to pay his respect to the great ṛṣi. He prostrated before the ṛṣi and said, "Oh Great Ṛṣi, what good fortune it is for me to find you here in this forest. I am thirsty and hungry. I am tired and have lost all of my friends. I am lost as well. I don't even know where is Ayodhyā."

Viśvāmitra replied, "Welcome, oh King. I am so pleased that you have come, and that I can be of some assistance. Go to that stream over there, wash and change into these dry clothes. I will prepare some food for you, and after you have taken refreshments and rest, I will show you the way back to your home."

The King replied, "You are so kind, oh Great Ṛṣi. You have been so gracious to my ancestors, and what a kindness you are performing for me."

And Viśvāmitra said, "Think nothing of it."

As he was instructed, King Hariścandra went to the stream and washed. He changed his clothes and took a drink of cool, clear refreshing water. Then he returned to the muni's her - mitage. There he ate delicious food and succumbed to the magic that surrounded him.

After taking rest he said, "Viśvāmitra, I am so pleased with your seva, the selfless service which you offer with the greatest of love. I am so greatful for the way you have saved my life and made me comfortable even in the pathless forest. You have put me in the best possible position, and that is the best sign of friendship: to always think of your friend's advantage. Choose from me some wish."

Viśvāmitra replied, "Oh King, I am a Ṛṣi, a Muni, living in the forest performing tapasya. I personally need nothing. But you see, I have a daughter who is of marriageable age now, and there is a young man to whom I wish to give this daughter in marriage. But I don't have a dowry. King, could you give me something for a dowry, so that I can perform the marriage of my daughter?"

The King said, "Mahārṣi, I am the King of Ayodhyā, the richest man in the country! I have more than ample wealth so that you can give your daughter in marriage. Not only that, but you were so kind to send my father to heaven. You freed Śunaḥśepha from the sacrificial post. You even freed me from the terrible curse of disease given by Lord Varuṇa. Mahārṣi, anything I can do for you, you have only to ask. I will be honored to give you the dowry for your daughter's marriage. You just tell me the amount. I personally will make sure that the sum is paid."

Then Viśvāmitra asked, "Oh King, you would never change your mind, would you? Once you have given your word, would you ever make your word become untrue?"

Hariścandra responded, "No, I am Hariścandra, the King of Ayodhyā. I have never spoken a lie since the day of my birth. I give you my word. I would never make my word become untrue. I will provide the dowry for your daughter's marriage."

Viśvāmitra said, "King, thank you very much for your most noble offer, but you see, it is almost night time. We don't want to return to Ayodhyā through the winding paths in the dark of night. We may become lost. Why don't you stay here tonight? Tomorrow morning, after a nice breakfast, I personally will escort you to Ayodhyā. There you can put on your kingly dress once again, and then you can give me the dowry that I need."

The King said, "Viśvāmitra, Mahāmuni, your hospitality knows no limits! You are the noblest of the Aryan race. It is from kind behavior such as yours that our country has grown and prospered. It is because we have such leaders as yourself amongst the Brahmiṇs. Please consider me to be your humble servant."

Viśvāmitra prepared a bed for the King, and that night they took rest.

They awoke in the morning and after bathing, they performed their morning prayers. Having completed their worship, they ate breakfast, and then began the journey along the twisted paths that led through the dense forest towards

Ayodhyā. When they came to the edge of the forest, Hariścandra looked down across the open valleys. There in the distance, he saw his city of Ayodhyā, and his heart lept for joy! Now it was Hariścandra who escorted Viśvāmitra, and when they arrived at the gates of the city, the entire population came out to greet their King. Everyone had been so worried because the King had not come home in the night. All the ministers came to greet their returning King. And as a conquering hero, Hariścandra proclaimed to the public that his safety and well-being were all due to the gracious hospitality of the Great Ṛṣi, Viśvāmitra.

He invited Viśvāmitra into the palace, washed his feet and made many presentations to him. Then he took his own bath, changed his clothes, and returning to the Great Ṛṣi he said, "Now Viśvāmitra, please tell me what can I do to please you. Anything you want. I am so pleased with the assistance you have given to me, to my ancestors, and to my kingdom."

And Viśvāmitra said, "Oh King, please remember your promise to me of last night. I need a dowry to give for my daughter's marriage. Please provide me the dowry."

The King Hariścandra replied, "Oh Great Ṛṣi, take any amount of dowry that you want. Take any amount of wealth that you need. Please fulfill your objective. You have been so gracious and so kind to me and to my family, and have been a benefactor to all the citizens of my country, as well as all of my ancestors. Just tell me what you want."

Viśvāmitra said, "Oh King, please give me the entire kingdom, including all the wealth that you possess."

Hariścandra was stunned. Viśvāmitra looked at the expression on the King's face and said, "Oh King, is there something wrong? Is it that you don't want to give me the entire kingdom? Just a few moments ago you spoke so magnanimously: 'Take what you want, Mahāṛṣi. Take what - ever you want!' Oh King, if you don't want me to have what -

ever I want, just say you made a mistake. Just tell me that you are not going to keep your word, and I will give it all right back to you."

The King stammered for a moment and said, "Oh no, Great Ṛṣi. It was just surprising to me. You can have the entire kingdom!"

"Well, then," said Viśvāmitra, "Please, get out of my kingdom."

Hariścandra looked around the palace, gazing as though it was his last farewell. His wife, Śaivyā, and his son, Rohitaśva, came and said, "Father, my King, Sire: wherever our King goes, we will go with you. Truly, we are a family. We have no desire for kingdom or palace, when the King, himself, lives outside the city. We will go with you."

Hariścandra agreed and then said to his ministers, "Ministers, friends, I pray that you protect the kingdom and administrate wisely on behalf of Viśvāmitra. I renounce all authority to this kingdom!"

And Hariścandra turned to walk away. Viśvāmitra said, "Stop! King, I thought you gave me everything in the kingdom?"

The King said, "That is right."

Viśvāmitra said, "What about those jewels and ornaments you are wearing? How about the jewels your wife is wearing. Are those items also not part of this kingdom? Give me those, too."

They took off all their ornaments, and then started to leave once again.

Viśvāmitra said, "Stop! King, did you promise to give me everything, or did you promise to give me only a portion? If you only want to give me a portion, just admit that you don't want to give it all to me, and tell me that you are a liar, and you can have the whole thing back - all of it! But if you want to give me everything, those kingly vestments, all the clothes you are wearing; they are mine. Take them off, and put them here!"

"Get these people some beggar's rags!" Viśvāmitra ordered the ministers.

Hariścandra, his wife and his son, took off the fine silks and embroidered satins and kingly vestments, and put on the sack clothes of a beggar, and once again started to leave.

Just as they got to the palace gate, Viśvāmitra said, "Stop! King, do you really want me to have this kingdom and this wealth, or do you not?"

The King replied, "I've already given you everything I own. What more do you want?"

And Viśvāmitra said, "I am a Brahmiṇ. When you give a gift to a Brahmiṇ, you must give some dakṣiṇa. Where is my dakṣiṇa? I sent your father to the heavens. I freed Śunaḥśepha from the pillar. I even freed you from Varuṇa's curse of disease. Look at all the dakṣiṇa you gave to Vasiṣṭha, all the wealth and honor that you gave him. Do you expect me to accept a gift without dakṣiṇa?"

Hariścandra said, "Ṛṣi, you can see that right now I don't have anything. How can I give you dakṣiṇa?"

"That is for you to consider. If you don't want me to have these gifts, take them all back and tell me you lied. But if you don't want to be a liar, give me my dakṣiṇa!"

"But Ṛṣi, I have nothing to give you. Give me some time, and I'll give you your dakṣiṇa."

"How much time do you need?"

"Give me one month."

"Okay. One month! But I want my dakṣiṇa! If you don't give my dakṣiṇa in one month, I am going to curse you!"

Hariścandra was struck with fear. Who wants to incur the curse of a ṛṣi? Who knows what evil will befall him, if the ṛṣi gives his curse? And yet, how can he be untrue to his vow?

Perplexed by this situation, Hariścandra set off into the

forest, accompanied by his wife and child. For several days they wandered in the forest, eating berries from the trees, often times unable to provide any food at all. Ultimately they came to the city of Benares. Just as they arrived there, Rohitaśva, the little boy, started to cry, "Daddy, I'm hungry. Don't we have anything to eat?"

And Śaivyā, the wife said, "Oh what a pity this is! Look at our position now. We have nothing to feed our crying child. The great Hariścandra, the Emperor of all of India, the King of Ayodhyā, the most noble of all the Aryans, who has never told a lie, has now been reduced to this position."

Just then, Viśvāmitra came. "Okay King, your thirty days are over. The month is finished. Give me my dakṣiṇa, or I'll curse you!"

Hariścandra said, "Oh Great Ṛṣi, please. The sun is still in the sky. The thirty days are not yet finished. Wait at least until the end of the day!"

Viśvāmitra said, "Very well, I'll wait until sunset. But if you don't give me my dakṣiṇa, then you can either take back all of your wealth, and admit you are a liar, or I'll curse you!"

Hariścandra turned to his wife Śaivyā and asked, "What shall we do? What shall we do?"

Śaivyā, that dharmic wife, replied, "Oh King, the noblest man I have ever met, so firm in your resolve of truth, I bow to you. A King is not allowed to beg. A King is not allowed to do business. And you have no weapons or arms with which to fight. You have only one way to get the money that is needed."

"What is that, my beloved?"

"Sell me."

The King fainted with shock. "Sell my wife? What a horrible situation have I been placed in! What a despicable character I must be to even contemplate selling my wife. A man's first duty is to protect his wife. Oh wife, what a terrible thing you are advising me to do!"

"No King, there is no other way! Quickly, the time is running out! You must sell me in order to pay the ṛṣi his dakṣiṇa. Otherwise he will curse you. Who knows what difficulties we will have? I know you will come and get me someday, and bring me back. Once again we three will dwell together again in Ayodhyā. Please don't lose time! Sell me, oh King."

Hariścandra walked into the market place. He began to call, "Hear ye, hear ye! Who wants to buy this fine dharmic woman? She is endowed with all qualifications: she can cook, she can clean, she can sew, she can do all the works of the household. Who among you good citizens can take compassion on this poor sinner of a man who has been reduced to such a deplorable situation? Help me! Take pity on me, and buy my wife!"

Just then one Brahmiṇ came and said, "What kind of a man are you that you want to sell your wife? Huh! What kind of dharma is this? You look like a noble man, a strong man; like you could do a good day's work! What kind of a man are you that you are going to sell your wife? Ha! All right, how much do you want for her? Let me see her teeth. Well, according to our customs, a woman like this will bring a price of 10 baskets of gold. Here, take your money, and give me the woman!"

He handed the money to the King. Hariścandra took the money, while the Brahmiṇ started dragging his wife away. Just then Viśvāmitra appeared and demanded, "Give me my money! Are you going to pay me my dakṣiṇa or not?"

Hariścandra said, "Viśvāmitra, here are ten baskets of gold."

"Ha! Ten baskets of gold? Do you think that is enough for me? Was that some little tiny sacrifice I performed when I sent your father to the heavens? Was it a little sacrifice I performed when I freed Śunaḥśepha from the sacrificial pillar? Was it just a little sacrifice I performed when I freed you from Varuṇa's curse of disease? I'll take these ten baskets of gold, but bring me more. I'm not satisfied with this!"

"Wait Viśvāmitra, don't curse me now. The sun hasn't sunk to the horizon yet! There is still time."

Just then his young boy, Rohitaśva, started crying, "Mommy! Mommy! Where are they taking you? Where is my mommy going? Am I going to be without a mommy?"

The wife, Śaivyā, the Queen of Ayodhyā, said pitifully, "Oh Brahmiṇ, please be compassionate and purchase my son as well, so he can come with me. He can work. He will bring you materials for your sacrifices, he will pick the flowers for your worship, he will cut wood from the forest, he will do the laundry. Together we will work for you. Please Brahmiṇ, don't seperate a mother from her child."

The Brahmiṇ compassionately agreed, "Okay. According to our customs a boy like this, about this age, let me see his teeth...yes, they're good. Okay, you get another ten baskets of gold. Here take your ten baskets of gold, and give me the child!"

Hariścandra took the ten baskets of gold and the Brahmiṇ took the boy. He started to drag the two of them, mother and child, off towards his home. And the noble Śaivyā said, "I part with you, my King, with one prayer: Lifetime after lifetime I will come again and be the handmaiden of the great and noble King Hariścandra. Never was there a King so noble, or a man so firm in the principles of truth!"

"Come on, Lady!" said the Brahmiṇ, while he pulled on the rope, dragging off the wife and child.

"Give me my dakṣiṇa!" commanded Viśvāmitra.

"Here, oh Mahāṛṣi. Here is another ten baskets of gold. Please be satisfied."

"Ha! Ten baskets of gold? Was that a little sacrifice I

performed? Look at the honor and wealth you gave to Vasiṣṭha for performing the Rājasuya Sacrifice. And you are only giving to me these silly measely ten baskets of gold? I sent your father to the heavens! I freed Śunaḥśepha from the sacrificial pillar! I freed you from Varuṇa's curse! Give me more, or take back everything you have already given, and confess that you told a lie. Or I'll curse you right now!"

Hariścandra said, "Oh Mahāṛṣi, please wait! Wait a few minutes more! The sun hasn't set as yet. There is still time."

Viśvāmitra asked, "What else do you have left to sell?"

And Hariścandra replied, "ME!" He began to call, "Does anyone want to buy this worker? I am selling myself into slavery. Circumstances put me in this position. Will anyone purchase me?"

Just then, the King of the Cāṇḍālās, the outcasts who work at the cremation grounds, was coming home in a drunken stupor, having completed his day's work of burning dead bodies. He asked, "Who is this that calls out, 'Will anyone buy me?' You can be a good servant for me to help me burn dead bodies. I'll buy you!"

Hariścandra said, "No, I am sorry. I can't work for a cāṇḍālā. I am a kṣatriya King, the Emperor of Ayodhyā, and I am not permitted to become the slave of an outcast, to burn dead bodies in the cremation grounds."

And the cāṇḍālā said, "So then you told a lie? When you advertised yourself for sale, you didn't say anything about only a special caste being able to purchase you, nor that you would only do some special kind of work. You said, and very loudly and in public, 'Does anyone want to buy this worker?' Now you are lying by adding extra conditions. Isn't that true? Are you going to tell a lie, Hariścandra?"

"No, I am not going to tell a lie."

"Then I can buy you?" asked the cāṇḍālā.

"Yes, you can buy me."

"Well, according to our customs a King of this height and weight and good physical condition is worth twenty baskets of gold. Here, take your price!"

Hariścandra took the price.

Viśvāmitra immediately took the money and said, "Okay, King, your debt has been paid!"

Instantly the clouds broke apart and the Gods showered flowers upon the earth! Hariścandra was showered with flowers, and he was freed from the debt!

The cāṇḍālā said, "Okay, Slave, carry my bottle of wine! You will come to work for me in the cremation grounds. Your job will be to burn the dead bodies, and collect the fees, and insure that I get paid my money." And he put Hariścandra in charge of the cremation grounds. Hariścandra would take the dead bodies that came in and put them on the funeral pyre. He would stack up the wood and light the fire. Pretty soon he began to act as his fellow workers would behave. He would take the cloth from the dead bodies and wrap it as a turban around his own head. He would take the garlands from the bodies and wear them himself. In all ways he began to act just like a cāṇḍālā at the cremation grounds, and he forgot all about the dream of his ever having been the King of Ayodhyā.

Meanwhile, his dharmic wife Śaivyā, was always badgered by the Brahmiṇ's wife. The Brahmiṇ's wife was never satisfied with any work that she performed. "You didn't wash this clean! You didn't cut this vegetable properly! You didn't cook nicely! You didn't iron my cloth properly! You didn't sweep here! You didn't do this! Your kid is eating too much! You're making a mess! You never work! You're always sitting around, you lazy good-for-nothing! Why did my husband spend so much money to bring me home a servant like you!" she continually rebuked her in a thousand ways.

Every night Śaivyā, the noble queen, would finish her duties, and would rub the feet of the Brahmiṇ's wife, and then she would rub the feet of the Brahmiṇ. She was always the last to go to sleep and the first to rise from the bed. She never had enough to provide for her child. And in this way she forgot all about her life as the Queen of Ayodhyā.

Some time passed. The mistress of the house would frequently beat her child, Rohitaśva, and never give him enough to eat. He was always dressed in tattered rags. One day Rohitaśva went into the forest with the other children to collect wood for the Brahmiṇ's fire sacrifice. As he went into the forest collecting sticks and twigs, he bent down to pick up one piece of wood near an anthill. A large cobra rose out of the anthill and struck the boy, who fell to the ground dead. The other boys ran to the Brahmiṇ's house to tell the maid Śaivyā, "Your son was just bitten by a snake, and he is lying dead on an anthill in the middle of the forest!"

Śaivyā was struck with sorrow and began to cry. The Brahmiṇ's wife said, "Why are you making such a noise? It's inauspicious to cry at sunset! This is the time for worship. Stop making that noise!"

And Śaivyā, the maid, said, "Dear Mistress, my son was just struck by a snake and is lying dead on an anthill in the middle of the forest. Please let me go and bring his body to the cremation grounds to perform his last rites."

The mistress replied, "Huh! Not only have I lost the price of the son for which I paid, but now I am going to lose your labor for the rest of the day on top of it! Can you imagine that? You cheater! You ripped me off, just as though you had stolen from me. I paid the price in gold for that kid, and I paid for you, and now you want to go off to look for the dead child? I lost the child; that's my bad fortune. But now I am supposed to lose your labor for the rest of the day in addition? You finish your work, Maid, and then you can go! I'm not giving you the day off for this!"

Śaivyā washed all the dishes until it was late in the night.

Then the Mistress of the house said, "Here. Here's a load of laundry. I want this folded and pressed before morning."

Śaivyā folded and pressed the laundry and when she finished, it was very late in the night.

Then the Mistress said, "Oh Servant, come here and rub my feet until I go to sleep. After I've fallen asleep, you can go look for your son. You make sure you are back here in the morning to start work on time. Don't cheat me for the price I paid for you!"

The Queen of Ayodhyā massaged the feet of her Mistress, who slowly fell asleep. Then Śaivyā ran out of the house all alone in the dark of night, and went off to the deep, dense forest to find her child. With much terror in her heart, she searched for her son. "Where is the body of my son, Prince Regent of Ayodhyā? Where is he who was born in the luxury, pomp and respect of the King of Ayodhyā, in the wealth of the Emperor of all of India?"

Throughout the night she searched the whole of the forest. Then in the darkness of the night she found the body lying still upon the anthill, covered with ants. Raising up the body, she held it to her breast and began to cry, "Oh my son! You were born to be the King of Ayodhyā, and here you are dying as a pauper, alone on an anthill in the middle of the forest? What fate is this? What are the ways of the Gods? What karma has reduced us to this status?"

She was crying when she started to carry him to the bank of the river in search of the cremation grounds. As she was passing outside the city gate, two policemen saw her carrying the dead body, and they said to one another, "Ah! This is she, the witch who kills children in the middle of the night! Certainly she has just killed another child and is taking the victim to her place to eat. She is a Rakṣāsi, a cannibal!"

The queen replied, "No, I was the Queen of Ayodhyā and this is my son. We were sold into slavery to the Brahmiṇ and his wife, and my son was bitten by a snake. He died on an anthill in the forest, and now I am taking my son's body to burn in the cremation grounds."

And the policemen replied, "What nonsense are you speaking? Now on top of committing this heineous crime, you are telling us ridiculous lies? Come with us to the magistrate!"

They bound her and took her to the magistrate in the middle of the night. The magistrate rose from his sleep. "What is this?" he inquired.

"This is the demoness who kills the children of our city. We found her with this dead child. She was taking this dead body to her place to eat."

The Magistrate said, "Condemn her to death! Take her to the cāṇḍālā at the cremation grounds and have him cut off her head and light her funeral pyre."

They brought her to the leader of the cāṇḍālās and said, "Cāṇḍālā, execute this woman, and burn her remains. She is the demoness who kills children in the night. We found her with the evidence. She was carrying the dead body of a child she had just killed, getting ready to eat the remains. Now, slay her."

The cāṇḍālā said, "Wait. I am a man of affluence. I don't do this work myself any more. Let me call my servant, Hariścandra. Hariścandra! Come!"

Hariścandra came. "What is it, Sir?"

"This demoness has been condemed to death, and it is the Magistrate's order that we perform the execution. He has ordered me to do it. You are my servant. I order you to slay this woman!"

"Oh Cāṇḍālā, it is not my dharma to kill a woman. Please ask anyone else to do it."

"I told YOU to do it! What do you mean it's not your dharma? You sold yourself to me. You promised to obey me as your master. What do you mean? Your dharma is to do what I say! You slay this woman! Take her to the cremation grounds, and cut off her head. Either that, or admit that you are a liar! You are not telling the truth, and you don't want to be my servant! Admit that you took the money from me under false pretenses, in which case you are not true to your word!"

Hariścandra said to the woman, "Come." Even then he couldn't recognize who she was. Nor could she understand who he was, as he was covered with the cloths and garlands from dead bodies, the dust and smells of the cremation grounds.

He took her to the cremation grounds, where she said, "Oh Cāṇḍālā, I understand that you are required to execute me. This is your duty; this is your dharma. You are bound to perform as you have been ordered. But I have one small request to you. Please, before you kill me, my son was bitten by a snake, and his dead body remains lying outside the city gates. I was just bringing him here to this cremation ground in order to burn that body. I request you to please allow me to bring his body here to perform the last rites. Then you can do with me as you please. I promise I will not run away. Just let me bring the body, perform his last rites, and then you can slay me."

Hariścandra agreed, "All right, go and bring the body."

The Queen went to get the body, and it was almost dawn when she returned to the cremation grounds along with the dead child. Hariścandra was sitting, waiting for her. She said, "Oh Cāṇḍālā, my words are not false. See, I have brought this body of my dead son. Now please help me to perform the last rites for this dear departed child. Build a fire, and cremate these last remains."

Hariścandra said, "Dear Lady, please understand that I am not the proprietor of this cremation ground. I cannot perform or allow any cremation in this cremation grounds without giving the proprietor his fee. You must give me some gold in order to perform the funeral rites."

The lady replied, "I have no gold."

"Well," said the cāṇḍālā. "You must go get some. I can't perform against my dharma. How can I perform this cremation without giving the proprietor his fee? That would be untrue. Are you sure you don't have any gold?"

Just then the Queen touched her locket, which is an ornament that married women wear. She said, "Yes, Cāṇḍālā, I have some gold. But this ornament was given to me by my husband, and I can't part with it until I part with my life. Please burn his body, then cut off my head, and then you can take the gold. In that way I will pay the fee for the sacrifice. You will have accomplished all the purposes: you will have performed the last rites of my dead child, you will have fulfilled the orders of the cāṇḍālā and the Magistrate by executing me, and you will have taken the fee to pay the proprietor of this cremation ground!"

Hariścandra looked at her and said, "I am sorry. My dharma does not allow me to take gold from a dead body, especially a dead woman. To kill a woman and then take the gold from that body: that is not my dharma! You must think of some other way."

Śaivyā began to cry, "What fruit of karma brought us to this position? What karma puts me in such a circumstance? Look at my son, Great Prince, Rohitaśva, lying dead on a funeral pyre. Where is the whisk that used to fan him? Where now is the umbrella that used to stand over his head to protect him from the sun, the wind or the rain, the insignia of his royalty? Where is the Great King Hariścandra, the most honorable of all men, who never told a lie? Where is he at this time of adversity, to help his family out of this difficulty?"

When Hariścandra heard the cries of his intended victim, he looked at her very carefully and asked, "Hariścandra? What do you know of Hariścandra? Where did you hear the name Hariścandra?"

Śaivyā said, "Hariścandra, the Greatest King among Kings; the most truthful and honorable man to set foot on this earth? Hariścandra is my husband!"

When Hariścandra heard those words, he was amazed. And he said with incredulousness, "You are Śaivyā, the Queen of Ayodhyā?"

The queen looked at him in amazement. "How did you know my name? Cāṇḍālā, please tell me, how did you know my name?"

The cāṇḍālā replied, "Because I am that very man, the King Hariścandra!"

The queen looked at him, covered with the garlands of dead bodies, the cāṇḍālā of the cremation grounds, and she fainted. When she regained consciousness she said, "You? The cāṇḍālā of the cremation grounds? You are the King Hariścandra, the most noble and honorable amongst men? Oh, what has fate brought to our family? My son is dead, and I am about to executed. The great and noble King Hariścandra has been reduced to the state of a cāṇḍālā, burning dead bodies in the cremation grounds? Why have the Gods put us to such a test?"

Then Hariścandra thought, "Come, my Queen. This is enough. Let us light the pyre for our son, Rohitaśva, and we, too, will follow him to the heavens. Let us join him in leaving this world."

Hariścandra began to light the fire, when Viśvāmitra came and said, "Oh Cāṇḍālā, what are you preparing to do?"

Hariścandra replied, "My wife and I shall now enter the funeral pyre. I have paid my debts. I owe no one. What pain our life has become, no one can know. Now we shall ascend to our final rest."

Viśvāmitra said, "All throughout your life you never renounced truth. Now, even in the face of the greatest adversity you remain stedfast in your vow of truth. You will sacrifice your life before you sacrifice truth! Vasiṣṭha was right. You are a man who has remained One with truth. I accept my defeat from the Great Guru, Vasiṣṭha. I return to you your kingdom, and admit that Truth is indeed the strongest force on earth. Now, please take your leave from the cāṇḍālā."

Just then the cāṇḍālā appeared. Hariścandra looked at him and said, "Oh Cāṇḍālā, please free me now from my debt."

Then he watched as the cāṇḍālā became Lord Śiva. And Śiva said, "Yes, Hariścandra, you are free from all debts."

Then Viśvāmitra said, "Let us call the Brahmiṇ and his wife and ask to be pardoned for any debts for your wife and child."

The Brahmiṇ and his wife came, and Hariścandra said, "Please, free us from the debts of our karma."

Then he watched as the Brahmiṇ became Lord Viṣṇu and his wife became Goddess Lakṣmī. They blessed him and said, "Yes, you are all free to go."

Then Viśvāmitra said, "Now, Hariścandra, I give you my blessings and free you from all debts. I accept defeat from Vasiṣṭha. Truth is indeed the strongest force of the universe!"

Just then Vasiṣṭha came to join the assembly, and he said, "Viśvāmitra, today you have become a Brahmā Ṛṣi! Today you have exhibited the most important quality of a Brahmiṇ, compassion and forgiveness. So long as you had lived in the egotism of your own attachments, along with anger and without humility, thinking that you could control events through your own will-power, you could not become a Brahmā Ṛṣi. But by forgiving Hariścandra, you have exemplified the true quality of a true Knower of Supreme Divinity, and now I certify your attainment!"

Then the heavens parted and Indra and all the Gods came and said, "Hariścandra, you have earned an everlasting place in heaven. Come to heaven with us!"

Hariścandra said, "Oh Gods, oh Munis, oh Gurus: the power of a King comes from the people of his kingdom. You cannot seperate a King from his nation. Every righteous deed a King performs, he performs on behalf of his nation. Therefore, if I have attained any merit from any act I have performed, it is not for my personal salvation. It is for the salvation of my nation. And if you will take me to heaven, you must take my entire kingdom along with me."

Indra said, "Now wait a minute, King. That is impossible! Look at your kingdom! Some of your people are sinners, some of the people are saints; most of the people are in between. Some of them have few merits, some of them have greater merits; how can everyone go to heaven?"

Hariścandra replied, "Just take all the merits that I have obtained and divide them among my people. Instead of one man going to heaven for a long time, let us all go to heaven for one day! Give of my merits: if somebody needs a little bit of merit, let them take a little; if someone needs a lot, let them take a lot. Let them all take what they need, and we will all go to heaven for one day together."

And Indra said, "Okay, I agree to this."

Hariścandra became a King once again, and his clothing, ornaments and crown were all restored to him. Śaivyā was dressed as the Queen of Ayodhyā, and Rohitaśva was brought to life and dressed as the Crown Prince. Then the three of them mounted on an aerial car, along with Vasiṣṭha, Viśvāmitra and the Gods, and they travelled through the air to Ayodhyā. When they came down in the middle of the city, the ministers came running out from the palace. The whole city came together to greet the King, and with such joy they welcomed the royal family.

The King asked, "All right my family of the nation: who wants to go to heaven? Anyone can come if you like to go to heaven for a day. Finish all of your affairs, pack your bags, clean up all your old karma, and come along!"

And some of the citizens said, "I can't leave my attachments!" And other citizens said, "YES! That is a great idea! Let's go!" And some others said, "I have so many possessions that I don't want to leave."

So everyone who so desired, put their affairs in order, and gave away their house and property to whomever they wanted, and they gave away their businesses to whomever they wanted, and they took care to complete all of their affairs. Then the King Hariścandra, along with his wife and child and all the citizens of his kingdom who so desired, ascended to heaven, where they spent a day in the Bliss of Infinite Consciousness.

## The Story of Gaṅgā

On the Full Moon Night of the Month of Kārttik, Rādhā and Kṛṣṇa, along with the Gopis, Gods and Goddesses, Yakṣas, Kinnaras, Gandharvas, and Apsaras, all engaged in the Rāsa Līlā, the divine dance and drama of immortal nectar. When Sarasvatī sang her beautiful song, Brahmā became so delighted that he offered some jewels and gems to her, and likewise Mahādeva and Kṛṣṇa and all the Gods and Goddesses made presentations to her in thanks for the beautiful song that she sang.

Then Brahmā requested, "Śiva, would you please sing us a song?"

When Śiva began to sing, everyone became enraptured by the sweet quality of his music. The song was so enchanting that Rādhā and Kṛṣṇa merged together in rāsa, they became so filled with nectar, that their union took a liquid form and became known as Gaṅgā. Gaṅgā was born from the union of the Rāsa of Śri Kṛṣṇa and Rādhā.

Gaṅgā grew up into a beautiful young lady, and she was very lovely. One day, when she saw Kṛṣṇa sitting by himself, Gaṅgā became very amorous, and sat down beside him. Being filled with desire, she looked at him coyly, with so much love and desire in her eyes. Just at that time Rādhā came there with all her attendants. She walked right up to her place beside Kṛṣṇa, looked with angry red eyes at Gaṅgā, who immediately got up, and then she took her seat.

She said, "Kṛṣṇa, we are women. We are naturally simple, and even-tempered by nature. Why are you exciting this young girl to passion and lust? I have seen you do it many times before, and I'm not going to stand for it any more! I saw you in union with Virājā, She who is Free from Passion or Attachment. When She who is Free from Passion or Attachment was making love to you, Consciousness was in union without attachment.

"But when you heard me coming to see you in union with your beloved, out of shame you ran away, and Virājā quit her body and became a river, which even to this day flows near Jagganāth, Puri.

"When I went back home, you went again to Virājā, and called her, 'Oh Virājā, Oh Free from Passion or Attachment!' And hearing your voice she came out of the river to assume her divine form again. And you united with her and gave her your seed, and from that seed was born Sāgar, the Ocean.

"Another day I saw you in Union with Śobhā, Radiance. And when you saw me coming, again you fled. Śobhā, Radiance, also out of shame, quit her body and went to live with the Moon. That is why the Moon has Radiance. And then you divided her radiance and gave some of it to gems and jewels, some to gold, some to precious stones, some to the faces of beautiful women, some to the bodies of kings.

"I saw you again in union with Prabhā, Lustre. Also out of shame, Prabhā left her body when you ran away. Then you divided her nature and gave some of her qualities to fire, some to the Gods, some to the Sun, some to lions and some to men.

"One time I saw you making love to Śānti, Peace. Oh Kṛṣṇa, Divine Consciousness, you were so absorbed in Union with Peace, enjoying yourself to the utmost. But when you heard the sound of my footsteps coming, I saw you run away. Śānti, too, quit her body out of shame, which you divided and distributed some to the forest, some to Infinite Consciousness, some to the Divine Mother, some to the sādhus, the pure sattvic beings, and some to Dharma.

"Another time I saw you in union with Kṣāmā, Patience or Forgiveness. You didn't even notice me coming, and when I came, I saw the two of you in union together. Your body turned black with shame. Kṣāmā also quit her body, and you divided her among the dharmic and religious persons, and among the Gods, ṛṣis and sādhus.

"Now I fully understand what you are intending to do with this young girl, Gaṅgā! I do not agree to this type of behavior! To think that you would act like this in our own home, no less! You are constantly flirting with every female who comes by. You have no respect, no shame! You do everything in your power to incur my wrath. And now in my anger, I am going to swallow up this Gaṅgā in one sip!"

When Gaṅgā understood how Rādhā might manifest her anger, She took refuge at the feet of Śrī Kṛṣṇa. She withdrew all the waters of the three worlds into His feet, and hid there. Immediately all the waters of the entire earth, the heavens and the atmosphere became dry. Everyone became thirsty. There was no water anywhere. All the waters were with Gaṅgā hiding in the feet of Kṛṣṇa.

Then all the people of the earth were extremely thirsty. They cried out to the Gods in their agony, "Please save us! The Earth Herself is parched from lack of water. All the plants, animals, all living beings on the earth, all that is, needs water. Please help us!"

The Gods came to Rādhā and Kṛṣṇa and sang a great hymn of praise. Hearing the supplications of the Gods, Rādhā and Kṛṣṇa asked of them, "What is your difficulty?"

Quickly the Gods responded, "Where is Gaṅgā? Without Gaṅgā we shall all perish from thirst. Even at this very time, all life on the earth is crying out for water. Please, if you know why Gaṅgā is hiding, reveal her hiding place and the cause of her withdrawal. We will quickly remove her every adversity, so that She will once again nourish the hearts of creation."

Kṛṣṇa replied, "Gaṅgā is hiding in my feet for fear from Rādhā's anger. Tell Rādhā not to be angry with her, and I am sure that she will come out to solve your difficulties."

Brahmā said, "Rādhā, you are Gaṅgā's mother. You cannot harm your own daughter. Please let her come to nourish creation. We will give her to Nārāyaṇa as his wife, and she will also marry Śiva. She can also marry Sāgar, the Ocean, and in every way we will keep her away from your Kṛṣṇa. But please, you must consent to let her come out of hiding. Without Gaṅgā we shall all perish!"

Rādhā agreed, but Gaṅgā was still afraid to see the anger in her face. Then Brahmā put his kamandalu, the mendicant's water pot, just beside Kṛṣṇa's feet, and Gaṅgā came out from her hiding place and directly filled up his water pot.

Brahmā took that water pot to Nārāyaṇa and said, "Nārāyaṇa, Gaṅgā is a most beautiful Devī. I saved her from the wrath of Rādhā's jealousy. She has come here of her own accord to seek refuge with you, so please marry her according to the rules of the Gandharva form of marriage."

Nārāyaṇa was very pleased to accept Gaṅgā as his wife. Then they spent much time together in happy enjoyment.

So Lakṣmī, Sarasvatī and Gaṅgā were the three wives of Nārāyaṇa, representing the three guṇas or qualities of Nature in union with Consciousness. Lakṣmī is pure and peaceful Sattva; Sarasvatī, firey and aggressive Rajas; and Gaṅgā, foolish and docile Tamas. All were equally loved and all were equally close to Hari, and all existed together in the same house in harmony.

But one day Gaṅgā looked amorously at her husband, Nārāyaṇa, with a smile on her lips. When Nārāyaṇa saw this, he was startled, and he smiled back at her. Lakṣmī saw this incident, but didn't take any offense. Sarasvatī, however, being firey by nature, became extremely angry. She began to shake all over, and in many ways her anger became known.

Lakṣmī, who is of pure and peaceful quality, began to console Sarasvatī in many ways, but the rajas of Sarasvatī could not be appeased. Her face became red, and she trembled with feelings of passion. She began to scold Nārāyaṇa. She gave him such a tongue-lashing for his behavior.

When Nārāyaṇa had received the brunt of Sarasvatī's rebuke, he paused for a moment, and, realizing that this was not the appropriate time to give an answer, he went outside to let the matter cool down.

When Nārāyaṇa left the room, Sarasvatī became fearless, and becoming abusive she called Gaṅgā names and proclaimed, "I will destroy your pride today!"

With much anger she rose and grabbed Gaṅgā by the hair and started to pull at her, trying to strike her. Lakṣmī intervened to try to stop the fighting, and Sarasvatī became violent and cursed Lakṣmī: "Seeing the inappropriate behavior of this shrew, you are standing by like a tree saying nothing in my defence, or with your wishy-washy way, like a river with no course of your own, you are not speaking out to right this injustice; I curse you! You go down to earth and become a tree and a river!"

The Sattva Lakṣmī didn't say anything in reply. She held

Sarasvatī's hands and remained silent. But the foolish Gaṅgā became charged with anger. Her lips began to quiver seeing the fiery nature of the red-eyed Sarasvatī, and Gaṅgā cursed her in return. "You, too, become a river and go to the earth, to the abodes of men, and wash away their heaps of sins."

Receiving the curse of Gaṅgā, Sarasvatī also replied with another curse to Gaṅgā: "You, too, go to the earth and become a river, washing away all the sins of humanity!"

When Nārāyaṇa returned into the room, he found that his three wives had all been cursed by each other, and he said to them: "Obviously the world is needing you now, and you should all go and incarnate on earth. When by taking one wife a man does not become happy, imagine how painful it must be to have many wives. When the house is full of quarrels, where will a man go to seek his peace? The forest is better for him than his own house. The pains of disease or venom are bearable, but the words of a quarrelsome wife are hard to bear. Those who are under the control of the moods of their wives, will never find any peace until they leave the body. I am in no need of many wives. Gaṅgā, you go become the wife of Śiva. Sarasvatī, you go and marry with Brahmā. Let the Sattva Lakṣmī stay here with me. He who has a chaste and obedient wife will attain peace and prosperity, will fulfill his Dharma and attain to Liberation. One man with one wife will be the natural way of peace and harmony. Many wives will be a burden to all."

Then Nārāyaṇa called Brahmā, and said, "Brahmā, you brought Gaṅgā here to be my wife. This is your responsibility. Now I am sending her to Śiva. Please take her back and give her to Śiva."

Gaṅgā got back into Brahmā's kamandelu, and Brahmā took her with him.

## Kapila Muni curses Sāgar's sons

Virāja's son, Sāgar, grew into one of the strongest Kings of Ayodhyā. He had dominion over the entire earth. One time, when he was performing the Aśvamedha Horse Sacrifice, Indra came and stole the horse. Sāgar's sons immediately chased after him.

Indra fled with the stolen horse, and left it tied to the gate of Kapila Muni's aśrama. When Sāgar's sons reached the aśrama, they found the stolen horse tied to the gate. Entering inside the aśrama, they began to abuse Kapila Muni: "Why did you steal our father's horse? You have disrupted the sacrifice, which is certainly not the conduct befitting a Brahmiṇ. Now we shall punish you and take back our father's horse."

Kapila Muni became very angry and said, "I didn't steal your father's horse! Why are you barging into my aśrama and disturbing my meditation? I don't know anything about your horse!"

The boys said, "That is a highly unlikely story, Muniji! Here is the horse right here. Now we are going to punish you. Not only are you a thief, but you're also a liar! Here you are caught with the stolen horse, and still you deny any knowledge! Certainly you will be punished severely for this misbehavior!"

Kapila Muni said, "You doubt the word of a Brahmiṇ! I said 'I didn't steal your horse!' I told you, 'I know nothing about your horse,' and still you are insulting me and insisting on punishing me? You are not believing the word of a Brahmiṇ? I curse you!"

He picked up some water in his hand and he pronounced the curse, and throwing the water at the boys, all the sixty thousand sons of Sāgar were immediately turned into ashes.

When Sāgar heard the news of the death of his sons, he

began to cry. Leaving his sacrifice, he retired into the forest to do tapasya. After some time Brahmā came to give him darśana, and asked Sāgar why he was practicing tapasya.

Sāgar inquired, "How can I be reunited with my sons?"

Brahmā said, "You will take birth as the ocean, and when Gaṅgā comes to the earth, she will marry you. When she rushes forward to mix her waters with yours, she will pass the spot where the ashes of your sons now lie. Being touched by her purifying waters, the souls of your sons will attain salvation, and the remains of their ashes will be brought to you in the sea."

Sāgar was extremely pleased with this news, and he began to perform even greater tapasya in order to ask Gaṅgā to come to the earth. He was not successful in his lifetime, and leaving his human form, Sāgar took birth as the ocean.

His successor, Anśuman, continued the tapasya to bring Gaṅgā to the earth, but he, too, was unable to complete that objective. Anśuman was followed by Dīlip. Dīlip, too, performed tapasya for the same purpose, but he, too, was unsuccessful. Dīlip's son was Bhagiratha, who also performed tapasya to bring Gaṅgā down to the earth.

He stood on his one foot, reciting Gaṅgā's mantras throughout thousands of years. Oblivious to the rain, wind, sleet or snow, Bhagiratha continued his discipline without fail. Daily he used to recite the excellent hymn of praise to Gaṅgā, which was composed by Nārāyaṇa himself, with intense devotion:

शिवसङ्गीतसम्मुग्धश्रीकृष्णाङ्गसमुद्भवाम् ।
राधाङ्गद्रवसंयुक्तां तां गङ्गां प्रणमाम्यहम् ॥ १

**śivasaṅgītasammugdha śrīkṛṣṇāṣaṅga samudbhavām I**
**rādhāṅga dravasaṃyuktāṃ tāṃ gaṅgāṃ praṇamāmyaham II**

Enchanted by the singing of Śiva, Śrī Kṛṣṇa and Rādhā were bathing in the perspiration of their union. To that Gaṅgā born of that sweat, I bow down in obeisance.

यज्जन्म सृष्टेरादौ च गोलोके रासमण्डले ।

सन्निधाने शङ्करस्य तां गङ्गां प्रणमाम्यहम् ॥ २

**yajjanma sṛṣṭerādau ca goloke rāsamaṇḍale I**
**sannidhāne śaṅkarasya tāṃ gaṅgāṃ praṇamāmyaham II**
Whose birth took place at Rādhā's festival of sentiments (Rāsa) in the regions of Light, who always resides with Śaṅkara, to that Gaṅgā I bow down in obeisance.

Brahmā was so pleased with Bhagiratha's devotion that he came and awarded the desired boon. Gaṅgā will come down to the earth and wash away the sins of man. But She will come down to the earth with such force that she will wash away the earth itself. Brahmā said, "Call upon Lord Śiva to marry with Gaṅgā. From that union he will be able to take some of the force away from her so that her falling to the earth will not destroy the creation."

Then Bhagiratha began a great tapasya for Lord Śiva, and after thousands of years Śiva was pleased and gave the vision to grant the boon. "Śiva, please take Gaṅgā as your wife. Unite with her and take away her force so that she does not destroy creation."

Śiva agreed to marry her and to take her waters onto his own head in order to let them come down to earth at a lessor speed. Then Gaṅgā could fall to earth without washing away all of creation.

Then Brahmā said to Gaṅgā, "Everything is arranged. You will marry Śiva, as Nārāyaṇa has spoken. Also you will have to go down to earth and wash away the sins of men, according to the curse of Sarasvatī. Then you will unite with Sāgar, the ocean, and together you will purify and nourish the earth."

"But," objected Gaṅgā. "If I go down to earth to wash away the sins of men, then my waters will become polluted.

Certainly I will become foul and an object of hatred and scorn for all. If I purify the sins of men, who will purify me?"

Then Brahmā thought for a moment and replied, "As many sādhus and pure souls who come to your banks and sing the names of the Divine Mother, or of Kṛṣṇa or Rāma or Śiva, or any other names of the divine, their divine chanting will purify your waters and make them the object of the greatest respect. In fact no pūjā will be complete without the offering of your waters. No matter where worship is being performed, your presence will be invoked."

Then Gaṅgā was very happy, and she agreed to Brahmā's arrangements.

### Bāli and the Vāmaṇ Āvatār

Once upon a time there was an aśura named Bāli. He was an extremely Dharmic and truthful man, even though he was an aśura and a representative of the forces of duality. He observed the code of ethics and stood by his word with the steadfastness of truth and honor.

At this time he was making the sacrifice by which he would become Lord of the Earth. He was doing a great tapasya which was frightening to all of the Gods, and all of the Gods assembled together and said, "If Bāli becomes the Lord of the earth, then he will make everyone on earth neglect us Gods and worship the forces of division. We must do something to stop this tapasya. You know Śiva. You know Brahmā; even Viṣṇu is liable to give him the boon of his choice if he does not waver in his sādhana. We must find a way to disrupt this yajña, and to make sure his worship is without fruit."

The Gods went to Vaikuṇṭha, the home of Lord Viṣṇu. After singing a great hymn of praise to Lord Viṣṇu, the Gods said, "Oh Lord, Bāli is doing a yajña by which he can become the Lord of the earth. We must find a way to stop him. If he is successful, he will teach mankind not to worship the Gods, and he won't stop until everyone is so tangled up in the webs of karma, that they will all say, 'Who has time for worship or meditation?' Please help us Lord."

Viṣṇu thought for a moment and then replied, "I've got an idea. Certainly I can put a stop to the threat of Bāli's taking over the earth. Gods, I shall help you in your purpose."

Bāli was sitting by the sacrificial fire, offering the mantras by which he could attain his desired objective. Viṣṇu assumed the Vāmaṇ Āvatār, the form of a dwarf. He was dressed as a Brahmiṇ, wearing a mālā of sacred beads around his neck. He was shining with the light of tapasya, radiant with light. And he walked into the sacrificial area beside the blazing fire.

Everyone was completely amazed. The light of the little dwarf was even greater than that which emanated from the sacred fire. When Bāli saw the radiance of the guest who had come to bless his sacrifice, in majestic tones he welcomed the dwarf and thanked him for giving the blessing of his presence. "Ask me for a boon," he submitted in kingly fashion.

The dwarf, Vāmaṇ, replied, "I am so pleased with the devotion you are showing in this sacrifice. I have every intention of blessing you with the highest attainment. You see, I am a poor Brahmiṇ, and I need a piece of land of my own where I can maintain my body. Though this body is small, whenever I want to sit to perform some great tapasya, some - one might come along and cause me to vacate the space which I have been occupying. Oh King, if you would like to grant me one boon, then please give me a little space to keep my body."

The King Bāli replied, "I am the King of the nation, ruler of the largest lands and estates. When I complete this sacrifice, I am going to be the Lord of the Earth. I will have at my command villages, towns, cities, countries. Yes, even nations obey my every order. You choose any amount of land that you want, and I shall grant it to you for sure!"

Then the Vāmaṇ Āvatār thought for a moment and said, "Oh King, you can see that I am not a very large man. Really I am quite small. I am a Brahmiṇ, and my karma makes me meditative, and I only want to practice tapasya. I don't have the temperament to be the chief of a village, or to run the administration of a town, or even to govern cities or states, not to think of nations or empires. I just want enough land so I can sit in my asāna in meditation without being disturbed! Oh King, please give me that much land as my foot covers three times. I ask you for three steps of land."

The King said, "Holy Brahmiṇ, I am the Ruler of nations, about to become the Lord of the entire earth, ask for villages for your sustenance, ask for great tracks of land for your aśrama, ask for cities for your devotees, you can have whole areas of mountains, lakes, fields, blooming with the abundance of nature! What will you do with three steps of land?"

"Please excuse me, King. I just need a place to put my body. I am not concerned with storing up treasures for the future. I am a Brahmiṇ. My only job is to worship God, not to run countries or cities of men. Now, if you want to grant me my wish, allow me to pace off three steps of land, and that will be my place."

The King went to his minister to seek his advice. He said, "Minister, a Brahmiṇ has come, radiant with a shining aura. I asked him to choose a boon from me, and he asked for three steps of land to call his own, so he could do tapasya without fear of being disturbed. I told him to take a whole village or even many villages, or any amount he liked. He replied that he is a Brahmiṇ and he wants to do tapasya. He does not want to be burdened with administration of other people's lives, he is not a tax-collector, nor a banker, nor a politician. All he wants is a space of his own where no one has the right to disturb him in his meditation. What do you think?"

The Minister replied, "Don't trust him. There is something funny about all of this. No one has controlled his greed to such an extent. Don't do it!"

The King said, "I already gave my word that I would give him any amount of land that he would like, and I am bound by that promise. If I don't fulfill my promise, and if I turn out to be a liar, I will lose all the merits that I hope to attain by this sādhana. So I am really obligated to give him the three steps of land."

The Minister said, "If you commit some sin, it is possible to make atonement. So if you commit the sin of not fulfilling the promise of your vow, then you can make atonement for it. But don't give him three steps of land! Something is not right!"

The King said, "I am very much afraid to incur the wrath of a Brahmiṇ by denying the promise that I have already given. He might curse me in his anger, and put me into a worse position then I am in right now. I think I had better give it to him."

The Minister took his leave with great reluctance.

The King returned to the Brahmiṇ and said, "Okay, radiant Brahmiṇ. I concede your wish. Choose the three steps of land as you desire."

Suddenly the dwarf form of Lord Viṣṇu began to grow in immensity until his foot covered the entire earth. And he said, "This is my first step. All the earth belongs to me."

He kicked his foot up into the air, and that foot permeated the furthest reaches of the heavens. And he said, "This is my second step. All the heavens belong to me."

And he turned to the King Bāli and said, "Oh King, with my first step all the earth belonged to me. With my second step all the heavens belonged to me. Where else is remaining for me to put my third step? What is left for me to claim as my own?"

Bāli, the King, bowed to the feet of Lord Viṣṇu and pointing to the top of his own head said, "Right here, my Lord. Please put your foot on my head."

Then Viṣṇu put his foot on Bāli's head, and that, too, became the property of the Lord.

Well, when Viṣṇu's foot went up through the heavens and went through to the other side of infinity, Brahmā was sitting up there in his residence in the Satya Loka. He was contemplating and singing the Vedas, when suddenly the foot came right up through the edge of infinity, and entered into the Satya Loka, whereupon Brahmā exclaimed, "Oh my Goodness! It's Viṣṇu's foot! What a wonderful blessing!" And he took his kamandelu filled with the waters of Gaṅgā, and began to pour those pure waters over Viṣṇu's foot in an offering of hospitality which is the duty of any householder. As he washed Viṣṇu's foot, the waters came dripping down, and Gaṅgā took flight through the cosmos.

She came off from Viṣṇu's feet and she started to gain velocity in her trip down to the earth. She passed by the seven ṛṣis who were meditating in the heavens, the constellation of the Big Dipper: Vasiṣṭha, Viśvāmitra, Gautam, Bharadvādja, Atri, Jamadagni and Kaśyapa. She washed past all of them, and none of the ṛṣis could slow down her force. She kept on coming with such speed that they all feared they would be washed away by her, so they sent her over to Drūva, the North Star or Pole Star.

Drūva exclaimed in terror, "Help! I can't stop the force of that rushing water!"

By now Gaṅgā was falling at tremendous velocity, and she was so strong everyone ran from her path in terror. "She will wash away anything in her way. No one can stop Gaṅgā!"

They all began to pray, "Śiva, please take Gaṅgā as your wife. Unite with her, and take away the force of her power. Then send her down to the earth in a nice way, so she doesn't create any harm."

Then Śiva assented, "Okay, I'll come and save the universe."

Fearlessly he took his seat right in the middle of Gaṅgā's path, and let her fall right onto his head. Hitting his head, the force was broken, and she spilled over and came down to the earth in order to fulfill the blessing given to Bhagiratha. That is why one of her names is Bhagirathi.

Gliding over the earth, she washed all of the sins of men away. In her course down from the mountains, she nourished and purified the earth. As she crossed the plains and wandered across the great land of Bhārat, the Land where the Light of Wisdom always Shines, she came across the ashes of the sixty thousand sons of Sāgar, the Ocean, who were burned to death by the curse of Kapila Muni. As soon as her purifying waters touched those ashes, all the souls of those sons were liberated, and rose up into heaven. Gaṅgā picked up the ashes of those sons and carried them to the Ocean.

When the Ocean saw that Gaṅgā was coming and carrying the ashes of all his departed sons, his heart leapt with joy! He was so happy. He remembered the boon he had received of being able to marry with Gaṅgā, and he accepted his beloved wife and allowed her to mix her waters with his in loving embrace.

## Vedavatī Curses Rāvaṇa

Pulastya Muni had a son named Viśravas. Jayā and Vijayā took their third incarnation as the sons of Viśravas and his wife Keśinī. They were known by the names of Rāvaṇa and Kumbhakarṇa. They had a third brother named Vibhīṣaṇa, who was dharmic by nature and a great devotee of the Lord.

The three brothers went off to perform severe austerities, to propitiate the Lord Brahmā for the attainment of powers. At last Brahmā came and advised them to request boons. Rāvaṇa was granted ten heads, so he would be invincible to the Gods, and he could become the ruler over the earth and heaven. Kumbhakarṇa desired Indra's seat on the throne of heaven, but Indra prayed to the Goddess Sarasvatī to please sit on his tongue, and in the place of Indra's seat, he requested Nidrā's seat, meaning he will always remain asleep. At Rāvaṇa's request, Brahmā allowed that Kumbhakarṇa could be awakened for one day, and then he would go back to sleep again. Vibhīṣaṇa asked for eternal devotion to the feet of Rāma.

With the strength of these boons, the demons took over the rule of heaven and earth. Rāvaṇa commanded his forces to oppress the followers of dharma, and the demon armies subdued all the Gods, ṛṣis and sādhus and made all subservient to the throne of Laṅkā. Then Rāvaṇa took all the treasures of the three worlds for himself, and took pride in causing pain to all who followed the path of truth. The very name Rāvaṇa means "To cause to cry."

The King Hrasvaroman had a son named Kuśadvaja. The Goddess Lakṣmī herself took birth in his house and was named Vedavatī, the Embodiment of Wisdom. When Vedavatī became a young lady, she took blessings from her father, Kuśadvaja, and went into the forest to perform tapasya. She chanted divine mantras with the most sincere devotion, and became beautiful with the radiant aura of her austerities.

One day Rāvaṇa saw the beautiful Vedavatī and became stricken by passion. He grabbed her by her arm and proudly said, "I am Rāvaṇa, the Causer of Sorrow to the Gods! I am the Ruler of heaven and earth, and the Possessor of all things beautiful. Therefore, you come with me to become an ornament of my palace."

Vedavatī replied in anguish, "Sinner! I am a pure woman, and cannot be made the object of your lust. You have defiled my body with your impure touch. Thus I cannot bear to wear this contaminated body any longer. But I promise that I will return to become the cause of your destruction!"

So saying, Vedavatī dissolved her body in the fire of meditation, as did Satī leave her body before Dakṣa's yajña.

The evil King Rāvaṇa demanded exorbitant taxes from all the citizens of the universe. Even the Gods sent a tribute of taxes to Laṅkā. Then Rāvaṇa sent messengers to the ṛṣis telling them to pay their taxes. The ṛṣis replied that they owned no property, and therefore were unable to pay. Rāvaṇa still demanded his taxes, whereupon the ṛṣis declared that the only thing they had which is their own is their blood. Therefore, they slit their bodies and extracted blood to send to the King. They put all of the blood into a container, which they gave to Rāvaṇa, and Rāvaṇa left the container in the custody of his wife Mandodarī. He instructed his wife not to eat of the contents of that container as it contains poison, but out of curiosity she disobeyed her husband and tasted the blood of the ṛṣis. Immediately she became pregnant and gave birth to a baby girl. Fearing her husband's anger, she placed the new-born child back into the container from which she had taken the blood.

Hearing of the ṛṣis' curse that "This blood will cause desolation to the country wherever it is kept," Rāvaṇa sent the container to be buried in the Land of Mithilā, in order to cause the destruction of King Janaka, an ardent upholder of dharma. The box was buried in a field in Janaka's land, and severe drought ensued in the land. The citizens suffered great hard - ships due to want for water, and the Brahmiṇs instructed the King to perform a yajña in order to bring the rain. During the yajña the King plowed a field to the chanting of vedic mantras, and while the bullocks were pulling the plow, the plow head (Sīt) became lodged in some strong solid substance beneath the surface. When the ministers uncovered the obstruction, they found the container which housed the infant child. Thereafter, Janaka named the girl Sītā, She who has manifested from the Sīt, and taking the baby home, he raised her as his own.

Meanwhile, all of creation cried out for a deliverer from the oppression of Rāvaṇa.

## Nārada's Curse

One day Nārada was roaming in the Himalayas, when he came upon a beautiful stream. The sight of the mountains and the rivers, the forests of trees, filled him with inspiration and he sat down and began to meditate upon the Lord. Fearing that the celestial sage was about to usurp his authority, Indra sent the God of Love along with his accomplices to try to disturb the meditating muni. The God of Love tried with his every capacity to excite the mind of the meditating muni, but Nārada was so deeply attuned that he could not be disturbed.

Recognizing his defeat, the God of Love fell at Nārada's feet and begged forgiveness. Nārada, who was undisturbed by the matter, gave his blessings, and Love returned to heaven to tell Indra and all the Gods about what happened. Everyone in heaven was amazed and all praised the sage and Lord Viṣṇu upon whom he was meditating.

Thereafter, Nārada went to see Lord Śiva, and told him all about this experience of defeating Love. Śiva replied, "This is wonderful that you have told me, Nārada, but don't ever let Viṣṇu hear of this incident."

Nārada assented and took his leave.

It was sometime after this occasion, when Nārada happened to meet Lord Viṣṇu. Viṣṇu inquired about Nārada's adventures and what was new in his life. And without thinking or remembering the words of Lord Śiva, Nārada proceeded to narrate the entire affair. Viṣṇu immediately apprehended that pride had welled up in Nārada's heart. No one can defeat Love, except Śiva. One may win a small battle, but only Śiva can attain to victory. Then Viṣṇu thought, "I must root out this egotism from my devotee's heart." Then the Lord set his Māyā into operation.

King Sīlanidhi had a beautiful daughter named Viśvamohinī. One day Nārada went to visit the King, where - upon the King introduced this beautiful daughter to Nārada and asked, "What will be her future?"

The sage looked at the girl and understood, "Whoever will wed this girl shall become immortal. He will be adored by all creation for all time." Then Nārada told the King that the girl is nice and her future will be Okay.

Nārada left and he thought, "I must devise some plan by which this girl will choose me as her husband. I know! I will ask Lord Viṣṇu to make me the most handsome man. I will go to her Svayambara with Viṣṇu's blessing, and surely Viśvamohinī will choose me."

Nārada went to Vaikuṇṭha and sang a hymn of praise to Lord Viṣṇu. Viṣṇu said, "You seem to be somewhat anxious, Nārada. What is the cause of this disruption of your peace?"

"Lord Viṣṇu," answered Nārada. "I have fallen in love with a beautiful princess. She is to be married soon, and I have come to get your blessings so that I will be the most handsome man at her Svayambara, and Viśvamohinī will certainly choose me. Please grant me the most beautiful appearance."

"Didn't you defeat Love just the last time we spoke? Now you are wanting a special boon to win a bride? Okay, I grant you the boon. You will have the most distinctive appearance of all the suitors at the Svayambara." So saying, Viṣṇu turned Nārada into a monkey.

Nārada was sure he was the most handsome man, and most confidently he strode into the Svayambara Hall. He was sure that the princess would choose him. After all, he did receive the boon from the Lord of the Universe.

The Princess took the wedding garland in her hands and began to walk around the room. All the Kings and princes began to beckon to her in their hearts. Nārada sat up straight and tall, so proud of the beauty with which he had been blessed, sure that the Princess would choose him. The Princess came before him, and much to Nārada's surprise, she turned her eyes away in disgust, and walked on to choose another.

Nārada was stunned with amazement. "How could she have passed me up? Certainly I am the most beautiful man present. Who else has received Viṣṇu's blessings?" Just then he heard two servants of Lord Śiva laughing behind him. "How could that monkey hope to be chosen as a suitable bridegroom?" they laughed.

"What monkey?" questioned Nārada somewhat doubtfully.

They laughed even harder. "You, Monkey! Don't you know what you look like? Go look at yourself in a mirror."

Nārada rushed outside and ran to see his reflection in the pond. Anger pulsed through his veins when he realized Viṣṇu's trick. He picked up some water into the palm of his hand and held it aloft. "So you want to humble my pride by making me a fool? Viṣṇu I curse you! As you have made me bereft of my wife today, you too, will know the pain of separation from your wife! As you have made a fool of me by making me look like a monkey, you will have to seek the assistance of monkeys in achieving your purpose, and monkeys will become your best friends!"

Accepting Nārada's curse, Viṣṇu withdrew his Māyā. When Nārada realized that he had been the victim of Māyā, he was filled with remorse. Viṣṇu, however, reassured him, and Nārada left for the Satya Loka praising God.

## Rāma

In days of old, when Svāyambhuva Manu had reached his fourth stage of life, he and his wife Satarūpā went to the forest to practice austerities. They performed severe disciplines for a long period of time, whereupon Lord Viṣṇu was pleased with them. He appeared before them and instructed them to ask a boon. They requested the Lord to incarnate on this earth as their son, and the Lord agreed.

In his next life Svāyambhuva Manu incarnated as Kaśyapa Muni, the Father of Creation, and his wife Satarūpā became Aditi, the Mother of the Gods. From the God of the Sun, through the generations of Ikṣvāku, the Kings of the Solar Dynasty reigned in Ayodhyā. Bhagiratha's son was Raghu, the King of Ayodhyā for whom the Family of Raghu is named. Raghu's son was Ambriṣa, and Ambriṣa's son was Ajā. Then Daśaratha followed as the King of Ayodhyā. Daśaratha was the incarnation of Svāyambhuva Manu, and his first wife, Kausalyā, the manifestation of Satarūpā.

Meanwhile, all creation was praying for the Lord to take birth in order to rid the world of evil. The Gods went to Vaikuṇṭha and prayed for Lord Viṣṇu to manifest. They reminded the Lord of the Worlds of Bhṛgu Muni's words, "'Viṣṇu, I curse you! Again and again, whenever righteousness recedes before unrighteousness on this earth, whenever dharma becomes weak while adharma is strong, then you will have to incarnate in the womb of woman, to be born upon this earth, to fight with the forces of iniquity, and once again establish the standards of morality and piety by which humanity is distinguished from the other animals!' Lord, we are extremely pained by the behavior of Rāvaṇa. The earth can no longer bear his burden of sin. Rāvaṇa has won the boon that he is invincible to all except for men and apes. You had promised Svāyambhuva Manu and his wife

Satarūpā that you will become their son. They have already taken birth as the King of Ayodhyā, Daśaratha and his wife Kausalyā. You please take birth as their son, while we Gods will assume the forms of monkeys and bears in order to help in your divine task."

Lord Viṣṇu agreed, and all the Gods prepared to assist him in their various roles.

Daśaratha had two other lovely queens, Sumitrā and Kaikeyī. Desiring children, the King requested Ṛṣi Śṛngī to perform the yajña of Atharva Veda which produced a pot of sweet rice pudding. This pudding was shared among the three queens, and they all became pregnant. Kausalyā gave birth to the noble Rāma first. Then Kaikeyī gave birth to Bharat and Sumitrā gave birth to Lakṣman and Śatrughna.

The four sons grew up in the palace filled with joy and love, and completed their education in the hermitage of Guru Vasiṣṭha. Returning from their studies as grown men, the Muni Viśvāmitra requested Daśaratha to send his two sons Rāma and Lakṣman to help protect his sacrifice from the oppression of Rāvaṇa's forces. Daśaratha tried his best to dissuade the ṛṣi from taking the two young men who were as yet inexperienced on the field of battle, but Viśvāmitra insisted. Then Rāma and Lakṣman followed the muni into the forest where they killed Taḍakā, a cannibal demon who had troubled many ascetics. Rejoicing at the death of the demon, Viśvāmitra initiated Rāma into the use of many divine weapons with which he could slay the demons.

Rāma and Lakṣman protected Viśvāmitra's sacrifice by slaying Subāhu and his forces, and with one arrow sent the demon Mārīcha flying thousands of miles beyond the sea. Thereafter the two brothers followed the muni to Mithilā, the City of King Janaka, to witness the spectacle of Sītā's marriage. King Janaka had proclaimed that whoever could lift the bow of Śiva would become the husband of his daughter.

On the way to Janaka's City, Viśvāmitra told Rāma and Lakṣman the story of the descent of Gaṅgā, and Rāma redeemed Ahalyā from the curse of Ṛṣi Gautam. Gautam had cursed her to become a stone because she slept with Indra. Reaching Mithilā, the King Janaka greeted them with great respect, and gave them a fine resting place in the royal apartments. Viśvāmitra sent Rāma and Lakṣman to the royal gardens to pick fresh flowers for his worship. There in the garden Rāma saw Sītā on her way to pray in the temple of the Divine Mother, Gaurī. When Sītā saw Rāma and Rāma saw Sītā neither could think of anything else. Each recognized the other as an eternal partner. Sītā prayed to Gaurī to make Rāma her husband, while Rāma promised that there would never be another to rule his heart.

In the Svayambara Hall, the great bow of Śiva lay upon the dais in the center. Kings and princes had gathered there from all the worlds. Even Gods had come from heaven to witness the marriage of Sītā. One after another they all tried to lift the mighty bow of Śiva, but none were successful. Then Viśvāmitra gave his order to Rāma. "Rise, Rāma, lift the mighty bow, marry the princess, and put an end to the suffering of Janaka."

Rāma arose in the midst of that assembly. He lifted the bow as if it were a twig, bent the bow to fix the bow string, but with a mighty roar the bow snapped in two. Sītā came forth to garland her husband, and Lakṣman was married with Janaka's younger daughter Urmilā, while Bharat and Śatrughna were married with Janaka's nieces Māṇḍavi and Śrutakīrti.

The four sons returned to Ayodhyā along with their wives, and the entire kingdom rejoiced. Then Bharat and Śatrughna went to visit their maternal grandfather in the far off Country of Kaikeya. During their long absence, the King Daśaratha had a lengthy conversation with Ṛṣi Viśvāmitra in which the ṛṣi expounded on the duty of a parent to make the children capable, and then to quickly hand over the management of daily affairs to the children so that the parents can pursue liberation of the soul. Inspired by the ṛṣi's instructions, Daśaratha discussed the matter with Guru Vasiṣṭha, and at the Guru's direction, summoned all the citizens and tributary Kings to an assembly.

In the assembly it was unanimously voted that Rāma become the King, and Daśaratha was very pleased at the people's decision. Guru Vasiṣṭha said that the next day would be the best time in order to perform the coronation ceremonies, and that another auspicious astrological configuration would be far off. Therefore, all arrangements were made, even despite Rāma's objections as to the absence of his brothers.

Kaikeyī's maid servant, Mantharā, was dismayed by this proclamation. She thought that this decision was made purposely while Bharat was away in order to deprive him of the kingdom without his objection. Neither could she desire her mistress Kaikeyī to become the servant to her rival wife, nor could she see Bharat cheated out of his kingdom. Therefore she instigated the feeble minded Kaikeyī to scheme in conspiracy against the King's orders. Kaikeyī accepted the maid servant as her foremost well-wisher, and thus made her a guru to get the throne for Bharat.

The King had previously offered her two boons, which she had declined to accept at that time, saying that she would ask another day. Tricking the King into swearing upon an oath of his love for Rāma that he would fulfill her wishes this night, Kaikeyī asked for the throne for her son Bharat, and that Rāma be banished to the forest for fourteen years, while Bharat consolidated his power. The King was caught in a moral dilemma of whether to give up his son or to give up his truth.

In the morning when Rāma learned of this dilemma, he

immediately determined to act in such a way as to prove his father right. He would not let anything stain the glory of his beloved father. Therefore, he gave up the kingdom at a moment's notice and prepared to go to the forest. When Sītā learned that her husband was going to the forest, she, too, prepared to leave. "Wherever my husband goes, and in whatever way he lives, there I shall be by his side to serve him with all of my Love and Devotion," she said.

Hearing that suddenly Rāma and Sītā were not to be crowned as the Royal Couple of Ayodhyā, in great anger Lakṣman desired to revolt against the injustice of the King. Rāma scolded him for his misunderstanding, and requested him to stay in the palace to care for the royal family in his absence. But Mother Sumitrā sent Lakṣman to be the servant of his brother. "If your brother Rāma is in the forest," she proclaimed, "then you have no work in the palace."

So Rāma, Lakṣman and Sītā went into the forest and began to visit the ṛṣis and sādhus. There they heard the complaint about the oppressive behavior of the demons, and Rāma undertook the vow to protect all the beings of the forest. For thirteen years they roamed the pathless forests and met with saints and sages, imbibed their teachings and protected their religious rites. Wherever they went, they made war against the tyranny of evil, and destroying the demons, they made the forests safe. Rāma, Lakṣman and Sītā received the blessings of many great saints like Bharadvaja, Atri and Anasūyā, Śarbaṅga, Śabarī, Sutikṣṇā, and Agastya. There were also many others, too numerous to mention.

Meanwhile, the King Daśaratha gave up his body pining for his son, and when Bharat learned of all that had happened, he refused to accept the kingdom. He began to administer the kingdom on behalf of Rāma, until the period of exile would be over.

Dwelling in the Pañchavatī during their last year of exile,

Rāvaṇa's sister, the demon Princess Sūrpanakhā spied the hermitage of the three. She became struck by passion upon seeing Rāma, and changed herself into a beautiful form in order to seduce him. Rāma declined her invitation, as did Lakṣman as well, whereupon the insulted demon princess turned herself into an ogre and prepared to eat Sītā. Then Lakṣman cut off her nose with a broad bladed sword.

The wounded Sūrpanakhā appealed for protection to her brothers Khara and Dūṣana, who were the rulers of the bordering area. She claimed that Rāma and Lakṣman had attacked her without provocation, and that they were mounting an attack on the authority of the throne of Laṅkā. Khara and Dūṣana immediately attacked, and Rāma killed them along with their entire army.

Then Sūrpanakhā went to Laṅkā to summon the aid of Rāvaṇa. She told the King Rāvaṇa that two men were attacking his kingdom, and that along with them was a very beautiful woman who should become the adornment of Rāvaṇa's palace. At Sūrpanakhā's instigation, Rāvaṇa conspired to steal Sītā.

Rāvaṇa ordered the master magician Mārīcha, Taḍakā's son who had already tested the strength of Rāma's arrows, to assume the form of a golden deer. In this captivating form, he lured Rāma and Lakṣman from the hermitage. Seizing the opportunity, Rāvaṇa assumed the dress of an aged sannyāsi, and entered the aśrama to steal the unprotected Sītā. Rāma and Lakṣman killed the false demon in the disguise of a golden deer, and fearing they were the victims of deceit, they rushed back to find the empty hermitage.

They were roaming from forest to forest in search of Sītā when Satī came down from Kailāsa to test them. In this way they searched in many places until they came upon the demon Kabandha. Slaying the demon in a pit of fire, they liberated the Gandharva who had been cursed by the Muni Durvāsā.

Then the Gandharva directed them to Mataṅga Muni's aśrama in order to meet Mātā Śabarī.

Finding Mātā Śabarī, Rāma and Lakṣman accepted her humble hospitality, and instructed her in the way of pure devotion. Then Śabarī confided her Guru's parting words before he left his body many years before when Rāma and Lakṣman and Sītā had first arrived in Chitrakūṭa. Śabarī had asked if she could come with him, but her Guru Mataṅga Muni had replied: "Not now. Don't waste this opportunity. Rāma and Lakṣman will come here in search of Sītā. Please tell them that Hanumān and Sugrīva will help to get her back. They will be found on top of the Ṛṣyamūka Mountain." Since that time every day Śabarī had prepared for their coming. Now, taking the blessings of the Supreme Lord, she ascended to join her Guru.

Rāma and Lakṣman found the Ṛṣyamūka Mountain, met Hanumān and formed an alliance with Sugrīva. They assisted Sugrīva in winning back his kingdom, and crowned him the King of the mighty Country of Kiṣkindhā. Then the monsoon rains came and Sugrīva spent this time in consolidating his authority in the new kingdom, while Rāma and Lakṣman remained for four months on Ṛṣyamūka Mountain, thinking of Sītā and waiting for the rains to stop.

During this time Nārada came to Rāma and told him, "I know the means to insure complete success. Perform the Navarātri vow of worship in the Fall, in the month of Aśvin. Fasting for nine nights, make jāpa of the mantras of the Divine Mother and perform the Homa ceremony at the sacred fire. If you perform in this way with sincere devotion, you will certainly defeat Rāvaṇa and be reunited with Sītā."

Rāma learned the method of worship from Nārada, and observed the performance in meticulous detail. On the evening of the eighth lunar day, the Goddess Bhagavatī was pleased with his worship, and the Divine Mother made Her presence manifest and offered him boons. "Oh Rāma, you are the incarnation of the Supreme Lord. You will slay Rāvaṇa and be reunited with your wife Sītā. It is for this purpose that the Gods had requested you to incarnate in this very form. Now the purpose of divinity must be fulfilled."

Receiving the boon from the Divine Mother, Rāma sent out the armies of monkeys in the four directions to search for Mother Sītā. In the fulfillment of this purpose, Hanumān leaped across the ocean to find Sītā, and burned the golden City of Laṅkā to the ground.

Now cognizant of her whereabouts, Śrī Rāma gathered his huge army of monkeys and bears on the shores of the sea, and while the monkeys and bears built a bridge across the great ocean, Rāma worshipped Lord Śiva. Receiving Śiva's blessing, Rāma took his army across the expanse of ocean. Arriving at the fortress of the golden city, one by one Rāma and Lakṣman and the other soldiers of the monkey armies defeated the great warriors of Laṅkā. Ultimately Rāma killed Rāvaṇa, and anointed Vibhīṣaṇa the King of Laṅkā. Having freed Sītā, Rāma, Lakṣman and Sītā returned to Ayodhyā where Rāma was crowned the King.

With the reunion of the family, the entire kingdom of Ayodhyā rejoiced. Soon Sītā became pregnant, and ṛṣis and munis from the forests came to Ayodhyā to bless the royal family.

One day, it was late at night, after the King had retired, a woman came to the palace gate seeking the help of the King. The guards at the gate told her that it was late and the King and Queen had already gone to sleep. Would she please return in the morning. The lady went away, but did not return the next day.

When King Rāma heard of the incident, he wanted to know who was the lady who had been denied his assistance, and what was her problem. Had she found a resolution? "As long as the citizens are not comfortable," said Rāma, "a King has no right to sleep in comfort. It was not right to send the lady away. You should have awakened me. Now, go find that woman. Find out her problem, and find a resolution."

Rāma sent his spies throughout the kingdom to search for that woman, but he was not satisfied with the answers that they brought. Then he determined to go himself. Disguising himself as a village businessman, the King wandered from village to village to listen to the talk of the people. Everywhere among the citizens it was the same. The lady who had come to the palace had been the washerman's wife. She had gone to the market in a nearby village, but when she was coming home in the night it began to rain. The boatman told her that it was unsafe to cross the river during the rainy night, and bid her to stay the night until the rain ceased. He then took her across the river in the morning. When she arrived home, her husband was angry. "You see," he said, "this is what happens when the citizens follow the example of their King. Rāma thought nothing of taking Sītā back, even though she had lived all those months with the demon King Rāvaṇa. Now, every woman will have an excuse to stay out all night whenever she pleases, and the husbands will have nothing to say. Well, I am not a King. So far as I am concerned, if my wife stays out all night with another man, she might as well spend the rest of her life there!"

Many of the citizens agreed with the washerman. Rāma was plunged into an ocean of despair. Seeing the dejection on her husband's face when he returned, Sītā asked the cause of his difficulty. Rāma could tell her nothing, but Sītā looked deeply within and understood the entire situation. "My Husband and my King," she spoke. "A King is pledged to his people. How can you let the shame of one woman cast its shadow upon the integrity of the throne? Royalty must remain completely true in order to maintain the trust of the people. A

King who does not enjoy the people's trust has no right to occupy the throne."

"But Sītā, that woman was innocent, and she has already gone away to another country. My shame is that she was denied justice while I rested at my leisure. Besides, even if my soldiers brought her home to her husband, if the husband has no trust, could they keep the couple living together?"

"I am not talking about the washerman's wife," answered Sītā. "There is nothing more you can do for her. I am speaking of Sītā, your wife. Your attachment to me allows the citizens to doubt the integrity and the purity of the King of Ayodhyā. Look at the examples of your ancestors. Remember how generous King Śibi was:

Once the Gods appointed Indra and Agni to test his generosity. Indra assumed the form of a hawk and Agni appeared as a pigeon. The pigeon flew into the King's court and took refuge with the King, hiding in his lap for protection. The hawk followed and insisted that the pigeon was its lawful food, and without food he and his family will die. Recognizing the duty of a King to protect those who take refuge in him, King Śibi offered the hawk any other food. The hawk replied that he would only be satisfied with an equal weight of the King's flesh to serve as his meal. Then the King placed the pigeon on a scale, and began to cut pieces of his own flesh and put them on the scale to match the equal weight. But no matter how much he put, the pigeon grew heavier. Then King Śibi was about to cut off his head and to place the entire body on the scale, when Indra and Agni took their divine forms, and blessed the King and made him whole again.

"My King, look at the example of the King Hariścandra, who gave away his entire kingdom, sold his wife and child into slavery, and even became a Cāṇḍālā in the cremation grounds in order to protect his truth. Even your own father, King Daśaratha gave up his own son, his kingdom and his life in order to honor his promised word. Even you, Rāma, gave up everything to undergo extreme hardships in the forest in order to maintain your father's word. Do not let all these sacrifices be wasted. Do not destroy the reputation of the Solar Dynasty. Do not let the question of your wife's purity or the attachment to your own comfort stand in the way of your duty to your people!"

"Then what must we do, Sītā?"

"There is only one possibility, my King. I must go."

"Sītā must go? Impossible. I can give up my life, but I cannot give up my Sītā."

"No, Rāma. The King is pledged to his people. He must be a sannyāsi who sits on the throne. He has nothing of his own. Everything he has is maintained in trust for the people. You cannot leave that duty. Nor can you betray that trust. Now you must allow Sītā to return to the forest, while Rāma protects the people of his nation. I have only one prayer as I leave: time and time again I will gladly take birth to become the wife of a divine husband like you. But please, in our future births, let us not know so much pain as we have in this life."

Sītā left to the forest and took refuge in the aśrama of Ṛṣi Vālmīki. Vālmīki made her welcome with respect, and Sītā began to pass the days of her pregnancy in the forest hermitage. Meanwhile, life in the palace became devoid of lustre. Rāma became a dispassionate ascetic, sleeping on the floor on a mat of kuśa grass, even amidst the luxury and splendor of Ayodhyā.

## Lavaṇaśura

One day Chyavana Muni came to Rāma's court seeking protection. The wicked King of Mathura, Lavaṇaśura, had been terrorizing the ṛṣis of the forest. Now, it was no longer safe for sādhus to meditate in the forest. The aśura had killed many munis and had imprisoned others, and there was no refuge for dharma in his kingdom. Could Rāma help?

Rāma's youngest brother, Śatrughna, requested, "May I be given the opportunity to serve?"

Rāma agreed and performed the coronation of his younger brother as the King of Mathura. "After you slay that wicked King of Evil, the people will need efficient administration to guide their systems in the way of dharma. Therefore, you must become the King."

Rāma presented Śatrughna with many weapons, and bade him to follow the instructions of the ṛṣis. He also told his brother that en route to do battle with the aśura of Mathura, that he should take the blessings of Vālmīki Muni.

King Śatrughna set out with his army towards the hermitage of Ṛṣi Vālmīki. Arriving at the ṛṣi's aśrama, the army made its camp, while King Śatrughna went to take darśana of the Muni. The Muni made him welcome with respect, and asked the King to help him in the performance of one rite. Just that morning two noble princes of the Solar Dynasty had taken birth in the aśrama. Would Śatrughna help in the birth ceremony? With great delight the King performed the ceremonies of birth, and blessed the children.

Śatrughna took the blessings of Ṛṣi Vālmīki, and set off to assist in the service of Chyavana Muni. With the blessings of the sages, King Śatrughna killed the evil Lavaṇaśura, and the descendants of the Solar Dynasty began to reign in Mathura.

## Lav and Kuś

Rāma and Sītā's two sons, Lav and Kuś, grew up in Ṛṣi Vālmīki's aśrama with their Mother's loving care, but the identity of their father was never disclosed to them. Their lives were filled with blessings, and the Guru Vālmīki taught them the use of every weapon known. They became masters of all the subjects of a King's dharma, and they learned to sing the entire story of the Rāmāyaṇ composed by Ṛṣi Vālmīki.

Sītā passed her days in the aśrama life, performing all the chores by herself, fetching wood, cooking, cleaning, and raising her children. Never did her mind swerve from her devotion to the feet of Rāma. Rāma passed his days administering the kingdom, and living as a sannyāsi even while on the throne. The entire royal family was overcome with sadness because of Sītā's absence. With the royal family in sorrow, the people could not be happy, and even though there was abundance and peace and justice, there was no joy or delight.

One day the citizens came to the King Rāma with a request that the royal family conduct a celebration. Far too many years have passed with nothing to look forward to; even though there was peace and prosperity throughout the land, the citizens desired to participate in a grand festival. Thus the people were so happy when the King agreed to perform the Aśvamedha Yajña. Arrangements were made for the sacrifice, and all the citizens and neighboring Kings were invited. Again there was excitement in the air of Ayodhyā.

Then the people began to speculate, "A King is not allowed to perform any religious sacrifice without his wife. A wife is an equal co-sharer in any dharmic activity. Therefore, if Rāma is going to perform the sacrifice, he must have a wife. Who knows where Sītā is, or even if she is? It must be that our King is going to marry again."

When news of this rumor reached to the King, he was beset with woe. "How can the people be so hard hearted?" he thought. "Sītā has never left my heart even for a moment, and they are thinking that I will marry another."

Then Rāma had a golden image of Sītā prepared, and placed it on the dais where he would sit. All the citizens marveled at the steadfast esteem in which Rāma held Sītā. They proclaimed, "Our King has given a great honor to all women by this act. He never doubted Sītā even for a moment, yet he sacrificed his own happiness and hers because of the doubts of his people. What an honor for a people to have such a King."

Guru Vasiṣṭha officiated at the ceremonies, offering oblations into the sacred fire while chanting Vedic mantras. A golden crown was placed upon a white horse. Upon the crown was inscribed the challenge: "Recognize the sovereignty of Ayodhyā, or prepare to do battle." The horse was set free to roam wherever it pleased, followed by a large army. The horse wandered around the entire subcontinent, and nation after nation surrendered to the supremacy of Rāma.

Finally, the horse and army were returning to Ayodhyā where the sacrifice would be completed. It was the last night of the journey, and the entire army had camped nearby the hermitage of Ṛṣi Vālmīki. Then the playing children spied the horse. Reading the challenge written upon the golden crown, Lav and Kuś took the horse. The soldiers guarding the horse, told the boys to give it back, but the two young ṛṣis replied, "Tell Rāma that we will like to talk with him. Ask him to come get the horse himself."

The soldiers became enraged, "We can't tell the King to come here because of two children playing in the forest! Give us the horse or we will punish you!"

"You punish us if you can!" cried the boys. "But we will not give up the horse until the King comes to get him."

The soldiers rushed forward to attack, but reciting a mantra, the ṛṣis made them unconscious. A few survivors ran to tell the Captain of the Guard what had happened. The Captain became very angry and scolded the soldiers for being afraid of two young boys. He came to where the ṛṣis were standing with the horse, and demanded it be returned. Receiving the same reply, he rushed forward to attack. Repeating the mantra, the ṛṣis made him unconscious as well.

Then King Śatrughna came to those boys. "Are you Rāma?" they asked.

"No, I'm Rāma's younger brother," he replied.

"We don't have any quarrel with you. Please go back and send your older brother to us. We have a question we would like to ask him."

"I can't tell the King to abandon all his other duties to come to the forest to answer the question of two boys! Give me the horse, and you can come to Ayodhyā and ask the King yourselves."

"He's trying to trick us, Brother," said Lav. "Don't trust him."

"Don't worry, Lav," said Kuś. "I won't trust him. He's a very clever soldier. He could take us to the King and punish us without answering our question."

"No, King Śatrughna, we will not go with you to Ayodhyā. You please go back and tell King Rāma to come here!"

Śatrughna rushed forward to attack, but repeating the mantra, the ṛṣis made him unconscious as well. One after another, Lakṣman, Bharat, Hanumān and Sugrīva all were defeated in battle, and were put under the spell of the ṛṣis' mantras.

At last King Rāma came to reclaim his horse. Just when the opposing sides were about to begin their battle, the Ṛṣi Vālmīki returned to the aśrama to intercede. "Boys, why are you fighting with our King? The King is the father of the nation. Fighting with your King is like fighting with your own father. Put down your weapons!"

Lav and Kuś put down their bows and arrows, and bowed down to their guru, Ṛṣi Vālmīki. "Now," continued Ṛṣi Vālmīki. "Why did you take the King's horse?"

"We wanted to ask one question of the King," replied the boys, and we were afraid he wouldn't answer us if we went to him."

"What is that question?" asked Rāma.

"King, we have heard from our Guruji that Śrī Rāma is the ultimate example of dharma, and never deviates from his duty at any time. Then what dharma allows a man to abandon his faultless, lawfully wedded wife alone in the forest, while he enjoys a kingdom, just because some people spread a foolish rumor? We learned from our Guruji that a man is supposed to protect his wife under every circumstance. Then how can you be the example of dharma, letting Sītā go alone into the forest? What dharma is this?"

"The dharma of Kings," replied Rāma. "A King is a servant to his people. He must be able to sacrifice everything for his nation, even his very life should it be required. Only then can one be fit to rule a nation. Only then can one be called a King."

"Then the fault of Sītā's exile is not yours. The fault lies with the people of Ayodhyā. Oh King, we're sorry for all the difficulties we have caused. Any punishment that you want to give us, we are ready to accept."

Lav and Kuś freed all the soldiers from the spell of the mantras, and Rāma took the horse and returned to Ayodhyā to complete the sacrifice. Then at their Guru's order, Lav and Kuś went to Ayodhyā and began to sing the Rāmāyaṇ. On every street corner, in every square of the city, the story of the heroism of the King and the purity of his wife made the people cry. Many citizens repented for their part in exiling

Sītā and depriving the royal family of happiness because of a foolish rumor.

Then King Rāma asked the two ṛṣis to sing the entire story of Rāmāyaṇ as composed by their Guru before the assembly of the royal court. Lav and Kuś captured the hearts of every - one present, as they sang the entire history of Śrī Rāma. They told of the birth of the four brothers, their education in Vasiṣṭha Muni's aśrama, how Rāma broke Śiva's bow and won Sītā, of their exile in the forest, the stealing of Sītā, the defeat of Rāvaṇa, and return to Ayodhyā. They sang of the washerman's wife and Sītā's exile, and everyone who heard their song was amazed at the profundity of their knowledge and the depth of their devotion. None could resist falling in love with them.

At the conclusion they sang of their own birth in the Ṛṣi's aśrama, of Sītā's purity and the hardships of her life in exile. "The people have betrayed their queen with untruth, and it is time that Devī Sītā be called back from the forest and given the honor of her rightful place in the palace. She is our Mother, and we are the sons of Rāma. We bow down to our Father." The two boys prostrated before the throne of the King of Ayodhyā.

Rāma said, "Before you can make a claim to the throne of the Kingdom of Ayodhyā, there must be some proof given to the people that you are the true and rightful heirs. Ask your mother to come tomorrow to testify that you are my children and have a right to this kingdom."

The next day Sītā appeared before the assembly of the royal court. All of the citizens of Ayodhyā were present to hear the testimony of Sītā. Then Sītā said, "If I am true, and I have never swerved from devotion to the feet of my husband Śrī Rāma, then let the Earth open up beneath my feet and liberate me from manifested existence. I have never told a lie, and I have never had any relationship with any other man. If

I am true, then let the Earth open up beneath my feet and liberate me from manifested existence. Lav and Kuś are the sons of Rāma. They are true princes of Ayodhyā, blessed at their birth by King Śatrughna. If I am true, then let the Earth open up beneath my feet and liberate me from manifested existence."

Suddenly the earth began to rumble beneath Sītā's feet, and then it split apart. Just before Mother Sītā descended into the bowels of the earth, she said, and these were her last words, "Rāma, of all men that have ever walked the face of this earth, you are the most noble. Again and again I will incarnate upon this earth wherever you manifest, only to enjoy the privilege of being your wife."

The earth swallowed Sītā, and Lav and Kuś joined their father Śrī Rāma in protecting the citizens of Ayodhyā.

## Mahā Biṣa and Gaṅgā

Many years ago in the family of Ikṣvāku, there lived a great King by the name of Mahā Biṣa. Mahā Biṣa was an extremely devoted King, and he had developed such spiritual powers that even the Gods became envious of him. He was so steadfast in truth and so honorable in nature, that he could change his consciousness at will. He developed such poise and will-power that he could ascend to heaven whenever he wanted.

One day when he was visiting in heaven, he happened to see Gaṅgā. Gaṅgā looked very beautiful. He stared at her, and Gaṅgā stared back. Brahmā happened to see this and said, "Hey, Mahā Biṣa, Great King, this is not the kind of conduct we encourage in heaven. If you're going to behave like this, why don't you go down to earth and be a man. Gaṅgā, you too better go down to earth and be born as a woman, and both of you get all this personal relationship business out of your systems. Then you can come back to heaven."

Both Gaṅgā and Mahā Biṣa were very sorry, but they had to obey Brahmā's order. As they took their leave, something very interesting happened.

There were eight Vaśus. The oldest of the Vaśus was named Dyau. Dyau means the Heavens, as in the mantra 'Śānta Dyau, Śānta Pṛthiviṃ.' Pṛthu was another one of the eight Vaśu brothers. His name means the Earth. One day the brothers happened to be wandering near Vasiṣṭha's hermitage, when Dyau's wife saw Nandi, the cow.

"What a beautiful cow. Whose cow is that, and what special qualities does it have?" she asked her husband.

Dyau replied, "Whoever drinks the milk from that cow, their youth will never end, and they will live for at least ten thousand years."

Then Dyau's wife said, "My dear husband, I have a beloved friend, who would be so grateful to drink that milk. Please get that cow for me. We can take some milk from the cow so my friend can be free from all disease. Then she can live for ten thousand years and be young and beautiful. We, too, can drink from the milk!"

Dyau called all his brothers together and said, "Brothers, let's take that cow."

So the brothers took the cow away and began to milk her. Just then Vasiṣṭha woke up from his meditation and, looking around, thought, "Where is my cow?" He looked all over the aśrama, but the cow wasn't there. Then he sat in meditation again and thought, "Where could my cow have gone?" In his meditation he saw, "Oh my, the Vaśus have taken my cow!"

Immediately he went to where the Vaśus were staying, and he took some water in his hand and exclaimed, "You have stolen my cow! You guys have behaved like thieves. I curse you! Go down to the earth and live amongst men!"

The seven Vaśu brothers said, "We aren't responsible. It was our older brother who told us to do this. We were just obeying his orders, so it's not our fault! We just went along with him. Why should we be cursed, and how can we be freed from this horrible curse to live on the earth among men? Men are so insensitive, and life on earth is filled with anxiety. Please give us a way to be free."

Vasiṣṭha said, "Okay, you seven brothers will be freed from the curse within one year. But Dyau, you are truly the guilty party; you are going to live a long, long time on earth, and it's not going to be pleasant. You'll atone for your bad behavior." Vasiṣṭha left, taking his cow.

Just when the Vaśus were on their way to earth, they saw Gaṅgā also en route to the earth. They asked her, "Where are you going, Gaṅgā?"

Gaṅgā replied, "I was cursed by Brahmā to go to the earth."

The Vaśus said, "We also were cursed to go to the earth by the Muni Vasiṣṭha, Mother. Would you do us a favor?"

"Surely, how can I help you?"

"Mother, we are Divine Beings, residents of heaven, raised on nectar all our lives. We don't want to take birth in any ordinary earthly womb. Would you consent to be the mother who gives us birth?"

"Of course," agreed Gaṅgā.

And then they added, "Mother, Vasiṣṭha said we could be freed from the curse of taking human birth within one year, so we have another request for you. As soon as we are born, drown us in the river of your waters."

Again Gaṅgā agreed and said, "Okay, that plan will work. As soon as each of you will be born, I will drown you in the river, so you can go back to heaven quickly. I'll do this in order to release you from Vasiṣṭha's curse." This was the plan upon which they agreed.

## Viśvāmitra and Menakā

Before Viśvāmitra had become a Brahmā Ṛṣi, there were many, many obstacles put in his path. For thousands of years he had strived in the path of realization and self control, but Indra constantly looked for ways to deflect him from the goal. One time when Indra was sitting in heaven reflecting upon this dilemma, he thought, "You know that Viśvāmitra Muni is performing such a strong tapasya of asceticism, certainly he will try to come here and take over my throne. I must put some obstacle in his way to humble him, and to thwart his efforts."

Considering thusly, he called Rambā, the Apsara, or seductress of the Gods who manifests beauty. He said, "Rambā, go down to the earth and seduce Viśvāmitra and make him pay attention to you. Cause him to stop his tapasya, and to stop trying to ascend to the heights of heaven. That is my order! Take with you Love. Take with you Spring. Take with you the whole army of accomplices and any other assistance you may need, and make that ṛṣi stop his tapasya!"

As ordered, Rambā proceeded to the forest where Viśvāmitra was deeply engrossed in meditation. Suddenly the air became filled with the sounds of Spring, and birds began to chirp. Bees began to buzz, and there was a fresh fragrance wafting in the breeze. Soft music began to play. Rambā herself began to sing very softly and gracefully, and to dance with all gentility.

As the music became faster, Rambā began to dance more rhythmically. In every way she tried to entice the awareness of the ṛṣi from his one-pointed attention in meditation, but no matter how hard she tried, Viśvāmitra did not stir. Then Rambā went where the muni was sitting in yogic posture meditating, and she lay her head down on his lap. Nothing happened. She began to massage him and caress him and in other ways tried to wake him up to the allurement of her charming beauty.

When at last the muni woke up, he looked with astonishment at the marvelous beauty of the Apsara Rambā sitting with her head on his lap, who was inviting him and caressing him, and immediately understood the entire situation. Becoming very angry, he said, "What! You were sent here to break my meditation! That foolish Indra! Does he think I will fall for this?"

Viśvāmitra looked at her with such a fire of vengeance, that the Apsara Rambā was immediately reduced to a stone. And Viśvāmitra went back to his meditation.

Indra looked down from heaven and exclaimed, "Rambā! The gem of my household! The most powerful weapon that I have! Beauty was reduced to a stone by the power of the tapas of that ṛṣi! I can't allow any sādhu to perform such a discipline that can jeopardize my entire kingdom! Menakā!" he commanded. "Menakā, oh You who Vibrate with Knowledge!"

"Yes, my Lord," Menakā appeared with folded hands.

"Go down to earth and entice the mind of that ṛṣi!"

Menakā said, "Oh Lord, Rambā, the most beautiful amongst all of the Apsaras was turned to a stone by that ṛṣi! Please, Lord, I don't want to become a stone. Please don't send me! I beg of you, Lord, send anyone else. Send Gṛtachī or Tilottama, even Urvaṣi could be very effective. Send any - one, Lord, but please don't send me! I am afraid. I don't want to become a stone or to be reduced to ashes at the foot of a ṛṣi!"

"No, Menakā, this is a very important function. This is your job! Take any assistance you may need, but make that muni give up his meditation. Go!"

Menakā had no choice but to obey. As she prepared to go down to the earth, she summoned all the helpers of the heavenly arsenal. She began to pray: "Oh please Lord, protect me! I know the power of the tapas of this muni. Please don't allow him to turn me into a stone." And she called Love and said, "Love, please shoot your arrows at that ṛṣi at the appropriate time, and make sure to hit your mark! Make him fall in love with me, and please don't allow him to turn me into a stone!"

Menakā descended to the earth, and began to practice her magical arts of seduction. But try as she might, Viśvāmitra never even saw her, so steadfast was he in the discipline of his meditation. He never even once became aware of her presence. Menakā danced and sang. She cooked delicious food and tried in every way to captivate the senses of that meditating ṛṣi. She tried to perform worship to him even while he sat in meditation, but he was unaware of her presence. In every way she tried to capture the senses of that meditating ṛṣi, but with no success.

When Viśvāmitra finally rose from his meditation, she tried to skillfully place herself by his path. But time and again he walked right past her, without the slightest acknowledgment of her presence. The she began to serve that ṛṣi, and in every way to help him in the pursuit of his goals. She began to help him in his pūjā by picking the flowers for worship and making ready his asāna. Viśvāmitra accepted her service, but never once felt the slightest stir in his heart, nor did he even take notice of who was providing this seva.

Some time passed. One day Viśvāmitra went down to the river to bring some water, where Menakā was taking a bath. Just then the God of Love, recognizing this excellent opportunity, quickly placed the flower-tipped arrow into his bow, and let it fly with perfect accuracy. The arrow struck Viśvāmitra, and suddenly he took notice of Menakā, and he fell deeply in love. He tried to meditate, but noticed that his heart was full of agitation, and every time Menakā walked into his sight, his heart leaped for joy! Menakā began to rub his feet in the night, when he had finished his long sitting in tapasya. She would put scented oils in his hair, and came closer and closer, as they started to do tapasya together. Now they began to sit together for meditation. She began to participate in all of his pūjās, and became the most efficient helper that a sādhu could desire. In every way Menakā became the perfect helpmate, giving him her fullest surrender and support.

Some time passed. Viśvāmitra fell deeper and deeper in love and began to surrender to the wiley charms of the beautiful heavenly nymph, the Apsara who embodies the Vibrations of Knowledge. After some time, Menakā forgot all about the heavenly task for which Indra had sent her. She surrendered herself completely to Viśvāmitra as he did unto her. Soon they were married, and they were both filled with gracious joy!

## Śakuntala

Menakā became pregnant, and they performed the prenatal ceremonies from conception to the preparations for giving birth. Without even noticing it, little by little Viśvāmitra began to spend more time with his dear wife, and less and less time with his worship. He loved his wife so dearly.

Indra looked down from heaven and was pleased.

When the appointed time came, Menakā gave birth to a beautiful baby girl. Viśvāmitra was filled with delight! The child was radiant: conceived and nurtured in the deepest love and respect. Viśvāmitra performed the pūjās relating to the birth of the child, and became lost in the bliss of his house - holder's life.

Then Indra said to Menakā, "Your work is finished. You have destroyed his meditation and made him bound by attachment. My dear Menakā, you have been a perfect success! Now leave the child with Viśvāmitra, and come back to heaven."

Menakā, who had been lost in the bliss of marital fidelity, was suddenly called to the consciousness of the reality of her situation. "How can I leave my helpless new-born baby? How can I leave my husband who has surrendered to me fully and trusted me completely? What kind of dharma is this?" she asked in dismay. "This is not the dharma of a woman and a wife!"

Indra said, "You are not a woman nor a wife! You are an Apsara. Your job is to do the bidding of the Lord of the Devas, to captivate the minds of munis who strive to become Gods through their tapasya. That is your job. Do you think anyone who likes can approach heaven without possessing the special qualities demanded of the Gods? Absolutely not! That is why you Apsaras must teach humanity the lessons of humility, to let them know that all that lives must act in accordance with Nature. Now come back to heaven! Don't worry about your concepts of right and wrong. We can make atonement later for any wrong doing. But the Laws of Karma and the supremacy of Fate are inviolable. Now leave the baby with her father and come home!"

Menakā begged, "Lord, please give me some time. I can't. I can't leave this child! This baby needs the nurturing of a mother. How will I tell Viśvāmitra, who trusted me and surrendered his pure love to me without reservation. Certainly in the fire of his anger he will curse me and turn me into a stone, just as he did to Rambā."

Indra became angry, "If you don't come home right now, then I will curse you and turn you into a stone!"

"Oh Lord, please let me at least tell Viśvāmitra before I leave him and our child!"

"Okay, but don't delay!"

Menakā went to Viśvāmitra filled with sadness. "My husband, I must make a confession to you. Indra ordered me to come here to destroy your meditation. That was the purpose of our relationship. Now that we have a child and you are fully committed to the Householder's life, Indra has ordered me to come home. I know you are going to curse me for this and turn me into a stone. I am worthy of that. My behavior is not proper for a woman, a wife or a mother, and I deserve to be cursed. Please go ahead and curse me. It would make my conscience feel better, for receiving the proper fruit of the seeds of the karma I have sown. I would like you to curse me, because I know this treacherous conduct is improper. I love you very much, my husband. I love our child as well. But if I don't go back to heaven right now, Indra will cause me to become a stone. Swāmī, I would rather be cursed by a righteous husband, than by Indra for his unrighteous actions. Please go ahead and curse me."

Viśvāmitra looked at Menakā and said, "I am not going to curse you. You did your duty, and it is no fault of yours. You were successful at completing Indra's task, you have already destroyed my meditation. Now go to heaven! Don't get cursed by Indra, nor is there any need for you to be cursed by me. Go to heaven! I don't need you. You set out to break my meditation and destroy my tapasya, and you have been successful. So go! Take your child with you and go!"

"Husband, I can't take the child. The child has to stay here on earth. She is not of heaven. The child is born of earth."

"Then leave the child and go. Do what you have to do! Taking care of an infant child is the mother's responsibility. A father cannot give milk. If you want to go to heaven, then go ahead. Abandon your child in the forest. I'm going off to continue the tapasya you set out to destroy. I will show that Indra!" And Viśvāmitra stormed off into the forest to do tapasya.

Menakā began to cry. She made a bed of leaves on the earth, and laid the baby within. With great sorrow, Menakā most tearfully ascended to heaven. All alone in the forest, the infant child began to cry. A Śakun bird came and spread its wings over the baby, to protect the child from the midday sun. So the baby was at the feet, at the tala, of the Śakun bird, who, with wings spread wide, stood guard as a sentry.

Just at that time, the Ṛṣi Kaṅva was coming along the path with some of his disciples. "Stop!" he commanded. "I hear some noise over there amongst the leaves in the thickets of the forest." He walked over and looked down to see this curious sight, a beautiful, radiant young child being guarded beneath the spread wings of the great bird. He carefully reached down to pick up the baby, and held her close to his breast. He thought, "What a beautiful, divine child, all alone in this forest, with no one but a Śakun bird to stand guard as a sentry! Certainly this child will fulfill some great karma in history. I will take this baby home for my wife to nourish."

He took the baby home to his aśrama, and performed the natal ceremonies for the birth of the child. He gave her the name Śakuntala, She who resides at the feet of a Śakun bird.

Śakuntala grew up in the aśrama of the Kaṅva Ṛṣi. She grew up into a beautiful young lady, filled with the wisdom of the saints. As she grew into marriageable age, Kaṅva's wife said to the ṛṣi, "Ṛṣi, it's time that we started thinking about our daughter's marriage. Please find a suitable husband for her."

Ṛṣi Kaṅva said, "I shall go into the forest to do tapasya, and I shall meditate to find out who might be a suitable husband."

Then the ṛṣi along with many of his disciples went into the forest and began to practice tapasya. Just at that time, the King of Hastinapura, born of the Lunar Dynasty, the King Duṣyanta, came into the forest for hunting. One of his ministers told him, "Oh Great King, yonder lies the hermitage of the Great Ṛṣi Kaṅva. King, you should go and pay your respects. He is a great Vedic Ṛṣi, a very wise and honorable seer."

Duṣyanta went to visit the Ṛṣi's hermitage, and as he approached the aśrama, he saw the very beautiful Śakuntala. Immediately his heart was pierced. He stammered for a moment and then with considerable consternation said to the love of his life, "Oh Goddess, what are you doing sitting alone in this forest? What is your name? Who is your father? Where do you live?"

Śakuntala with complete poise replied, "Oh King, I perceive that your mind has lost its control. I am Śakuntala, daughter of the Ṛṣi Kaṅva who is my father, and the guru of this aśrama. I suggest that you wait some time for the ṛṣi to return, for he has gone into the forest to practice his meditation. When you will meet the ṛṣi, I am sure he will grant you the request for which you have come."

The King Duṣyanta was a young man, very handsome, a most noble King. He looked at Śakuntala and thought, "How can I wait? My heart was pierced the moment I set eyes upon her. I will surely die and give up my life if I have to wait even one more day before this Śakuntala is mine."

He boldly said, "Śakuntala, will you marry me according to the Gandharva law of marriage? I am sure your father will approve."

Śakuntala's heart was stolen away. That night Śakuntala went to visit the King's pavilion, where they performed the marriage ceremony. Having consummated the marriage vows, they made love and Śakuntala became pregnant.

In the morning, the King said, "Oh my dear Queen, I am required to return to my kingdom now. I must prepare a place for you. Please wear this ring with the royal insignia of my name inscribed upon it. I will be back within three days to get you." Handing over the ring, the King departed.

Just then, the Ṛṣi Kaṅva returned to the hermitage. Everyone came from the aśrama to greet him. "Where is Śakuntala?" he asked. "Surely my daughter would come to greet me?"

The mother said, "Śakuntala was out all last night. Today she hasn't eaten a thing, nor spoken a word."

"Bring her to me," said Kaṅva.

The mother brought Śakuntala. When Ṛṣi Kaṅva saw the look on Śakuntala's face, he closed his eyes and went deep into meditation. With his divine perception in the stillness of meditation, he came to realize the entire circumstance. He blessed his daughter and said, "Śakuntala will bear the sword of the lunar dynasty."

Śakuntala understood that her father knew everything. They decided to wait the three days for the King Duṣyanta to return for her, so that Kaṅva could welcome the groom with the devotion of a Vedic ceremony. Kaṅva was so pleased! With great joy he prepared a feast for all of the people of the nearby villages, a grand celebration in honor of the marriage of his daughter. Śakuntala was so deeply lost in thought, she could think of nothing else but the return of her husband. Those three days seemed like an eternity!

On the third day of her waiting, she was sitting on the bank of the river just gazing at the face of her beloved inscribed upon the waters. She was lost in meditation, unaware of any - thing else, when the angry Ṛṣi Durvāṣa came to the river. "Young lady," he said. "Which way is Ṛṣi Kaṅva's aśrama?"

There was no response.

"Where's the path to the aśrama?" he called out in a louder voice becoming filled with anger at being ignored. "I've lost the path! Where is the aśrama?"

Not a sound entered into Śakuntala's ears. She was so lost in her reflections, she merely gazed at the ripples of the water, and dreamed of the reunion with her husband.

Durvāṣa called again with even greater anger, "Young lady, I am calling you! Is this the hospitality that the ṛṣis of the forest show to Durvāṣa Muni? Don't you know my anger? Everyone fears my anger! Which way is the aśrama?"

Still there was no response.

Durvāṣa became filled with anger. He stooped down beside the river bank, scooped up some water in his hands, and called, "You have failed to show respect to an elderly sage! You have failed to show respect to a guest at your door! You have ignored the innocent questions of one in need! I curse you! The person that you are thinking about will forget you!" He threw the water at Śakuntala who remained totally unaware.

But two of her friends that were sitting near to her, witnessed the entire scene, and when they saw the muni storm off into the forest, they ran after him and said, "Oh Great Ṛṣi, please forgive our friend, Śakuntala. She was just newly wed and has been left by her husband. She was thinking again and again about her husband and when he will come. Please take back your curse! The aśrama is this way! We will give you all the hospitality we can offer you! Please Muni, take back your curse!"

Durvāṣa said, "Well, this is certainly better behavior than your friend showed to me. But once a curse has been given, it cannot be withdrawn. What I have said will come to pass. But because of your friendship, because of the humble way in which you are requesting me on behalf of your friend, I will give you the boon that a time will come when the person of whom she is dreaming, will find some object which will inspire her memory. Then the curse will be withdrawn." So saying, Durvāṣa Muni marched off into the forest.

The three days passed and became three weeks, and there was still no sign of the King. When three months had passed and there was still no sign of the King, Śakuntala was beginning to have some motherly symptoms and getting a little bit large around the middle. Her mother said to the Ṛṣi Kaṅva, "Oh Ṛṣi, I am beginning to doubt if the King Duṣyanta is really going to come back for our daughter. Maybe he has forgotten her completely. Now our daughter is showing signs of motherhood. It is time that we take her to the King's household, because if she is to bear his child, the child should be born in the household of the father, not that of the mother. This is even more important for this child is destined to be of the royal family. Ṛṣi, the time has come to send our daughter to her husband's home."

Ṛṣi Kaṅva called two of his disciples, "Accompany our Śakuntala to the King's palace, and tell the King he should accept responsibility for the karma he has performed, and to accept his wife according to our Hindu Law and traditions. It isn't right for a King to behave in such an irresponsible way, having a relationship with a Brahmiṇ girl, and then leaving her without another word. So now, oh King, do what is proper."

The two hermits escorted Śakuntala in their journey to the King's palace. The path wound through the dense jungle, and then to the edge of the forest. Soon they came to the banks of the Jamuna River. The three passengers sat down in a boat in order to cross the river. As the boatman was pushing the boat across the river, Śakuntala was playing with the waves in the water, skimming her hand over the surface, and splashing and enjoying the coolness of the spray. She didn't even notice when the ring slipped from her finger, and sunk into the depths of the great river.

When they finally arrived at Hastinapura, the hermits from the forest wandered through the great bazaars until they came to the King's palace. The ṛṣis requested to speak with the King, and when they were escorted into the audience chamber, they said, "Oh King, we have been sent by the Great

Ṛṣi Kaṅva, who sends this message to you: 'Oh King, now you should take your wife, Śakuntala, and you should fulfill your responsibilities as a husband and a father. She is pregnant with your child, and the child should be born in your own house. Now, oh King, please do what is proper to uphold the Law of Dharma, as well as the honor of my daughter.'"

The King Duṣyanta looked at Śakuntala and turning to the ṛṣis said, "You are saying that this is my wife? I don't recall having any marriage. Please tell me where we were married and when? Who was the witness? I have no recollection whatsoever! What kind of nonsense is this?"

The ṛṣis were unable to convince the King. They said, "Oh King, we are ṛṣis from the forest. We would not lie to you. You married this daughter of ours, this innocent girl from our aśrama. Now take your wife, or we will return to the ṛṣi and tell him that you refused to take your wife, in which case she will be blamed, and we won't take her either. She will be shamed and will be required to live alone, exiled in the forest. Now, oh King, take your wife!"

The King replied, "I don't know what you're trying to pull here, but I assure you there is some deceit! I never saw this woman before! You are just trying to find a husband for your unwed daughter! I never had any marriage with this girl. Well, this King is not going to stand for these unjustified accusations! Take your girl and get out!"

The ṛṣis were mortified, when Śakuntala spoke up, "Oh King, I trusted you and believed in you. How could I have thought that you would treat me with such disregard? Now I will show you the proof of our relationship. Do you remember the ring that you gave me? You had said to me, 'Keep this, my Beloved. I shall return for you within three days. I am going only to make a place ready for you.' Now, oh King, see the ring!"

She held up her hand to show the King the ring with his

insignia, but looked with amazement as she saw that the finger was empty!

The King said, "What ring do you wish to show me? Show me the ring! If you have a ring, show it to me!"

Śakuntala said incredulously, "I don't know where it has gone!"

And the King became angry and said, "Neither do I! Show me the ring if you want to prove that I am your husband! What a wanton woman you are. You are trying to use subterfuge and trickery in order to make me responsible for your wanton ways. Get out of my palace! This is an outrage! Go back to the Ṛṣi Kaṅva and ask him to show me the ring!"

Then the ṛṣis turned and said, "Oh King, we believe this girl is telling the truth. We believe you will receive the fruit of your karma. This dishonored girl is not coming with us. If you do not take her, she will be required to find her own way!"

The two hermits turned and departed to their own aśrama.

Śakuntala wandered into the forest alone and in great distress. Looking down from the heavens, Menakā could not stand to see the plight of her daughter. She descended to the earth and escorted her daughter to the aśrama of Ṛṣi Kaśyapa, who was her father. Menakā introduced the grandfather to her daughter and prayed to Kaśyapa that he take care of her. Receiving his assurances, she returned to the heavens.

Receiving a respectful welcome from the high-souled munis, Śakuntala stayed in the aśrama. Kaśyapa said, "All who are distressed are welcome at the hermitage of the ṛṣis. You may stay here, bear your child here, and we will be pleased to accept you into our community."

Śakuntala gave birth to a son, and the Jāta Karma, the natal ceremonies were performed. The son was named Bhārat, a name of the Sun, meaning He who manifests the Light of Wisdom and the Warmth of Devotion. Śakuntala raised the child in the muni's aśrama, and she taught him all the branches of knowledge. She taught him how to take wood from a tree and to make it smooth and then make it wet; how to warm it over a fire and bend it into a bow; how to cut the little branches from the trees into straight, strong arrows. She taught him how to shoot the arrows so that they never miss their target. And Bhārat became the greatest archer of all India.

She also taught him the folklore of their heritage along with the inner meanings of the scriptures. Even in his early age he could quote mantras and their meanings, and in this way the young child grew up in the aśrama learning the lessons of how to protect the Dharma.

One day a very strange circumstance occurred. A fisher - man was fishing in the Jamuna River, and in his net he caught a big fish. When he brought the fish home, he cut it open, and inside the fish's belly he found a gold ring. On the ring was inscribed the name Duṣyanta. He thought, "This is such a priceless ring and the name of our King is inscribed upon it. In no way should I keep this. I shall bring this to the King right away. Maybe he will even give me a reward for my trouble. If I do not, I might get into trouble."

Immediately the fisherman went to the King's palace, and said to the guard, "Guard, I must see the King."

The guard said, "What do you mean, Fisherman, you want to see the King? At this hour of the day, without an appointment, what do you want to see the King for?"

The fisherman said, "I have something very important that I must give him, and I must give it to him personally."

The guard called the minister, and the minister came and said, "Fisherman, why do you want to see the King?"

Then the fisherman replied, "As I was out fishing yesterday, I caught a fish. And when I cut open the fish, I found a ring inside. I believe this may be the King's ring, and I want it to be returned to him. I want him to know that I didn't steal it, but I found it inside a fish."

The minister took the fisherman directly to see the King. After the fisherman told his story to the King, the King looked at the ring and immediately remembered Śakuntala. "My dear Śakuntala, my wife, where is my wife?" He was so happy he gave the fisherman a very generous reward for finding the ring and bringing it to him. Then he called his ministers and said, "Ministers, send soldiers all throughout the kingdom. We must find Śakuntala, my wife. She came here to me after I broke my promise that I would return to her aśrama to get her within three days. She came here, and I insulted her. I sent her away! Oh my goodness, what difficulties she has experienced. What an insult I have committed!"

He sent all the ministers along with his army to search throughout the entire kingdom. He was filled with sorrow and remorse. He sat in his temple praying, "When will they find my Śakuntala?"

After some time the ministers came back and reported, "King, we have searched all throughout the kingdom, and we have not found your wife. We sent messengers to the Ṛṣi Kaṅva's aśrama, but nobody knows anything about her. No one has seen hide nor hair of her since that day when she left here after you didn't recognize her. Who knows if she is dead? Who knows if she is lost in the forest? Who knows if she may have mounted upon a funeral pyre and burned herself to death after having received that terrible insult? But we can not find your wife!"

Duṣyanta the King was filled with sorrow. For many days there was no light and no joy in the King's palace, only sorrow and suffering and remorse. Little did he know that his forgetfulness was due to the Ṛṣi Durvāṣa's curse.

One day his minister said, "Oh King, you can't sit around your palace like this suffering. You are the Inspiration and the Light of the people. Come, let's go hunting and forget these troubles."

The King quite lifelessly agreed and said, "All right, but my heart isn't in the hunt."

Nevertheless the King went hunting with the minister and his own personal guard. They went deeper and deeper into the forest in the pursuit of their objective, until the King sighted a wild boar. Thinking that it would be a fit trophy for him, he started to chase after the animal. The boar took off running through the underbrush into the most dense part of the forest, and the King gave chase. The boar was running, while the King was riding on his horse faster and faster. In this way the King left his hunting party, and he went into an unknown part of the forest. The boar ran near the aśrama of Kaśyapa Muni, and ducked into a grove within the aśrama precincts.

The King came riding on his horse in hot pursuit. He drew his arrow, ready to shoot, when suddenly a young boy came out from the aśrama and stood before him commanding, "Stop, oh King!"

The King pulled his horse to a stop, even while he kept his eyes on his target, the boar, who was trying to hide in the ṛṣi's grove.

"This is the forest of Kaśyapa Muni's aśrama, oh King, and there is no hunting allowed here. This animal has taken refuge in our aśrama, and we are the priests of this aśrama. It is our duty to protect those who come to us seeking refuge. Therefore, please, oh King, turn around and go back. You cannot slay an animal in this locality."

"Young hermit," the King replied. "I have no fight with you. Why are you telling me to go back? I am the King! This forest and all other forests in my kingdom are mine. I am in pursuit of that animal, and I am going to kill that animal. You can't stop your King from killing an animal in his own forest."

The young hermit said, "Oh King, you have become much too proud of your strength and your possessions. Please remember that the King's duty is to protect his citizens. Do not use your strength to oppress others. This boar happens to be a citizen of your community. You yourself should protect him. But as you are not protecting him, therefore, it becomes my duty as a hermit of the forest to protect those who are oppressed. This boar has taken refuge within the precincts of this aśrama, and King, he who has taken refuge in the Lord must be protected at all costs. In order to fight with him, you will have to fight with me first!"

The King said, "Child, you are a little boy! I can't fight with a little boy, especially a hermit from the forest."

The young boy said, "You are a great King, and it is the duty of the Brahmiṇs to protect their King. But it is also the duty of Kings to protect the Brahmiṇs, especially as they are the source of right instruction. So please, oh King, protect our dharma, protect the Brahmiṇs, and leave this oppressed animal, who has sought refuge in this aśrama."

"Stand aside!" commanded the King.

The little boy drew an arrow in his bow.

The King said, "I can't fight with a young boy like you. Put down that bow, or I'll take my sword and smash your bow!"

The King raised his sword. The boy let his arrow fly, which cut the King's sword to pieces. The King looked at the boy with astonishment. "I am Duṣyanta, Emperor of the Lunar Dynasty. Who is this little boy to cut the sword from my hand?" He raised his bow and drawing back an arrow commanded, "Stand aside, Brahmiṇ boy! I am going after that boar!"

Just then, the young boy let his arrow fly, which broke the King's bow to pieces. He took more arrows and he made a silhouette of the King's body in front of the tree before which he was standing. The boy said, "Oh King, the kṣatriya Kings have a lot of power. But the Brahmiṇ sages of the forest have even greater powers. It is from the blessings of the Brahmiṇs, that the kṣatriyas reign. Don't abuse your kingly privileges, or

I will have no recourse but to take your life."

Just then, Śakuntala came running out of the aśrama. "My son, stop! You are not allowed to raise your weapon against your own father!"

The King looked in amazement. "That's my son? Śakuntala! My wife! I am so sorry for what I said to you! I am sorry for not recognizing you when you came to me! And this is my son?"

Duṣyanta hugged Bhārat, his son, and pleaded with his wife for forgiveness. Then Bhārat and Śakuntala joined Duṣyanta as he sat on the throne of Hastinapura. What prosperity the kingdom enjoyed while Duṣyanta was the King! And when Bhārat became the Crown Prince, appointed to be the successor to the King, the entire empire rejoiced. Bhārat conquered all of India from the Himalayas to the great sea, and made all the Kings of India subservient to the throne of Hastinapura. In his older age, Duṣyanta went to the forest to practice tapasya, and ultimately he ascended to heaven.

## Bhārat Gives the Throne to Śantānu

Bhārat became the King of Hastinapura, which is now known as Delhi, and what a King he was! Even today the Land of India is called Bhārat, the Land where the Light of Wisdom always dwells. During Bhārat's reign there was peace and happiness throughout the kingdom. His rule was filled with a righteous respect for Dharma.

As Bhārat advanced in age, one day he went to his mother and said, "Mother, I have nine sons. Which of them should become the next King?"

Śakuntala answered, "The one most fit among them."

And Bhārat said, "Mother, I am having difficulty determining which among my sons is the most fit to become the King."

His Mother replied, "Go ask Ṛṣi Kaṅva what to do."

So Bhārat travelled to Ṛṣi Kaṅva's aśrama, and bowing down to the Ṛṣi's feet he said, "Oh Ṛṣi, you are the father of my knowledge. Be a Light to me in my darkness. I am having difficulty determining which of my sons is most fit to become the King of Hastinapura as my successor."

Kaṅva said, "Look within. God will certainly give you the answer."

Then Bhārat went into the forest and began to meditate. After some time of deep, deep meditation, he became illuminated and he returned to his kingdom in Hastinapura. Calling an assembly of all the vassal Kings, all the noblemen, the ṛṣis, gurus and Brahmiṇs of his kingdom, he wisely proclaimed the discovery of his knowledge. "A King has three duties to his people: the administration of law and justice; the protection of his people; and the preparation and appointment of a fit successor. By God's grace, my kingdom has been prosperous, it has been safe and the rule of justice has prevailed. My first two duties as a King have been fulfilled. Now, as for the third duty, to appoint a fit successor, I have decided that none of my nine sons are appropriately fit. Therefore, in Bharadvādja's aśrama, there is a young man named Śantānu. I have seen in a vision that he will be the next King."

Having received Brahmā's curse, Mahā Biṣa had been reborn as Śantānu. Śantānu was brought from the muni's aśrama and was crowned Prince Regent and Heir to the Throne of Hastinapura. When Bhārat left his body, Śantānu became King, and he began to reign in Hastinapura and to conduct the administration of justice and order. He was a great warrior, and without difficulty was able to protect the frontiers of his kingdom.

## Śantānu Marries Gaṅgā

One day Śantānu went hunting into the forest, and as he rode in his chariot along the River Gaṅgā, out from this River Gaṅgā rose a most beautiful woman, the Divine Gaṅgā Herself. Śantānu looked at Gaṅgā, but he could not remember their former love affair. He became mesmerized by her lovely radiance. Gaṅgā looked at Śantānu and recognized him as Mahā Biṣa, even in his present body.

Śantānu said, "Oh Beautiful One, my heart is filled with love. I don't know what has inspired this, but please become my wife."

Gaṅgā replied, "King, I would love to become your wife, but only if you accept one condition."

Śantānu requested, "Oh Lovely, Beloved of my Heart, give me any conditions you like. I will accept any condition, if only you will consent to be my wife."

Gaṅgā said, "First, you must hear my condition and make me the promise that you will fulfill it, and then I will agree to marry you."

Śantānu said, "You have only to ask."

Then Gaṅgā said, "Whatever I like to do, I will do, and you will never stop me. The day you stop or question me, or in any way put any impediment or obstacle to my performing exactly as I see fit, that day I will leave you immediately."

And Śantānu said, "My beloved, there is nothing that you could want to do for which I would have any hesitation. You have stolen my heart. I agree you can do anything that you like. I surrender to you completely."

Śantānu and Gaṅgā were married, and Śantānu became lost in the bliss of lovemaking. He would make love to Gaṅgā all the time, and she responded with the most sensuous, gracious acceptance. They had the most beautiful relationship, and Gaṅgā became pregnant. The King was overwhelmed with joy! Performing the prenatal ceremonies, he fed all the people of his kingdom and gave tremendous dakṣiṇas to the Brahmiṇs. Everyone gave their blessings.

When the child was born, the King's heart leapt with joy. The maidservants from Gaṅgā, his queen, came to the King and cried, "Bidai! Avinandana! Greetings, oh King! A son has been born unto you this day! Congratulations!"

Then the King looked out from his window, and he saw Gaṅgā carrying the son, the newborn infant, to the river bank. She threw the child into the raging waters, and the child drowned! The King stared on in disbelief. "Evil woman! You killed my son!" he thought. And yet he did not say a word.

After some time, Gaṅgā became pregnant again. The King was filled with joy! An heir to the throne! After the child took birth, he watched Gaṅgā take that newborn baby as well, carry it down to the bank of the River Gaṅgā, and dropped it into the waters to watch it drown. The King's heart broke into two. And so it transpired with the third, fourth, fifth, sixth, and the seventh child! Each time he watched as his beloved wife took the infant child, the heir to the throne, his own flesh and blood, to drown the child in the waters of the River Gaṅgā. The King stared on in disbelief.

The seven Vaśus had already been freed from their curse of human birth as Vasiṣṭha allowed them, when the eighth son was born. When the eighth son, Dyau, was born, and the King looked out the window to see Gaṅgā taking this son to the bank of the river to receive the same fate as his brothers, his heart could bear it no longer. He ran to the river and jumped in front of her and said, "Stop! You can't do this! You have killed all my seven sons. What did they do to you? What are you doing, you evil woman? You are destroying my entire family! Stop this madness!"

And Gaṅgā said, "Now King, you have broken your vow. You promised never to question me or to stop me from what I want to do. Therefore, I am leaving you. I will take this son with me and nurture him in the forest. When he has grown up, strong and independent, I will give him back to you. For now, he requires his mother's love and nurturing. But just so you may know, the eight Vaśus had been cursed by Vasiṣṭha Muni that they must take birth on this earth. Seven of them were granted the boon that their sojourn would be completed with - in one year. As per our agreement, those seven Vaśus have gone back to heaven by my actions. Now this last child is yours. He will be known as Gaṅgeya, he who was born from Gaṅgā. Also we will call him Devavrat, Vow of the Gods. After you take your child again, I shall return to my heavenly abode. King, remember your curse as Mahā Biṣa. You must remain here to fulfill your karma."

Suddenly Śantānu was stunned into recollection. His mind became lost in memories so distant, and he disdained to think of the promise he had broken with his wife, Gaṅgā. Even as he thought of his own loss and his attachment to his sons who had gone and to his wife who was going, he also recalled his friendship with the Gods and of their plight at being cursed to come to earth. He gazed at Gaṅgā in silence, and watched as she disappeared into the wilderness along with her baby.

Gaṅgā took the child into the forest, and taught her son how to be a King. The child grew up strong and healthy and knowledgeable, having studied with the finest Gurus available. He learned weaponry from Paraśurām; he studied the scriptures with Bṛhaspati, the guru of the Gods himself. Gaṅgā saw to his health and wealth and education as no earthly mother could possibly do. Devavrat later became known as Bhīṣma, the Protector of the Lunar Dynasty, the Regent of Hastinapura.

## The Birth of Matsyagandha

Many years ago in the Kingdom of Cheddi, there reigned a King by the name of King Uparichara. He had a very beautiful wife, whose name was Girikā, which means Of the Mountains. Girikā was such a radiant beauty filled with devotion, and she loved her husband very, very much. He, too, always thought of her.

One time Girikā finished her menstruation period, and after she took her bath, she was filled with desire. She went to her husband, the King, and said, "Husband, I would like to have a child."

Her husband replied, "Wife, I would love nothing better than to give you a child right now, but I have some other important function to perform that cannot wait. We are required to offer a memorial ceremony in honor of my departed ancestors, which necessitates certain types of meat to be offered in sacrifice. I am going to the forest to hunt. I must fulfill this myself, because the sacrifice is to honor my ancestors. This is the order from our Guru."

Girikā allowed him to go and she kept her patience. The King went into the forest hunting. After some time he got tired from riding on his horse, and he sat down under a tree to take rest. He started to think of the wonderful love that he shared with Girikā, and his heart opened up and he was so full of love. He thought, "How wonderful it is to have a wife come to me filled with love and desire. Everyone in this universe desires to be desired. When other people love us and desire us, we, ourselves, feel a greater strength and security. Then we can direct that energy into any noble pursuit. How blessed am I with such a love!"

As he sat there under the tree thinking of his wife, he became excited and he dropped his semen. Then he thought, "Oh my, I have lost all control in the contemplation of my beloved! Well, this semen should not be wasted. It should not go without bearing fruit."

He picked up the semen and put it on a leaf. He folded the leaf and called a falcon and said, "Oh dear Falcon, please bring this semen to my wife, Girikā. She is thinking of me, and I want her to know that I, too, am thinking of her. She wanted to have a child. Enclosed within this leaf is the child that she desired, so bring it to her forthwith."

Obedient to the King's command, the falcon put the leaf in his beak and rose up into the sky. He started to fly towards the Kingdom of Cheddi, towards the palace of the King Uparichara, where his wife Girikā was thinking about her husband. In the course of his flight, another falcon spotted him and thought, "Hmmm. What precious trophy does that falcon have in his beak? I want my share too."

A fight ensued in the middle of the air. The one falcon started to peck at the messenger with such great zeal, that he overturned the messenger falcon. The leaf fell from his mouth, and it fell right into the Jamuna River! Then both the falcons, realizing that their trophy was lost, gave up the fight and flew off in their separate directions.

A beautiful Apsara named Adrikā came down to the earth one fine beautiful spring day, and she decided to bathe in the Jamuna River. She started to swim and to splash and to frolic. She danced with the flowers and bathed in the sun and jumped into the water and splashed having such a wonderful time!

Sitting on the bank of the river was the angry Ṛṣi Durvāṣa. He was performing his Sandya Bandana, his daily prayers, and he was making jāpa. As he made jāpa, Adrikā the Apsara, being filled with love and joy, swam over and playfully grabbed hold of his feet. The ṛṣi woke up from his meditation with a start and angrily said, "What kind of a lady are you to interrupt my meditation? Don't you know I am the Ṛṣi Durvāṣa? No one can stand before my anger! You have a lot of nerve to interrupt my pūjā and my meditation, swimming around the river like a fish! I curse you! You become a fish!"

Adrikā, the poor Apsara started to cry. "Oh Ṛṣi, I didn't mean any harm to you! Why would you do such a thing as to curse me and make me into a fish? I am an Apsara, a beautiful servant of the Gods. I am not a fish! Ṛṣi, be compassionate! Compassion is the grace of the Brahmiṇs. Please tell me, how can I be freed from this curse?"

Durvāṣa looked at the young lady who was radiant with beauty, Adrikā, and he said, "This fish will give birth to two human children, and then you can go back to heaven."

Adrikā the Apsara looked incredulous. "What! How can a fish give birth to a human? Not to speak of one human but to two humans?"

The Ṛṣi Durvāṣa said, "So it has been spoken, so it shall be. Be a fish."

The Apsara was immediately turned into a fish. Really it wasn't so bad. She even began to enjoy being a fish. She would swim along the banks of the Jamuna River, and listen to the mantras being chanted by the holy men who sat there. She began to frolic in the holy waters of the river.

One day as she was swimming around, she spied a strange looking leaf. "This leaf is not from a forest around here," she thought as she picked up the leaf in her mouth. Suddenly she swallowed it and became pregnant with the semen of the King of Cheddi! As the days went on, her belly got bigger and bigger and bigger. Finally she had trouble moving around in the river. She grew larger and larger so that she couldn't swim as fast as she used to, being in that pregnant condition.

One day a fisherman cast his net into the River Jamuna, and Adrikā, the fish, was powerless to swim away. The fisherman hauled in the net and found this huge, beautiful fish. He took the fish home, cut open it's belly, and was amazed by what he saw. Inside the womb of the fish he found two human children! One was a boy and the other was a girl. The fisherman thought, "I have been fishing in these waters all my life, but I have never seen or heard of anything like this in the history of fishing!" Meanwhile, the Apsara, Adrikā, was freed from her curse, and she returned to heaven.

The fisherman performed the natal saṃskāras, holding a great feast, gave dakṣiṇas as gifts to the Brahmiṇs, and welcomed the children to their new life on the earth. Then he thought, "What shall I do with these children? This is the most amazing thing I've ever seen or heard of in my life! I would like to keep the boy, who is such a beautiful and noble child. But this baby girl smells so bad, like a horribly rotting fish. I would like to throw her back into the waters, because I can't stand the smell!"

Just then a voice called in rumbling clouds from heaven above, "Fisherman, Das Rāj, do not throw this child away! Her son is destined to be a King!"

"What!" cried the Fisherman. "The son of this foul-smelling girl will become a King? Then I shall take these children to the King."

The fisherman took the two children to the King Uparichara, the King of Cheddi, and said, "Oh King, the most amazing thing in my entire career of fishing in the Jamuna River happened today. I never saw or heard of anything like it in my life. I caught a fish, the biggest fish I ever saw, and when I cut open the belly of the fish, I found these two human children: a boy and a girl."

The King looked at the two children with astonishment and said, "This girl smells like a fish, so let's call her Matsyagandha, She who Smells like a Fish. The boy is really beautiful and handsome. He looks like the son of a King. I will take the boy and raise him myself, and we will call him 'Matsya Rāj, King of the Fish. Fisherman, you take the girl back with you and raise her as your daughter. I will keep the son here with me and raise him as my son." And that is just what happened. Matsya Rāj grew up in the palace of the King, and Matsyagandha became the daughter of the fisherman.

Matsyagandha grew into a fine young lady. She had the most radiant beauty, but no one could get near her because she smelled like a fish! When she grew up, she became of great help to her father. She would help him mend the fishing nets and would help him row their boat. She would help him cook the food and help him to clean. And she became so filled with devotion, Matsyagandha grew into a radiantly beautiful girl.

## The Birth of Veda Vyāsa

One day the Muni Parāsara came to bank of the Jamuna River and said, "Fisherman, would you please ferry me across the river?"

The fisherman replied, "I am sorry, but I am busy right now. Please excuse me, Muni. I can't leave what I am doing at this time. If you can stand the smell, my daughter, Matsyagandha, will take you across the river."

The muni said, "I am in a hurry to get across the river. It doesn't matter who rows the boat. Let your daughter come take me across the river."

So the fisherman called his daughter, "Matsyagandha, please take this Muni Parāsara across the river."

Matsyagandha came and sat down in the boat, and the muni sat down in the boat across from her, while Matsyagandha started to paddle. As she was paddling across the river, suddenly the muni looked at her and said, "My dear young lady, I have this strange feeling of attraction towards you. I feel compelled to make love with you right now."

Matsyagandha was incredulous, "How can you say that? I smell so bad, like a rotting fish."

And Parāsara replied, "Well, that can be changed very easily. Through my yogic power and through my mantra siddhi, I endow you with beautiful fragrance. Your fragrance will be so captivating, that all animals for miles around will want to come just to smell you." And he did! Suddenly Matsyagandha emitted the most beautiful, enticing fragrance, which captivated all of life!

He said, "Now, let us make love! I can't explain why I have this feeling. I am a self-controlled ṛṣi from the forest, a seasoned sādhu having performed great austerities of renunciation. I can't explain why, but I just have this terribly wonderful urge to make love to you right now."

Matsyagandha said, "But Muni, Ṛṣi, you can't make love in a boat! You don't even know how to swim! What would we do if the boat tipped over while we are making love? How will you get to the shore? Control your self! At least wait until we get to the other side."

The muni said, "All right. But I understand that I am a muni. I have controlled my passions. There is some other reason that I am feeling these feelings. There must be some Divine Fate that is causing me to feel like this. I will wait until we get to the other side."

Matsyagandha paddled to the other side, and the muni said, "Come quickly! Let us make love!"

Realizing that there was no escape from the muni's passion, Matsyagandha said, "But Muni, it is daytime, and here we are on the bank of the river. Anyone coming down the path or by the river can see what we are doing. I will be greatly despised if we do this thing in public! My reputation will be ruined!"

Then the muni said a mantra and using his yogic power, he made it become night! He made clouds appear low in the sky, and then he said, "There, now it's dark and we are covered by fog. No one can see what we are doing."

And Matsyagandha knew there was no escape. So she said, "Muni, I am asking that you give me three boons for participating with you in this. The first is that my father will not know about this, and that my virginity will not be lost. The second is that the son born from our union will be powerful like you and intelligent, a knower of all the Vedas. And my third wish is that I will always have this beautiful smell and this enticing, youthful beauty."

And Parāsara said, "I grant you these three wishes! Your son will collect all the Vedas and classify them. He will be the author of all the Purāṇas, a repository of wisdom and knowledge, and he will be the chief expositor of the Sanātana Dharma."

So the muni lay down and had intercourse with Matsyagandha. When they were done, he went into the river, washed, and then departed into the forest. She became pregnant.

Matsyagandha began to get bigger and bigger and bigger! She went into her boat and paddled out to a lonely island in the middle of the Jamuna River. On this deserted island she gave birth to her baby son, but as soon as the child came out of her womb, he started to grow! And he grew and grew and grew into a full sized man, and then he said, "Mother! Praṇām. I bow to you. I am going off into the forest to practice tapasya. Thank you very much for being the vehicle of my entry into this earth plane. I have much karma to do, so I won't have time to stay here to assist you. Thank you very much for giving me birth. Please remember me at anytime you are in difficulties, and as soon as you remember me, I will come to do whatever you ask. But I have much karma to do now, so please take a bath and go home. I am going to perform my tapasya."

Matsyagandha was quite amazed at this, and she said, "I bless you, my son. Let your tapasya be fruitful." Because he was born on the dwīpa, on the island, his name was Dwaipayan. And because he was dark of complexion, his name was Kṛṣṇa; so his name was Kṛṣṇa Dwaipayan, otherwise known as Veda Vyāsa.

## The Wisdom of Veda Vyāsa

Matsyagandha returned to the fisherman's home. When she returned, her father noticed the beautiful scent. "Where is that scent coming from?" he thought.

As Matsyagandha came in through the door, he realized it was she who was emitting that fragrance, and he knew that it was the blessing of the ṛṣi. He hugged his Matsyagandha and blessed her, and he thanked the Ṛṣi Parāsara for having blessed his daughter with that beautiful fragrance. Then the fisherman lived very happily with his daughter Satyavatī.

Veda Vyāsa wandered off to the Sarasvatī River and began to perform tapasya. He studied the Vedas, and divided all the Vedas into various sections and classified them into four types of wisdom. The Ṛg Veda is the Wisdom of Hymns; The Yajur Veda is the Wisdom of Sacrifice; Atharva Veda is the Wisdom of the Definitions of Harmony; and the Sāma Veda is the Wisdom of Song.

He collected from each of the four Vedas a tattwa or basic principle, four principles which express the essence of the Vedas. From the Ṛg Veda came forth the principle Prajñānam Brahmā, the wisdom of nature is Supreme Divinity. From Yajur Veda came the principle, Tat Tvaṃ Asi, That thou art. From the Atharva Veda came forth the principle, Ayaṃ Atma Brahmā, this individual soul is the Supreme Divinity. And from the Sāma Veda, Ahaṃ Brahmāsmi, I am the Supreme Divinity. Taken together these four principles make a very beautiful poem: "Prajñānam Brahmā, Tat Twaṃ Asi; Ayaṃ Atma Brahmā, Ahaṃ Brahmāsmi." In various ways, Veda Vyāsa classified all the wisdom of non-duality and became the chief expounder of the Sanātana Dharma. Many years passed.

## The Birth of Śuk Deva

One day Veda Vyāsa was preparing to light the yajña fire. The yajña fire is traditionally established by rubbing two sticks together. One stick is laid down horizontally called Araṇi, and a pointed stick is placed into a little notch called Mantan Daṇḍa. Then one can rub the Mantan Daṇḍa into the Araṇi back and forth until the friction of the two sticks together will cause a spark of fire. That is how we give birth to a sacred fire.

One day Veda Vyāsa was sitting by his Homa Kuṇḍa, chanting the mantras and rubbing the Araṇi by means of the Mantan Daṇḍa. Just over his head there came a very beautiful Apsara by the name of Gṛtachī. Gṛtachī looked down at this beautiful hermit and became filled with passion and love. Veda Vyāsa looked up and saw this beautiful young lady filled with passion and love, and he too was struck with the arrows of love. He became passionate, and then he got angry and said, "I am not supposed to be passionate. I am supposed to be enkindling the divine fire."

He kept rubbing the sticks and chanting the mantras and felt himself becoming even more angry. He knew he was feeling passion inside, and therefore he was growing more and more angry. Gṛtachī got scared when she saw his anger, and she turned herself into a Śuka bird, a parrot, and started to fly away. Just at that time Veda Vyāsa got so excited he dropped his semen. The semen landed right on the two sticks. When the semen touched the place where the Mantan Daṇḍa was rubbing against the Araṇi, a spark of fire shot up into the air, out of which came Śuk Deva! He bowed down and said, "Oh Father, Namaste! I bow to you! Thank you and thank you again for bringing me into manifestation! Now tell me what I am to do?"

Vyāsa looked at his beautiful son and hugged him and surrounded him with all his love, holding him close to his breast! "My son, I am so pleased! I have a son! It is written in our scriptures that a man cannot attain heaven unless he has a son to pass down his wisdom to, and to perform funeral rites for him after he leaves. And now my life is fulfilled!"

Veda Vyāsa called all the Brahmiṇs and performed the Birth Ceremonies. He performed the First Feeding, and the Naming Ceremonies and said, "Son, you came when I saw the Śuka bird. I shall call you Śuk Deva, the God of Parrots, also meaning the God of Subtle Light or Radiance." Vyāsa performed all the religious ceremonies and rites of passage, all the saṃskāras prescribed by the Sanātana Dharma. He taught the child the wisdom of the Vedas, invested upon him a sacred thread and said, "Son, now the next step in the life of a Brahmiṇ is to live with your guru, serve the guru, and learn as much as you can. Please, when your learning is complete, come back to me. I am sending you to your guru's house."

Śuk Deva was sent to Guru Bṛhaspati's house, where he studied for twelve years. He memorized all the Vedas along with the explanatory texts and commentaries available, and when he was finished, he knew all the traditions of yoga and prāṇāyam. He knew how to meditate and how to keep his senses under control. He was in every way a pillar of the Sanātana Dharma, the Ideal of Perfection in Universal Wisdom and Harmony.

After the prescribed period of study was completed, one day Bṛhaspati came to Śuk Deva and said, "My son, you have learned as much as I can teach you. Give me my dakṣiṇa and go back to your father's house. You can't learn any more here."

Śuk Deva gave the dakṣiṇa to his guru and bowed down to his lotus feet. Now he was a man, and he returned to his father's aśrama on the banks of the Sarasvatī River. When Veda Vyāsa saw Śuk Deva coming towards the aśrama, he dropped everything and ran outside to greet him. He grabbed his son and kissed his head, and hugged him and kissed him again, and held him close. He was so glad to have him back. "My son, my son, you have come home!"

## The Discussion on Marriage

Some days after the celebration of the Samavārtan Ceremony, returning home after studies, with renewed spirit the father and son sat down together on the bank of the river, where they began to talk. Śuk Deva said, "Father, having lived with my Guru Bṛhaspati for so long, I have studied all the sciences, the various forms of knowledge, the Vedas and the forms of tapasya. I have learned what it means to do sādhana and to dedicate my life to God. Now, Father, what is your order for me? What is next for me to do in my life?"

Veda Vyāsa replied, "According to our Hindu scriptures, every being has four stages of life. You have completed your Brahmāchari aśrama in which you learn, and now the next stage is to become a Gṛhaṣṭha. Gṛha Avaṣṭha, iti Gṛhaṣṭha; he who lives in a house, is a householder. The duties of a householder are to make a contribution to society, and to store up something so that in our older age we won't be a burden to anyone else; to take care of our families, and to see to the progress and upliftment of the community. Thereafter, you can become Vanapraṣṭha, literally one who lives in the forest, and practically, a Vanapraṣṭha has one foot inside the house, and one foot outside the house. And then, quite naturally, one evolves from Vanapraṣṭha to Sannyāsi, someone who has established truth within. Satya Nyāsa Kariāte, He Who has established Truth Within is a Sannyāsi. So now my son, it is time for you to marry. Enjoy your life in this world, make your contribution to society, and I will be very pleased.

"You know everyone who comes to this earth plane has three debts of karma: Devaṛn, Pitriṛn and Acāryaṛn; debts to the Gods, debts to our ancestors, and debts to the Gurus or teachers of wisdom. The debt of karma to the Gods is discharged by making a contribution to all of life, by working for the upliftment of all existence, by helping others. The debt to the ancestors is paid by taking care of our elderly people the way we would want to be cared for when we are old, and by nourishing the next generation the way we want our world to become. And the debt to the Guru or teachers is discharged by acting in accordance with the wisdom that they teach. So now, my son, marry. Take a beautiful wife, enjoy your life, pay off your debts of karma. Free me from my debts of karma, and in this way you will fulfill the Hindu ideal."

Śuk Deva gave his reply, "Father, is there any pleasure that is not mixed with pain? Is it possible to have any kind of pleasure while never having any pain? Isn't it true that pleasure and pain are inseparably connected, and anyone who invites pleasure and seeks the pleasures of a beautiful wife, of a family, a home, or the comforts of good food, nice living conditions, is also going to find that pain is attached to those objects and relationships? I would think that freedom could come to someone who is tied to a pillar, but freedom will never come to a man who is tied to his wife and children. If someone is tied to a post, he can aspire or hope to be free, but if one is bound by the economic and emotional attachments of wife and children, he can never hope to be free. Is anyone free from their children? Even when they are grown is it possible to be free? They still call Mother!

"You know," continued Śuk Deva, "the noble ātmas, the noble souls, who really find pleasure in the Self, they never pursue sensual pleasure. They enjoy the pleasure of unity in Brahmāṇ. I took Bṛhaspati as my guru with the hope that he would show me the way to be free. But as I was watching even the Guru of the Gods, I saw that he was not free himself. I remember the time when his wife Tāra went to stay at Candra's house. Do you remember that incident? Tāra had a relationship with Candra, the Moon, and Bṛhaspati was so sad. He was crying all the time. 'When will my wife come home? She has abandoned me for the Moon!' Now, if the Guru is not free, how can he teach the disciple to be free?"

## The King and the Puṅḍit

Śuk Deva continued, "There is the story of a King, who was told by a puṅḍit, 'Do you know King Parikṣit was freed, received total liberation, just by hearing the Bhagavāt recited for seven days? You, too, should listen to the Bhagavāt.' The King said, 'All right, let me hear the Bhagavāt.' And the puṅḍit went every day and read the Bhagavāt for the King to hear. Then the King said to the puṅḍit, 'Puṅḍit, more than a week has passed since I have been listening to the Bhagavāt, and I am not yet liberated. Either there is something wrong with the book, or there is something wrong with the puṅḍit. Please tell me why I am not liberated. Which one is at fault?' The puṅḍit thought, 'If I say the book is wrong, he will ask me why I wasted seven days of his time reading it to him? If I say the puṅḍit is wrong, he will say, 'Why do I need this kind of a puṅḍit? Give me someone who is knowledgeable, who can illuminate me.' What shall I answer?'

"Then the puṅḍit said, 'King, I will give you the answer tomorrow.' The King said, 'You had better give me a satisfactory answer tomorrow, or I am not going to pay you any dakṣiṇa for the services that you have performed, nor will I use your services in the future.' The puṅḍit went home and was filled with sorrow and anxiety. 'What will I answer the King?'

"That night his young daughter looked at her father and asked, 'Daddy, you look so anxious. You look like you have been plunged into the world of worries. What is the problem?' The puṅḍit replied, 'The King told me that he did not get liberated from listening to the Bhagavāt for seven days. Now either the book is wrong or the puṅḍit is wrong. Which is it?' And he said you tell me tomorrow, or I will not pay for any of your services. You know what, my daughter? If the King does not pay me my dakṣiṇa, how am I going to buy the groceries and to pay the expenses to take care of our family? Now I am at a loss as to what answer I will give the King.'

"The daughter said, 'Father, that's easy. I've got the answer!' The father said, 'You do?' She said, 'Yes, Father, you just have to take me to the court tomorrow, when you go to see the King, and I will give him the answer.' Father agreed.

"The next morning they went to the King's palace. The King said, 'Okay Puṅḍit, why have I not become liberated? I have been listening to the Bhagavāt for seven days now. Either the book is wrong, or the puṅḍit is wrong. Which is it?' The puṅḍit said, 'Excuse me, King. My daughter wants to give you the answer to this question.' 'Your daughter? Okay, let her answer!' The young girl came to the King and said, 'King, I will give you the answer, but you must promise that you will cooperate with me, and do just what I will tell you to do.' The King said, 'All right, I'll cooperate.' The daughter said, 'Okay, tie me to this post.' The King said, 'Captain of the Guard, tie this girl to the post!' They tied her. 'Is it secure?' she asked. 'Yes, it is secure.' 'You see, I can't get away, can I?' They said, 'No, you can't get away.' She said, 'Okay, now tie the King to that post. King, you promised that you would cooperate, and that you would do what I said.' 'Tie me to the post,' the King ordered. They tied the King to the post, and the girl said, 'Is it secure? Can the King move?' The King said, 'No I can't move. I can't get away.' And then the little girl said, 'Okay, King, untie me.' He said, 'I can't untie you! I, myself, am bound!' She said, 'No, King, come and free me! Set me free!' 'I can't set you free!' he said. 'I myself am bound! How can I set you free when I am bound myself?' Then the daughter said, 'You bound my father with fear for money and payment. You bound him! How can he set you free until you release him?' And the King accepted the answer, and he gave the dakṣiṇa to the puṅḍit. When he liberated the girl, he became liberated himself. When we bind others, it is very difficult for them to set us free. How can they set us free when they themselves are bound?

## The Debate Continues

"So, Father, I don't want to marry, because I think that marriage is a bondage. You know I have this divine birth. I was born from the sacred fire, and not from any ordinary woman's womb. I am not longing for the pleasures of the world, I am longing for the pleasures of the soul. And those are not the pleasures that are obtained by marrying and having children, along with the financial responsibilies and the rest. It is very rare to get a human birth, especially to be born in the holy land of India, and even more so to be born in a family of Brahmiṇs, and even more so to be born from the sacred fire from such a father as Veda Vyāsa. Now I have studied the Scriptures and Vedānta, and I have had the honor of learning with such a Guru as Bṛhaspati. If beings such as ourselves cannot aspire to freedom, then who in this world can become free? So Father, please. I will do whatever you say, but please don't tell me to get married."

Veda Vyāsa gave his reply. He said, "Son, the house is not a prison from which one seeks to be freed. The house is the temple of your worship. Did you know that even the

Brahmācharis, the Vanaprasṭhas and the Sannyāsis, when they get hungry, they must come to do pūjā at the doorstep of the Gṛhasṭhas. That is why the Gṛhasṭha aśrama is called the highest of the aśramas, because the householder is the support of the entire society. So Son, don't be afraid of bondage. Allow yourself to make a contribution to this world. Look at Vasiṣṭha and all the other Great Ṛṣis. They all were married. He who does not take a wife, is certain to be maddened by the senses. These senses are like restless horses, and even though they may appear to be still for a few moments, at any moment they can jump and run away and take the mind with them. Son, get married. Fulfill your dharma through the appropriate karma, and gradually attain to the highest renunciation.

"Look at Viśvāmitra. Even practicing such tremendous austerities for so many thousands of years, when the beautiful maiden, Menakā, came before him, he forgot all his spiritual virtues in a moment, and engendered a daughter by her, Śakuntala. My own father, Parāsara, when he saw Matsyagandha in the boat, even though she smelled like a fish, he did not care. He lost the virtue, the stillness, the control of his thoughts, and his senses ran away with his mind. My Son! Get married! Fulfill your dharma, and go step by step from aśrama to aśrama."

Śuk Deva replied, "Father, you know a married man is always looking for money. Always he is in need of money! He needs money for this and he needs money for that. Therefore, he is always anxious. Look at Indra. Indra is Lord of the Heavens, and yet he is always anxious. He doesn't want any - one to conquer the heavens or become as great a sādhu as he. So he is always putting obstacles in the path of every seeker. Brahmā is not happy even though he has created this whole saṃsāra, or ocean of objects and relationships. Even Viṣṇu who has the beautiful Lakṣmī as his bride, even still he is not always happy and satisfied. He is repeatedly required to come down to earth to fight with aśuras. Śiva suffers incessant problems. Knowing fully well the truth of the world, why are you putting me into this terrible saṃsāra full of pains and agonies? Why are you sending me to get married?

"Father, there is pain in birth, there is pain in death, there is pain in old age, and there is pain in the life of the womb. But the pain arising from unfulfillable desire and greed is the most terrible of all the pains mentioned. A Brahmiṇ has only six activities in which to become engaged: learning and teaching; worshiping for himself and worshiping for others; giving what he can and accepting what is offered in love. That means that a Brahmiṇ has no other way to earn a livelihood, but to accept gifts from others. Can you imagine what a pain it is to dwell in expectation that after years of study, after years of tapasya, a Brahmiṇ is forced to wait for the generosity of others who are not even trained to appreciate his knowledge? Is there anything more regrettable than this in life? After studying all the Vedas and other scriptures and acquiring wisdom, ultimately the Brahmiṇs have to go to the rich and to praise them in the hopes that they may get some money with which they can feed their family?

"Whereas, if there is contentment in the mind and a man is alone without any obligations or responsibilities, he can somehow find something to satisfy his appetites. Father, please teach me the Wisdom of Eternal Truth, the way to perfect happiness. Tell me how my karmas can be completely fulfilled. Don't tell me about having children and having a wife and a house, nor about having bills and debts, nor about having to go out and beg for money to pay them off. Tell me how I can obtain silence and stillness in my mind, so that I don't need to get anything more. Tell me how this great ignorance of duality can be destroyed."

When Veda Vyāsa heard Śuk Deva's discourse, he became merged in a sea of anxiety, and began to think of what else could be done to convince his son of the truth contained in the path outlined by the scriptures. Śuk Deva looked at Veda Vyāsa filled with anxiety and said, "Oh my goodness, what power this Māyā has! Nothing is as strong as Māyā. You who divided the Vedas, defined the schools of the Vedas, who wrote the eighteen Purāṇas, who wrote the histories, the Bhagavāt, the Mahābhārat, and the Devī Bhagavatam, you are suffering from the ignorance and delusion of attachment. You want your son to have a wife. What pleasure is that going to bring you, Father? Seeing me bound for eternity in the saṃsāra of objects and relationships, is that going to make you happy? How can this wonderfully intelligent being become so deluded by Māyā? What a power this Māyā has that even the Great Veda Vyāsa, to whom the whole world looks for inspiration, is suffering from these delusions. This Māyā deluded Brahmā, it deluded Viṣṇu, it deludes Śiva and the whole universe. Who is there in the universe that is not fascinated under the influence of Māyā. I bow down to that Māyā. I take refuge in that Māyā. I will have only that Māyā as my own.

"Father, all this universe is like a net of delusion. Understanding this, remembering this, abandon your grief. Renounce your sorrow. To get a human birth in this Land of Karma is very difficult. Again to get a Brahmiṇ birth is extremely rare. And when I have attained this beautiful birth as a strong and healthy Brahmiṇ boy, who has studied the wisdom of the scriptures and Vedānta, and I have served many spiritual teachers, yet I still have this idea that I am bound by the world. Father, how can I get freedom? Even Veda Vyāsa is not free. And you are telling me to marry?!"

And his father replied, "My son, if you still don't believe me, please study the Devī Bhagavatam. In the Devī Bhagavatam are many stories, an anthology of our Hindu Dharma, the Sanātana Dharma, the Eternal Ideal of

Perfection in Wisdom and Harmony is expressed in the most explicit terms. Son, study the scriptures, and then tell me if you have made up your mind."

Śuk Deva studied the Devī Bhagavatam, and even after that, he still didn't want to accept his father's opinion. And Veda Vyāsa said, "My Son, I can tell your mind is made up. But before you take the decision to enter into the fourth stage of Sannyāsi, my Son, please go visit Janaka, the King of Mithilā. He is liberated while living in a body, and he is my disciple. Go ask him your question, and please, listen to his discourse. Then come back and tell me your decision. I will allow you to do as you choose. I promise you, my son. Just go meet with King Janaka."

### Śuk Deva Visits King Janaka

Receiving the blessings of his father, Śuk Deva began to traverse the Land of India en route to Mithilā. For a few years he walked over the plains and climbed the mountains, crossed streams and rivers. After some time he finally came to Mithilā, the City of Janaka. Outside the city gate was a soldier who ordered him, "Stop, please. I am required to know who you are, and what business you have in the city."

Śuk Deva looked at the soldier and replied, "I knew I was wrong in coming here. What a fool I was to believe that this King was liberated while living! To me being liberated means one sees everything as being the same. And yet this King has so much attachment that he puts soldiers outside the city to ask every prospective visitor, 'Who are you and what business do you have to come here?' I knew that it was impossible. I am sorry, soldier. I didn't mean to waste your time. I am going home right now."

The soldier replied, "Well, you have come such a long distance. I didn't mean to offend you. It's just my duty to ask."

Śuk Deva said, "I understand it's your duty, and that you meant no offense. A King is right in proclaiming such a duty. But that is not the type of proclamation that an enlightened being who sees everything as the same would make! What difference is it to him, who is a good person, or who is a bad person? He knows everywhere is Oneness, and good and bad are merely value judgements according to individual aspirations. What everything is becoming makes no difference either. A liberated being sees everyone and everything as being the same. Being enlightened means seeing everything is One! There is no duality, there is no distinction, no delusion. How can he be liberated, when he puts a guard in front of his city? It's impossible! Forget it! I don't even want to come into this city!"

The guard said, "Holy Brahmiṇ, I can tell that you are a very knowledgeable and respectable man. Please excuse me. Go ahead and enter the city."

Śuk Deva said, "I know the purpose of my visit is going to be fruitless. I have come to hold discourse with an enlightened King, but obviously instead of seeing Oneness everywhere, this man sees distinctions everywhere. Well, as long as you invite me with such courtesy, and I've come this far, I might as well go in and see the city."

So Śuk Deva walked into the city and looked into the market places. He saw normal people. Some of them were happy, and some of them were sad. Some of them were arguing, and some of them were debating the qualities of merchandise and the prices that they must pay. In various ways, various people were doing various activities. Śuk Deva thought to himself, "There doesn't appear to be any sign of an enlightened administration in this city to me. These citizens aren't so happy. These citizens aren't radiating the joy and the bliss of having an enlightened master as their King. They are just normal people, doing the same thing every normal person does. What kind of enlightened King is this? I knew I was wrong! My father gave me the wrong information; he was just trying to convince me to do his will."

When King Janaka heard that Śuk Deva, his Guru's son, had come into his kingdom, his heart was filled with joy! He immediately sent his ministers outside to meet Śuk Deva, and they escorted him to a beautiful palace. Then many beautiful young ladies from the palace came and prepared his bath. They gave him fresh clothes, and prepared delicious food for him. The ladies made a beautiful soft bed upon which he could rest. They put him on the bed and started to massage his feet. Śuk Deva was oblivious to the entire affair. When all the girls left, he sat in his yogic posture and went into meditation. Then he slept for a few hours.

At the break of dawn, he woke again to sit in meditation until the sun rose. Then he took his bath and waited for the King to call him. After a short time a messenger came from the King, "The King wants to see you. Please come."

Śuk Deva went to see the King. The King rose to greet him, "Oh Śuk Deva, please tell me, to what do I owe the honor of this visit?"

Śuk Deva said, "Oh King, for twelve years I studied Vedas and Vedānta, living in the aśrama of the Guru Bṛhaspati. When I returned from my studies at my Guru's aśrama, I asked my father, 'What work should I do now? What is my karma in life?' My father instructed me that I should marry and have children and free him from the debts of karma. I said, 'Father, for several years I have studied the knowledge of non-duality. I had a divine birth; I didn't come from any womb, but I came from the Divine Fire. Why should I marry and sell myself into bondage, when I am not seeking the pleasures of the body? I seek absorption in the soul.' My father seemed to be perplexed by anxiety and told me, 'No son, you should marry!' And when I flatly refused, he said,

'Okay, if you don't believe me, go to Mithilā to visit the King Janaka. After you talk to the King Janaka, I will allow you to make any decision you like. So King, I have come for your darśana. Please enlighten me. What are the duties of a man?"

Janaka replied, "I shall tell you about the path of liberation. After completing the studies as a Brahmāchari, one should bow to the guru and pay the dakṣiṇa. Then he should go home and marry. After marriage one should remain contented and free from desires, sinless and truthful, and earn a livelihood with a pure heart, live with justice and according to the dictates of conscience. And then when the children are self-sufficient, the stage of Vanapraṣṭha can be commenced, along with the practice of tapasya. Ultimately a developed soul can become a Sannyāsi, fully absorbed into the Truth of Supreme Divinity. That is the path of liberation proclaimed by our Dharma. See, a true seeker must complete his stages of life, the aśramas of life, one by one, step by step. No one should skip a step. He must complete the previous aśramas successively, and then enter into the next stage."

Śuk Deva asked, "But King, if the purity of detachment arises from wisdom within the seeker, is it still necessary for him to go through all the aśramas? Isn't it possible to quit everything and reside in the forest?"

Janaka answered, "No. Even though it appears that the senses have become still for a time, that doesn't mean that they will always be still for all time. Even in the state of Perfect Yoga, it might appear that the senses are under control. That appearance is not to be trusted. The net of desire is very difficult to be conquered, and it never dies. The mind is very difficult to control. Therefore, it is necessary to move step by step, aśrama by aśrama. Nobody jumps. See, even a householder who performs his duties without attachment can live in pure happiness, realize his own Self and attain liberation. You see, I am liberated while living and engaged in protecting this kingdom. I am not affected by pleasure or pain; still I continue to act.

"The material world is simply an object of sensory perception. And the soul which perceives it, is itself imperceivable. So tell me how can the perceivable creation bind the imperceivable soul? This is a logical impossibility. The Self which is changeless, without impurity, can never be bound by the changeful, visible, tangible material things. When the heart becomes pure and quiet, all things become fully pure and fully quiet. It is the mind that is the cause of bondage and freedom. It is not the body. It is not the soul. It is not the senses. The Self, the Soul of all, is always Pure Consciousness, and it is always free, so it can never be bound. Bondage and freedom reside only in the mind. So when the mind is at peace, the bondage of existence ceases. This individual Self, this individual existence is God. I am that God and nothing else."

"But, oh King," inquired Śuk Deva. "I have another doubt. How can a man be free from desires and the rewards from actions when he lives in the midst of this Māyā? This entire material world is always forcing the mind into delusion. Even acquiring the wisdom of the scriptures and discrimination to understand what is real and what is not, the delusion of the mind is not dispelled until one practices Yoga. How can freedom from desire and liberation come to a householder? The munis and ṛṣis who live in the forest controlling their diets, controlling their senses, living their lives as hermits and mendicants, they know the transient nature of this world. Even they fall victims to Māyā. Then what hope is there for you or I or anyone else who is acting and interacting in duality? When you are in this duality, you are bound by Māyā. The five elements go with you wherever you go, and these elements always bring us to Māyā, the delusion of duality."

Janaka replied, "What you say is true without a particle of

falsehood, Śuk Deva. You are right. The five elements: earth, water, fire, air, and ether, do exist everywhere. So even if you go to the forest, they will exist with you there. You will also be concerned about your staff, your seat, your blanket, or your cup. You will worry about where you will find water and wood. Enlightenment doesn't mean the complete cessation of thought. That state of Yoga, Citta Vṛtti Nirodh, the cessation of all modifications of Consciousness, is transient. Neither does Brahmā remain there, nor Viṣṇu, nor Śiva, nor any other embodied beings. Everyone returns to the awareness of duality. Enlightenment does not mean being free from manifestation, it does not mean being free from thought. Enlightenment means freedom from attachment!

"You see, your mind is filled with doubt. Therefore you are traveling in search of the cessation of your doubts. But you see, my mind is free from doubt. I am remaining here quite peacefully and cheerfully observing my dharma. 'I am not bound up by this world.' This idea gives me constant happiness of the highest degree. You consider that you are bound, and therefore you are in constant pain. No matter whether you go to the forest or you reside in your home, your mind will determine your state of bondage or liberation. 'This body is mine.' That idea leads to bondage. 'This body is not mine.' This knowledge gives freedom. So I tell you truthfully that all this kingdom, all this wealth, all the subjects for whom I perform administrative duties, none of this is mine!"

Śuk Deva was extremely inspired. "You are a sādhu," he said to the King Janaka bowing with respect. "A sādhu is a Master of Efficiency. You have become extremely efficient at organizing your life. I bow to you in respect for your wisdom."

Śuk Deva looked into his own heart and thought, "I can live in this world, and this world is not mine. I can act in this world, and the fruits of the action will not be mine. Then I, too, can become a Yogi of Karma, maintaining purity in action.

Even if I go to the forest with my stick, my pot and my blanket, I will be bound so long as the mind is not free. Whereas this King administering an entire empire on behalf of a higher power, is liberated."

Śuk Deva bowed before King Janaka and took his leave. With this realization, he returned to his father's aśrama on the banks of the holy Sarasvatī River.

## The Marriage of Śuk Deva

Veda Vyāsa came running to greet his son, and was so happy to see him. He immediately inquired, "How are you my son? What have you determined for your life?"

And Śuk Deva replied, "Father, as you wish I will perform. None of this is mine."

Then Śuk Deva submerged himself in the practice of Yoga. His father, Veda Vyāsa, arranged a marriage for him with Pibari, a very beautiful daughter of a ṛṣi. This beautiful young lady gave birth to four sons who were named: Kṛṣṇa, Gauraprabha, Bhūri, and Devaśruta. And then she gave birth to one daughter whose name was Kīrti.

Śuk Deva saw to the nurturing of his children, to their education and marriage, and maintained his strict adherence to dharma. When his children grew up and they were able to take care of themselves, he proceeded to Mount Kailāsa, where he started to meditate. Then he began to float into the sky. He developed all the eight siddhis. There he was, meditating high above, up in the sky above Mount Kailāsa. He began to radiate light like the sun. Suddenly he became merged into the Parabrahmā, the Paramātma. He became one with the Universal Soul, and vanished in the air!

Veda Vyāsa was much distressed. "My son, where did you go? Why did you leave me? You still have to perform my funeral rights! My son come back!" Veda Vyāsa was very sorry that Śuk Deva left.

One day Veda Vyāsa was wandering around looking through the heavens, "Where is my son Śuk Deva?"

Then Śuk Deva looked down at him from heaven and in a voice which rumbled like a cloud he said, "Father, there is no difference between you and me if you look at our soul. Why then are you weeping for me? Go home and perform tapasya."

Then Veda Vyāsa went back to his aśrama on the Sarasvatī River and began to practice tapasya.

## Śantānu Reunited with Devavrat

Ever since Gaṅgā took her son Devavrat and left Śantānu, the King remained very sad. After performing his duties as the King, every afternoon he would drive down to the banks of the Gaṅgā in his chariot, where he would sit in contemplation of his lost beloved, longing for just one sight of her.

Every evening, well after dark, he would return to his palace and in the despondency of his loneliness, he would sit throughout the night, lost in his suffering, and alone. In this way a number of years passed. The King had no joy in his life. He did not celebrate any of the festivals or perform any Pūjās or worship. He only sat alone in his own quarters. The citizens, like their King, had no joy and nothing to look forward to. Everyone seemed to be merely tolerating life, and waiting for something to change.

One day Śantānu went down to the bank of the Gaṅgā as usual. He sat down on his rock, where he looked out over the banks of the river, when he suddenly saw a most amazing sight. A flight of arrows came down and all of them stuck one into the other and created a dam which stopped the flow of the Gaṅgā. Suddenly there was a dam across the Gaṅgā made of the arrows from some unknown archer. Śantānu looked with amazement. The Gaṅgā had stopped.

The King was so surprised that he ran over to see this dam, when suddenly Gaṅgā appeared. He took a long look at her and said, "My beautiful, beloved wife, you left me, and now you have come again. What is this amazing thing? Who is it that can stop the flow of your waters?"

Gaṅgā said, "Look over there. That is your son Devavrat. This is an example of the knowledge he has attained. He has studied politics with Bṛhaspati, the Guru of the Gods. He has studied weaponry with Paraśurām. He has studied all the great branches of wisdom from the greatest teachers available. Now I am giving you a son fit to follow in your footsteps."

Gaṅgā called her son, Devavrat, and Devavrat came. "Yes, Mother."

"My son, please bow down to your father."

Śantānu grabbed his son, hugged and kissed him. Devavrat fell to his father's feet and made praṇām. Gaṅgā said, "Now my duty is complete. I am going to leave you both. I won't come to you anymore, Śantānu. Only when my son is deeply in need will I come to him." With those words, Gaṅgā entered into the river and disappeared from sight.

Śantānu was filled with joy to have his son, a companion and heir to the throne. Devavrat was in every way the most beautiful son he could imagine. He was a fine warrior, a sportsman and a craftsman. He was a great benevolent being and everyone loved him. To the delight of all Śantānu anointed Devavrat the heir to the throne, the Crown Prince, the next King of Hastinapura.

## Devavrat Becomes Bhīṣma

Even though Śantānu had his son and the people had a crowned prince, Śantānu's heart was not yet satisfied. There was still an empty place that longed to be filled. One day Śantānu went with his son Devavrat and their most trusted advisors and friends, to hunt. Śantānu went off in pursuit of some precious trophy by himself. He followed that game until he came to the bank of the Jamuna River where he saw Satyavatī sitting by her boat. Satyavatī had received the blessing from Parāsara that she would have the most wonderful scent and everlasting beauty. Satyavatī, Matsyagandha, the daughter of the fisherman, was sitting by the boat waiting to ferry passengers across the river. She was exuding her beautiful fragrance and her beauty was radiant. Śantānu went to Satyavatī and asked, "What are you doing here?"

Satyavatī said, "I am waiting for a passenger to ferry across the river."

Śantānu said, "Would you ferry me across the river?"

"Gladly, oh King," she replied.

Satyavatī ferried Śantānu across the river, but the King could not take his eyes from her the entire journey. When they reached the other side the King said, "I have made a mistake. Please take me back to the other side. I will pay you double the fare."

As Satyavatī paddled the boat, the King could see nothing but the beauty of this lovely young lady. Śantānu said to her, "I came here to this forest for hunting, but it seems as though someone has hunted me. I have become the target. Now there is only one person who can save the King of Hastinapura. That person is you, Satyavatī. Will you become my wife?"

Satyavatī said, "I would be honored to be your wife, oh King. But you must take permission from my father, Dāsrāj."

Śantānu agreed, "Yes, without hesitation I will go to your father and ask for permission to marry you."

Śantānu immediately went to Dāsrāj and told him, "Dāsrāj, I have fallen in love with Satyavatī. I wish to make her my wife."

Dāsrāj said, "What a wonderful opportunity for my daughter. But as father of the bride, I have one request. My daughter will marry you only if you will make her child the next King."

Śantānu said, "That is impossible. I have already anointed Devavrat. He is the most perfect person to be the King. He has already been installed as the heir to the throne. How can I steal the kingdom away from my own son who is qualified in every way, to give it to the unborn son of your daughter? I can't do such an injustice and still call myself the King."

Dāsrāj said, "Then you can't marry my daughter."

Śantānu got angry and stormed out of the house and returned to his encampment. His heart was sad. Every day he would go down to the bank of the Jamuna and look at Satyavatī from a distance, hiding behind a tree. Every evening, well after dark, he came home to the encampment of the hunting party. His heart was heavy. Devavrat went to him and said, "Father, what is the problem? Is it some problem with the kingdom? If it is, then as the Crown Prince of the kingdom I should be informed. Please share your troubles with me. Or is it a personal problem? As your son you should share your burden with me. Please Father, trust in me. Confide in me. Unburden your heart, and let's see if we can't find a solution."

The King said, "My son, a man cannot share everything. Neither can the King share everything, nor can a father share everything."

Devavrat said, "Then let's go home to Hastinapura. We have important matters to take care of there. We have hunted enough and spent enough time in the forest. Let's go back to Hastinapura."

The King Śantānu said, "No son, not now. Just a few more days."

Every day Śantānu went down to the bank of the Jamuna River and he watched Satyavatī as she did her work; rowing people across the river or sitting on the bank waiting for another passenger.

The King came back to the encampment late one night and retired to his tent. Devavrat, the King's son, called the chariot driver and said, "Charioteer, where do you take my father everyday?"

The charioteer said, "That's a private matter between your father and me. I cannot betray his confidence."

Devavrat said, "Charioteer, the King of our country is beset with sadness and a heavy burden. I am the Crown Prince and also his son. I must know what is the cause of his burden. What can I do to relieve my father of his sadness? Please, you must tell me where you take my father everyday."

"To the bank of the Jamuna River."

"Why do you take my father to the bank of the Jamuna River? What does he do there? "

"He looks at Satyavatī."

"The whole day he looks at Satyavatī? Did he ever talk to Satyavatī?"

"Yes. He did."

"Well, what did he say?"

"He said, 'I would like to marry you.'"

Devavrat again inquired. "What did she say?"

"She said, 'I too would like to marry you, but you must get permission from my father.'"

Then Devavrat inquired, "Did he ever meet her father? What did the father say?"

"Yes," said the charioteer. "The father said, 'You can't

marry my daughter unless her son becomes the next King of Hastinapura.' Then your father got angry and left. And every day he goes to the bank of the Jamuna and looks at her."

Devavrat said, "Take me to Dāsrāj. I want to meet Satyavatī's father."

In the middle of the night he rode to Dāsrāj's house. When Dāsrāj woke up in the night to see Devavrat, the King's son, he was most surprised. "What are you doing here?" he inquired. "It is a most surprising hour to see the King's son at my home."

"Dāsrāj, I've come to bring Satyavatī to my father."

"Oh, Crown Prince, you must know of my desire. I told your father that I cannot give my daughter to him unless her son would be made the King of Hastinapura. Your father said that he could not grant that wish. So then I could not give him my daughter as his wife."

Devavrat said, "The King was right in telling you that he could not grant that wish, because he already gave up that privilege. A King can only bestow his kingdom once. He would be dishonest to take that kingdom away from the person he gave it to, in order to give it to another. He gave that promise to me. So he couldn't give that promise again to you. Dāsrāj, I have the promise; the promise is now with me. And I give you the promise that the son of Satyavatī will become the next King of Hastinapura. I will not accept the throne if it means the happiness of my father. In all our histories, how many times we have found a father making a sacrifice for the happiness of his son. Now history will find an example of a son making a sacrifice for the happiness of his father. I will not accept the throne. I give my right to the throne to the son of Satyavatī."

Dāsrāj said, "What a noble son you are to think so highly for the happiness of your father that you are willing to sacrifice your kingdom. But what if your children don't agree?

What if your children raise the issue of a claim to the throne and with an army come to do battle with Satyavatī's son?"

Devavrat said, "You are absolutely right, Dāsrāj. I have no capacity to promise on behalf of my unborn children. But I do have the capacity to promise to never have children. So I, Devavrat, the son of Śantānu, hereby promise that I will have no children. I will never marry. I will never have any physical relationship with a woman."

When that promise was given, the whole earth shook. The Gods showered flowers down upon him. Dāsrāj bowed to Devavrat and gave to him the beautiful Satyavatī. Satyavatī got into the chariot with Devavrat and together they returned to the King's camp.

It was almost morning when they arrived. Śantānu was very anxious, wondering where his son had gone in the middle of the night. When Devavrat returned in the early morning along with Satyavatī, Satyavatī explained the entire circumstance of how Devavrat gave the promise that allowed her father to grant the permission to marry. Śantānu blessed Devavrat and said, "Devavrat, you have taken such a strong vow. You are Bhīṣma, the strong, the one of such terrific strength and noble character. I give you the blessing of Icchā Mṛtyu. You will only leave your body when you desire. You will be invincible to all beings. Never before was there a man so strong and steadfast in his vow, seeking only the happiness and delight of his father. Your name, Bhīṣma, will be eternal. You will be the strongest supporter of Dharma."

Again Bhīṣma promised, "Father, your sons through Satyavatī will continue your lineage. And no matter who sits on the throne of Hastinapura, I will always protect the King of this kingdom. This is my vow to you."

## The Marriage of Vicitravīrya and the Curse of Bhīṣma

Even with his beautiful wife, Satyavatī, Śantānu couldn't take pleasure. Always somewhere in his heart, both he and his wife felt their union came about as a result of such a tremendous sacrifice by their son. Bhīṣma was such a noble character who gave up so much for the happiness of his father, and yet the parents always dwelt in sadness.

Despite this sadness, Satyavatī and Śantānu had two sons. The first was Citrāṅgada and the second was Vicitravīrya. Even though he had two sons, Śantānu still wasn't happy. When Citrāṅgada was a young man, he was crowned the Prince Regent. Soon after this coronation, Śantānu died. Bhīṣma became the administrator of the kingdom and guarded the throne, while Citrāṅgada and Vicitravīrya grew up to be strong young men and heroic warriors.

One day Citrāṅgada, the King of Hastinapura, went hunting in the forest. During the hunt, he was attacked by a lion and he died right there on the spot. Then Vicitravīrya became the King of Hastinapura.

The King of Kāśi, which is now called Benares, had three beautiful daughters: Ambe, Ambike and Ambālike. When the time came for their marriage, he called for the Svayambara where the girls would choose their husbands. He invited all the Kings of India, princes and noblemen, who all came to Kāśi to participate in the festivities in which the three maidens would choose their husbands. But because of an old defeat that the ancestors of Kāśi had suffered at the hands of the Kings of Hastinapura, the King of Kāśi decided to insult the Kingdom of Hastinapura by not inviting King Vicitravīrya.

Bhīṣma became angry at this insult and, by himself, immediately proceeded to Kāśi. When Bhīṣma arrived at the Svayambara hall, the three girls were standing with the wedding garlands in their hands, waiting to choose their husbands. Bhīṣma entered into the hall in great anger, his bow drawn with an arrow and said, "King of Kāśi, you have chosen to insult Hastinapura by not inviting our King to be a part of this ceremony. Therefore, I am now taking all three of these girls to be the wives of the King of Hastinapura."

All the Kings assembled in the room drew their swords. Bhīṣma let his arrows fly which pierced through all the crowns of those Kings, and put those crowns at the feet of the King of Kāśi. Thereafter all those defeated Kings lowered their heads.

Bhīṣma said, "If anyone likes to fight, let them avail the opportunity right now. Otherwise I am taking these three girls with me."

Their father gave the order and the three girls got into Bhīṣma's chariot and were carried off to Hastinapura. When they arrived at Hastinapura, Satyavatī was so pleased to see the three girls coming, young brides for her son. When they were introduced to Mother Satyavatī, Ambe said, "Queen Mother, before Bhīṣma stole us away from the wedding ceremony, I had already fallen in love with Salvya. I had planned to give my wedding garland to him, but Bhīṣma came and at the point of an arrow stopped me from exercising my right as a princess in choosing my own husband. Therefore, if you will send me to the husband I have chosen, I will be very grateful."

Satyavatī said, "Of course, my dear. Bhīṣma will make all the arrangements to send you to Salvya immediately and with great honor."

Then they sent a contingent of the army as an escort to take Ambe to Salvyarāj, so she could marry the man of her choice.

Meanwhile, Vicitravīrya married the two sisters, Ambike and Ambālike. When Ambe reached to Salvyarāj's kingdom, she met with the King Salvya and said, "My dear, I wanted to marry you."

Salvya said, "This is a great insult. You were stolen away from me at the point of an arrow. I wasn't able to defend you then. How can you come back to me now as a gift from Bhīṣma? How can I accept you? I am sorry I cannot. My Dharma as a warrior King does not allow me to accept you as a gift from the man who had stolen you away from me by force of arms. You had better go back to Hastinapura.

Ambe became very angry. She went back to the court of Vicitravīrya in Hastinapura and she said, "King, Queen Mother, I want justice. Bhīṣma has ruined my life. He stole me away from my wedding ceremony when I had the wedding garland in my hand. I had already chosen the man to whom I was going to bestow my life. And now because of Bhīṣma, that man will not accept me. Now shall I spend the rest of my life as an unwed lady? I want to be married. King, order Bhīṣma to marry me. He is the one who ruined my life, and only if he marries me can it be restored to my satisfaction."

Bhīṣma stood up and said, "That's quite impossible. I have taken the promise that I will never marry."

"Coward! You stole me away from my wedding ceremony when I was holding the wedding garland in my hand, and now you are relying on that old promise to excuse your misbehavior. My lover wouldn't accept me because you stole me away from him. Now Bhīṣma, if you don't marry me, I promise I am going to become the cause of your death!" Thus speaking, she stormed out of the palace and went into the forest to perform tapasya.

## Satyavatī Calls Veda Vyāsa

In the palace Vicitravīrya was very happy with his two queens, Ambike and Ambālike. The three of them had such a beautiful relationship, each one paying honor and respect to the others.

One morning as Vicitravīrya was getting dressed to come to the hall of audience, he began to cough. And he coughed again. Suddenly he fell down and died. There was much mourning and sorrow in Hastinapura. The King was dead and there was no heir to the throne. Satyavatī called Bhīṣma.

"Bhīṣma, you must renounce your promise and take the throne."

"How can I renounce my promise, Mother. A vow given to the Gods is a sacred pact. I cannot renounce my promise."

"Then at least renounce your vow of celibacy and implant a seed within the two wives of Vicitravīrya, Ambike and Ambālike, so we will have a King."

Bhīṣma said, "Mother, I am sorry I cannot renounce my vow."

Then Satyavatī said, "Bhīṣma, please go to the forest and find my son, Veda Vyāsa. Bring him here to me. Tell him his mother is in need."

Bhīṣma went to the forest where he found the muni Veda Vyāsa sitting in an aśana on the banks of the Sarasvatī River. Veda Vyāsa said, "Blessings to you Bhīṣma. I know the reason for your coming."

Bhīṣma said, "Satyavatī is calling you."

Veda Vyāsa said, "I know my mother has need for me now. I will go with you. You are not her son, so there is no need for you to obey her order. But I cannot forsake the call of my mother."

Veda Vyāsa came with Bhīṣma to the palace of Hastinapura.

"Māte, Mother, I bow to you. Namaste. How are you?"

"Satyavatī said, "I am in terrible difficulties. Both of my sons have died. Bhīṣma has promised never to accept the throne and not to have any children. I need an heir to the throne. You are part of my family and I want you to have children by the wives of Vicitravīrya and produce an heir to the throne."

Vyāsa said, "Mother, I have been doing sādhana in the forest, and I am not prepared to do this act right now. Give me one year's time and I will come and help you."

"Satyavatī said, "I cannot wait one year. I need an heir as soon as possible. Do it right now."

Vyāsa said, "Mother, please understand the result of this."

Satyavatī said, "Whatever God wills to be, will be, but I cannot wait."

That night Vyāsa went to his room and Ambike was sent to sleep with him. She became startled with fright when she saw that old man with long matted hair, a long beard, thick wrinkled skin, wearing the markings and forest dress of a hermit. She closed her eyes, cringed, and began to shake.

In the morning, Satyavatī asked Veda Vyāsa, "How did it go?"

"Mother, she closed her eyes. She couldn't bear to see me. Her child will be born blind."

Satyavatī said, "Oh, this is terrible. I need a son who is capable of becoming the King. I can't have a blind King. I will send you the other girl, Ambālike."

The next night Ambālike came to visit Veda Vyāsa. As she entered into the room, she saw that old hermit with long matted hair and beard, and she became startled with fright and turned pure white with paleness.

In the morning Satyavatī came to Vyāsa and asked him, "How did it go?"

Vyāsa said, "Mother, just what I had feared. When

Ambālike saw my old tattered form she turned pale white with fear. As a result, her son will be an albino. He will be born pure white."

Satyavatī said, "This is terrible. I need a son who is suitable to become the King. I will talk with the girls."

When she talked to Ambike and Ambālike, and ordered them to go back into the room again, neither of the girls could go back. They said, "I am not going to do this deed. I don't care about the kingdom or the King. Let's send our maid servant."

So they sent the maid servant. She went to Veda Vyāsa, and bowed down and was so kind to him. She served him without thought for herself. He blessed her and said, "Your son will be the most Dharmic man of history. He will know all the rules of politics and understand all philosophies and will be the example of wisdom throughout the ages."

The three children were born. The first and oldest was Dṛtarāṣṭra. He was blind. The second was Pāṇḍu. He was pale. The third, the son of the maid servant, was Vidura. He was the wisest and most just and most noble of mankind.

The three children, Dṛtarāṣṭra, Pāṇḍu and Vidura, began to grow up under the tutelage of Bhīṣma. He taught them all he could about weaponry, statesmanship, politics and Dharma. They grew up to be fine, strong gentlemen. Dṛtarāṣṭra, the oldest, was blind. Pāṇḍu, pale in color, was very strong and heroic. Vidura was the wisest advisor there could be.

When the three brothers came of age, Bhīṣma brought them before the Queen Mother, Satyavatī. Satyavatī looked at her grandchildren who had grown up to become fine gentlemen. Bhīṣma said, "All right, Mother. Which one should be King?"

Satyavatī said, "Dṛtarāṣṭra is oldest, but he is blind. How can he be the King?"

Vidura said, "Mother, if I may give my advice, it's impos -

sible to have a blind King. We need a defender and protector of our nation."

Satyavatī said, "Yes, Vidura, I agree with you. Pāṇḍu will be the King." Pāṇḍu was crowned the King of Hastinapura, and he began to reign in the most Dharmic way. He cared for all of his subjects like his own family.

## Pāṇḍu Marries Kuntī and Mādrī

Once there was a King by the name of Surasena. He was related to the King of Mathura, Ugrasena, and a descendant from the royal lineage established when King Śatrughna killed the evil Lavaṇaśura. King Surasena had a very beautiful daughter, the princess named Kuntī. One day Kuntī's father called for her Svayambara, for her to choose her husband from among the Kings of India. King Pāṇḍu went to watch the marriage ceremony, and the princess took the garland of victory, walked around the entire hall, and then she chose Pāṇḍu. Pāṇḍu married Kuntī.

Kuntī had a very interesting story in her youth. One day, the great Ṛṣi Durvāṣa came to visit her father. Kuntī performed all the seva for the ṛṣi herself. She fanned him when he went to sleep. She prepared his meals and served him. She rubbed his feet in the night. She sat at his feet and listened to all his wisdom. Durvāṣa Muni was very pleased and said, "Oh Kuntī, I will give you a blessing. Choose from me one blessing."

Kuntī said, "Mahārāj, I don't know what to ask for. Please, you are trikāldasi, you know the past, present and future. Please give me that blessing which will benefit me in the future."

Durvāṣa thought for a moment and said, "All right Kuntī. I am giving you a mantra. By that mantra you can call any Deva and he will come and bless you with a child."

Kuntī thought that was a very strange blessing to give. She took initiation in the mantra and Durvāṣa left.

That night Kuntī was sitting in her room thinking about what kind of a mantra she had received. She wondered if it was true that if she called any Deva he would give her a child. She could not understand how that would help her in her future. She doubted that it could be true. She sat up the whole night thinking about it, and in the morning, just when the sun was rising, she looked at the sun and said, "I have to see if this is true or not, and whether or not it really works." And she pronounced the mantra.

Sure enough, Sūrya Deva, the Sun God, came right into her room. Sūrya said, "Oh Kuntī, you have called me. That is a very powerful mantra."

Kuntī said, "Oh yes, I am sorry. I did not want to disturb you. I just wanted to see if the mantra worked. You can go back now."

Sūrya, the Sun, said, "No. It can't be that way. Once you call me by means of this mantra, I would be remiss if I did not give you a child. So here is a child."

And Sūrya gave Kuntī the most beautiful, strong and heroic looking son, who was wearing a suit of armor and earrings that came from the Sun. Then Sūrya left.

Kuntī looked at the child and contemplated what she would do. Her whole family would be angry with her and no one would believe where she got the child. She took the child and said, "Oh child, please forgive me. I know you have a destiny of great karma ahead of you." And she put the child in a basket and set it into the river. The basket floated downstream.

Adhirath, who was the charioteer of the King, found the basket. The child was taken to the charioteer's house and raised as his own son. The charioteer's wife, whose name was Rādhā, had no other children, and she named the child Rādhe.

Rādhe grew up in the house of the charioteer. But Kuntī never told anyone the secret of her first and oldest son.

After their marriage, Kuntī returned with Pāṇḍu to Hastinapura. Then Pāṇḍu said to her, "My beloved wife, a King has many obligations. My first duty is to my people, and even before we enjoy the pleasures of our married life, I must protect the borders of our nation. So I am going to certify that all of our borders are protected and safe. I will return to enjoy our honeymoon just as soon as I can."

Pāṇḍu marched off with his army and conquered all of India. He made all of the Kings of India subservient to the throne of Hastinapura. When he came to the kingdom of Madras, the Crown Prince came out to meet him and said, "Oh King, I hope you accept our friendship."

Pāṇḍu was very happy and said, "Certainly, I accept your friendship."

Then the Crown Prince said, "Well then, you must accept a token of our friendship."

Pāṇḍu said, "I will gladly accept whatever gift you wish to give me."

The Crown Prince ordered, "Charioteer."

The charioteer dismounted from the chariot and came to where the prince was standing. "I am giving you to the King of Hastinapura. King Pāṇḍu, this is my charioteer, my dear sister, Mādrī."

Pāṇḍu looked at the beautiful young lady that was driving the chariot. He was so surprised. He said, "I would love to take your sister with me, but I am already married."

Mādrī said, "Well then, take me to the Queen Kuntī. I have already been given. Let's see if Kuntī will accept me or not."

Pāṇḍu replied, "Okay, get in my chariot. Crown Prince, please excuse us as we take your leave. We shall return to Hastinapura." Then Pāṇḍu and Mādrī returned to Hastinapura.

When Kuntī heard that Pāṇḍu had returned she was filled with joy. When she saw the beautiful wife that he had brought back with him, she was filled with surprise. But Mādrī came to Kuntī and bowed down and said, "My elder sister, please bless me that we can all live together in peace and harmony," and Kuntī was delighted to accept her into the family. So Pāṇḍu was married to both Kuntī and Mādrī. He and his two wives lived together in joyous harmony.

## The Curse of Pāṇḍu

Some days after Pāṇḍu's return to Hastinapura, Satyavatī said, "My son, it's time you take some rest. Pāṇḍu, you have only been working and fighting since the day you became King. Why don't you take your two wives to our forest retreat. We have a little house there, where you can have some time for yourselves."

Pāṇḍu said, "That's a wonderful idea. Now my kingdom is safe and well protected. Let me enjoy some private time alone with my family."

Before going to the forest retreat Pāṇḍu came to his elder brother Dṛtarāṣṭra and said, "Dṛtarāṣṭra, I don't want to leave my kingdom unprotected. Please in my absence, I want you to wear the crown. You will be the King in my place."

Dṛtarāṣṭra was so pleased to have the crown on his head. As soon as Pāṇḍu left, Dṛtarāṣṭra thought of ways he could keep that crown. The crown should have been his, and would have been his, if he had not been born blind. He was the oldest. He wondered why his karma treated him in this way, and he desired to keep the crown in whatever way he could.

Pāṇḍu went to take rest with his two wives. There in the forest they met the Ṛṣi Kiṇḍal. Many days were passed listening to the wisdom of Dharma from the mouth of the ṛṣi. After many days of learning wonderful wisdom and enjoying the great rest in the most harmonious way with his wives, a lion came near the hermitage where they were residing.

Mādrī said, "My husband, look at that lion over there."

Pāṇḍu immediately grabbed his bow and arrows and said, "Today I shall bring you back a trophy."

And he ran off into the forest. The lion led him on a great chase. Pāṇḍu ran close behind, but the lion hid himself in the thickest part of the brush. Then Pāṇḍu listened. There was a rustling in the leaves. Pāṇḍu drew back his arrow and let it fly. Suddenly he heard the sound of a human being crying out in pain. Pāṇḍu wondered what the sound was. He ran through the forest to where the arrow had landed. There he found that the arrow had pierced through the hearts of both the Ṛṣi Kiṇḍal and his wife.

When the dying ṛṣi saw Pāṇḍu he said, "What is this? The King is supposed to protect his subjects, and here I am a harmless hermit in the forest. This was my only time alone with my wife, and now I have been pierced by an arrow that was supposed to be protecting the subjects of Hastinapura."

The King said, "Forgive me, Ṛṣi. I heard the sound and thinking it was a lion, I let the arrow fly to the sound."

The ṛṣi said, "You didn't look and you shot the arrow, and you have killed both me and my wife! I curse you! Whenever you come to touch your wife, or if you ever hold a woman in close embrace, you will die just as I am dying now." Then the ṛṣi and his wife left their bodies.

Pāṇḍu stared in disbelief and shock. He returned to the hermitage and took his wives back to Hastinapura. Immediately he called an assembly of all the wise and learned beings of the kingdom. Bhīṣma, Dṛtarāṣṭra and Vidura assembled along with all the counselors of the court of Hastinapura. Pāṇḍu said, "Wise counselors of Hastinapura, it was an accident. But the arrow of the King has killed the ṛṣi and his wife. Now I must perform some penance to atone for this horrible sin of killing a Brahmiṇ. I am going to the forest to practice tapasya. Dṛtarāṣṭra, my older brother, you are currently the King. You remain King. I am going to do sādhana in the forest."

Everyone was very sad to see Pāṇḍu, Kuntī and Mādrī walk into the forest in bare feet. For some years they practiced tapasya, strong spiritual disciplines of yoga and meditation. One day Pāṇḍu had a dream. In the dream all of the ṛṣis were walking up to heaven. Pāṇḍu, too, wanted to walk with them into heaven. But they said, "Where are you going? You can't go to heaven, because you haven't paid your debt to the earth. Where are your children that will perform funeral oblations for you? You have no child. You have not nourished the next generation in a way to make the earth any better. How can you go to heaven?"

Pāṇḍu was very disturbed by this dream. When he woke up, he asked his wives, "What shall I do? I have no son. I can't go to heaven no matter how much tapasya I perform."

Kuntī said, "My Lord and husband, when I was a child I served Durvāṣa Muni. He gave me a mantra by which I can have a son by any God that I choose."

Pāṇḍu was so happy and said, "Use the mantra. Do tapasya. Bring a son for me."

Kuntī said, "Who shall I call?"

Pāṇḍu replied with great excitement, "Call Dharma. Ask him to be the father of our first son."

Kuntī sat in the forest and started to perform recitation of the mantra. Dharma came and gave her a son, and Pāṇḍu was so happy.

Pāṇḍu said, "Now Kuntī, call Pāvan, the Wind."

Kuntī sat again and called the Wind. The Wind came and gave her a son.

Then Pāṇḍu said, "Call Indra."

Kuntī sat again and called Indra. Indra came and gave her

a son. Then Kuntī taught the mantra to Mādrī.

Mādrī called the Aśvin twins and she gave birth to twin sons. The first son born of Dharma was named Yudhiṣṭhira. The second one, born of the Wind was named Bhīm. The third, from Indra, was Arjuna. The fourth was Nakula. The fifth was Sahadeva.

Meanwhile the blind King, Dṛtarāṣṭra, married Gandhārī, who bound her eyes with a cloth so that she would share her husband's darkness. Together they had one hundred sons. The eldest was named Duryodhana.

The five sons of Pāṇḍu grew up in the forest, learning wisdom at the feet of the ṛṣis. One day Pāṇḍu was sitting under a tree by a stream meditating, when Mādrī came alone to take her bath and draw water. She looked beautiful. She took her bath and was all wet and fresh. When she came back from the waterfall after drawing water, Pāṇḍu came to embrace her. Immediately he fell down and died. Mādrī and Kuntī were very sad that their husband lay dead in the forest.

The ṛṣis came to that place and performed the funeral rites, whereupon Mādrī climbed upon the funeral pyre, making herself a Satī, a woman who leaves her mortal body to accompany her husband.

### The Five Sons of Pāṇḍu Return to Hastinapura

Kuntī returned to Hastinapura along with her five sons, where Bhīṣma welcomed them home. Dṛtarāṣṭra, the King, gave the order that the sons of his brother should experience no difficulties, and will be treated as members of the royal family. But Duryodhana replied, "Those forest dwelling hermits have no place in my palace. This is my house, and they have no right to stay here."

Gandhārī said to the King, "Please explain to our son that this is their house too. They have every right to be here. Even

Yudhiṣṭhira is the oldest son of the authorized king. This kingdom rightfully belongs to him. Please remember, my husband, that your brother Pāṇḍu gave you that crown to wear on his behalf. Please explain this to our son."

Dṛtarāṣṭra replied, "Gandhārī, if I hadn't been born blind, then the kingdom would have been rightfully mine. How can I convince my son, when I, myself, am not convinced? He is the oldest son of the King. How can I tell him that this is not his kingdom? Why should he be deprived of his birth right, just as I have been deprived of mine? He was not born blind. Anyway, I will try to instruct him to live in harmony."

But Duryodhana wouldn't listen.

When the boys became a little older, Bhīṣma sent all the boys to study with Kṛpācārya, the family guru. Kṛpācārya said, "Yudhiṣṭhira is the oldest of the students, and therefore he will be in charge of the group." This made Duryodhana very angry, and he began to plot how he could get rid of these five brothers.

Gandhārī's older brother, Ṣākūṇi, was also very angry with Hastinapura. He had wanted his sister to become the wife of Pāṇḍu, and not the blind brother Dṛtarāṣṭra. Now Ṣākūṇi wanted Duryodhana to become the King, and he kept trying to poison the mind of the child. He often told him, "Your father should have been King, but he was born blind. His younger brother took the kingdom in his place. But you are the oldest son of the King. Who should take the kingdom in your place? You must make sure that the sons of Pāṇḍu don't take the kingdom away from you, as their father did from your father. You are the rightful successor to the King."

Everyone knew that Yudhiṣṭhira, the son of Dharma, was the eldest son of the family and the son of the first King and therefore the rightful heir to the kingdom. Not only was he the rightful heir, but also he was the most suitable and fit for guiding the nation.

One day when they were still children, Duryodhana invited Bhīm, the second son of Pāṇḍu, to eat rice pudding in which he had mixed poison. Bhīm fell unconscious, and was thrown into the river. When he sank into the river, some Nāgas from under the water came and took him to the King of the Nāgas. They said, "This boy was given poison."

The King of the Nāgas looked at the boy and said, "Whose son are you?"

Bhīm replied, "I am the son of Kuntī."

The King of the Nāgas said, "Kuntī is my grand-daughter." He immediately brought an antidote to the poison and fed it to Bhīm, who was freed from the poisonous effect. Then he took a great elixir and said, "Drink this, my son. This will give you the strength of ten elephants." Bhīm drank it down. "Now you had better go back home because your mother will be worried about you."

Bhīm returned to his home and told his brothers, "Duryodhana invited me to eat rice pudding, from which I got very sick. Then they pushed me into the river, where the Nāgas found me. They told me he had put poison in the pudding. I met our Great-Grandfather, who gave me some - thing to drink which he said will give me the strength of ten elephants."

Yudhiṣṭhira said, "Make sure nobody else knows anything about this. Don't tell anyone anything."

Droṇācārya became the teacher of weaponry for all the students. Of all the students he loved Arjuna the most, because Arjuna was always so cooperative and willing to learn. He practiced with his bow in the day and in the night, and Arjuna became a master of archery. In this way the boys grew up all together in the hermitage guided by Droṇācārya, but there was always a tremendous amount of animosity and fear between the sons of Pāṇḍu and those of Dṛtarāṣṭra.

When the boys graduated from school, their Guru

conducted a great convocation to show the citizens of Hastinapura what his students had learned. Each of them displayed their prowess with the various weapons they had studied. Arjuna shot arrow after arrow. He made it rain. He made the wind come. He made the fire burn with the strength of his arrows. Droṇācārya said to the assembly, "I hereby declare that in all of India there is no finer archer than Arjuna."

Suddenly there was a voice saying, "Stop! Droṇācārya! You have not given me a chance to display my prowess."

"Who are you, young man?"

"My name is Karṇa."

"Who is your mother?"

"If you want to judge who is the best archer in India, don't ask who are my mother and father. Don't look at my birth or my parents. Look at the way I shoot the bow. Look at the way I shoot my arrows."

Kṛpācārya replied, "No, this convocation is only for the children of Kings and princes, and not for anyone of any caste or any discipline. You are not allowed to show your strength here."

Duryodhana approached Karṇa and said, "I can tell you are a fine warrior, and I want you to be my friend. In my child hood my father made me the King of Aṅgadeśa, and I give that kingdom to you in exchange for your friendship."

Karṇa said, "What generosity! I pledge that for all of my life I will be your friend. This crown is for you; and the head that wears this crown is for you. You are the person who spoke up for me in my defense, and I will give my life for you."

Thus Karṇa and Duryodhana became very good friends. While Duryodhana was always plotting how he could get the kingdom and be appointed the Crown Prince, Karṇa was desirous of being acknowledged as the greatest archer of India. Yudhiṣṭhira continued in his path of Dharma. And all of the advisors, counselors and citizens of Hastinapura worried over who will become the next King.

## Yudhiṣṭhira Becomes the Crown Prince

Some time passed. Bhīṣma came to Dṛtarāṣṭra and said, "King, it is time to appoint the Crown Prince."

Dṛtarāṣṭra was most terrified of this time. He kept putting it off until he could wait no longer. Summoning all into the great assembly hall, he had to bow to the pressure of the community and the elders, and appointed Yudhiṣṭhira the next King.

Duryodhana fumed with anger. He couldn't wait until he found a way to get back at Yudhiṣṭhira. With the help of his Uncle Ṣākūṇi, he prepared a great palace in the forest made of pine pitch, hoping to entrap the five brothers in the burning cinders. He went to his father, King Dṛtarāṣṭra, and said, "Father, why don't you send Yudhiṣṭhira to the forest retreat, to meet all the citizens of the forest?"

Dṛtarāṣṭra agreed, "That's a wonderful idea."

Duryodhana said, "Why doesn't he take his four brothers with him? They can all accompany him. Even his mother, Kuntī, can go along too. Then all of the citizens will meet their new King, as well as the royal family. Not only that, I have personally prepared for them a new palace, where they will be extremely comfortable."

Dṛtarāṣṭra said, "How very thoughtful you are. Please call Yudhiṣṭhira."

Yudhiṣṭhira came and the King gave him the order, "You sons of Pāṇḍu go to the forest; all five of you, along with your mother. Spend some days with the forest-dwelling citizens of our country."

Yudhiṣṭhira was most pleased to receive this order. He was equally pleased to learn that Duryodhana had prepared a palace for his stay along with his family. Then Yudhiṣṭhira proceeded into the forest with his family and they went to the new palace.

"This palace has only one door and no windows," they said to one another. "This is very strange."

Then Vidura, the Prime Minister, found out about the plot to burn the entire Pāṇḍava family in the house made of pitch. He sent them a tunnel digger. The digger came and said, "Vidura has sent me to prepare an escape route for you. I must go about my work very quickly and quietly." All day and all night he dug until he prepared the tunnel.

Then one day Duryodhana sent the signal. "Tonight is the night."

Just as those enemies were about to set the house on fire, Bhīm called to Yudhiṣṭhira, "They have come. When they enter, we will set the house on fire ourselves."

Kuntī along with the four Pāṇḍavas went into the tunnel and began their walk to safety, while Bhīm took a torch to light the fire. All of those people who had come to set the house on fire were trapped inside as the house burned. Then Bhīm descended into the tunnel, and the five brothers made their escape from the burning house along with their mother Kuntī.

Bhīm and Arjuna were adamant that they would not stand for this insult to the Pāṇḍava family. "This is no way for family members to behave, to build a palace made out of pine pitch with no doors nor windows through which they could escape."

Bhīm and Arjuna decided immediately, "Let us attack Hastinapura."

"No," said Yudhiṣṭhira. "Don't you realize that when we attack Hastinapura, our Pitāmahā Bhīṣma will have no other recourse but to defend the throne? Don't you realize that our Guru Droṇācārya will have no alternative but to defend the kingdom? How about Kṛpācārya, the Guru of our family, won't he, too, have to defend the kingdom? Will you like to lift up your weapons against our Gurus? Against our Grandfather? Be patient!"

Then Mother Kuntī said, "My children, Hastinapura has given us nothing but sorrow. Could we think that they would give our family a house made of pine pitch in which to live? We have no need to return to Hastinapura. It's better that we remain as mendicants in the forest than to return to our capital city."

Adhering to their mother's wish, the five Pāṇḍava brothers dressed in the white cloth of Brahmiṇ ascetics and retired into the forest to protect the citizens of their country.

## The Marriage of Draupadī

One day the five brothers heard that King Draupad was calling for the Svayambara, the marriage ceremony of his daughter, Draupadī. Draupadī was a divine princess, born from the sacred fire itself, and the Pāṇḍava brothers could not resist attending and witnessing the wedding ceremony of Draupadī. In the dress of Brahmiṇs, they were invited into the assembly hall, where the Kings of India had congregated.

King Draupad announced, "I want my daughter, Draupadī, to be married to the finest archer in all of India." He took one wooden fish, and had it attached as a revolving target on the ceiling of the assembly hall. He put one pot of water in the center of the hall and ordered: "Lift the bow, tighten its string in place, then the archer will look at the reflection in the water and shoot his arrow above to hit the eye of the revolving target."

The Kings of India took their turns to try to hit the target, but none was able to even lift the bow. Duryodhana tried, but he failed to lift the bow. Then Karṇa, the disciple of

Paraśurām, stood up. He lifted the bow, tightened the string in place, and took aim. Then Draupadī said: "Stop, I don't recognize you as a King! Even though your friend, Duryodhana, has given you a kingdom, you are still the son of a charioteer! I won't marry the son of a charioteer." Karṇa sat down.

All the other Kings took their turns and no one was able to lift the bow. Then Arjuna, dressed as a Brahmiṇ, asked permission from his brother, Yudhiṣṭhira, "Please brother, may I take a turn?"

Yudhiṣṭhira gave his blessings. Then Arjuna took up the bow, looked into the water below, and let the arrow fly right into the center of the target. The garland of victory was placed around his neck, and Arjuna won the bride.

When Duryodhana learned that Arjuna had won the bride, he was both amazed and dismayed. He realized that the five Pāṇḍava brothers had not died in the fire. How is it that they are still alive? He drew his sword and raced forward to attack. Along with him came Karṇa and brother Duṣāṣāṇa. Duryodhana called to Draupad, "This assembly is only for kṣatriya Kings! How is it that a Brahmiṇ has been allowed to enter? This is not according to the rules! This is an insult to the Kings of India!"

Bhīm said to Yudhiṣṭhira, "Yudhiṣṭhira, take Nakula and Sahadeva away from here. I will keep them back." So Yudhiṣṭhira, Nakula and Sahadeva exited, while Arjuna guarded the bride and Bhīm stood as a pillar not letting any others pass. Then Arjuna took the blessings of King Draupad, and with his brothers they took their bride into the forest to make their escape.

When Arjuna came to the hermitage, their mother, Kuntī, was preparing food inside and he called, "Mother, we won the most wonderful thing today!"

And mother called out from the kitchen, "Share it between

the five of you!" When Kuntī turned to see what it was that they had brought, she was most surprised to find the Princess Draupadī. She became very angry and said, "What? Is a wife a thing that is possessed, to be won or lost according to the fortunes of time? Or is she a partner who shares in the inner-most secrets of your heart? Now, how will you live so that your mother's word will not become false, and so that you do not disgrace this princess who has given her life to your care?"

Just at that time Kṛṣṇa came, and when he was apprised of the situation, he explained, "This is no time for sorrow. Remember, Draupadī, in your last life when you performed austerities for Lord Śiva, and when Śiva was ready to grant you a boon you said, 'I want a husband who is the apex of Dharma, who is strong like several elephants, who is the greatest archer, the greatest swordsman, and has incomparable beauty.' Then Mahādeva said, 'All those qualities can't exist in one man.' And you replied, 'Śiva, you asked me what I want, and I told you.' Thereupon he said, 'Tatā-stu, I grant you the boon.'

"Also remember, Draupadī, in your incarnation as Sītā, when you were imprisoned in Rāvaṇa's aśoka grove, again you prayed to Śiva and said, "Give me my husband, give me my husband,' five times you repeated. Again Śiva granted that blessing. So you see, you have nothing to be sad about now."

So Draupadī became the wife of the five brothers, but actually she was the wife of Yudhiṣṭhira.

## Two Crown Princes

The time had come for the five brothers to return to Hastinapura. In their absence, thinking that Yudhiṣṭhira had died in the fire, Dṛtarāṣṭra had appointed Duryodhana as the Crown Prince. When Yudhiṣṭhira and his brothers, along with Kuntī and Draupadī returned to Hastinapura, they were greeted with great respect by Bhīṣma, Vidura, Droṇācārya and Kṛpācārya, but Dṛtarāṣṭra and Duryodhana were not content to see them return. Now two crown princes have been appointed as heir to the throne, and Dṛtarāṣṭra had to make a decision as to who would be the next King of Hastinapura.

Duryodhana went to his father and said, "Father, believe me, if you take away my right to the kingdom and steal my birthright to give it to Yudhiṣṭhira, I am going to kill myself. I am the oldest son of the rightful heir to the throne. There is no reason that you should take away my authority. You have already appointed me the Crown Prince. I will not allow Yudhiṣṭhira to have any portion of the kingdom!"

Yudhiṣṭhira, in consultation said, "Dṛtarāṣṭra, you are the King. You are the eldest member of our family. The decision is yours. Whatever you decide, I will abide by that. All I want is harmony and peace in our family."

The citizens, Bhīṣma, Vidura, the Gurus, Droṇācārya and Kṛpācārya, all voted in favor of Yudhiṣṭhira. But Dṛtarāṣṭra felt that he, himself, had been cheated out of the kingdom because of his blindness, and he didn't want his son to be deprived in the same way. Therefore, he decided to divide the kingdom in half. Duryodhana will stay here in Hastinapura and the Pāṇḍava brothers, led by Yudhiṣṭhira, will be given some land at the edge of the kingdom.

Everyone was sad to see the kingdom divided. When Yudhiṣṭhira took his five brothers in procession to the land that they were given, they were led into a barren desert with no water whatsoever. It was a wasteland, devoid of life, which was apportioned as their half of the kingdom.

## The Ancestry of Kṛṣṇa

In days of old, Kaśyapa Muni was performing a great yajña, and went to search for a beautiful cow whose milk would be suitable for this sacrifice. As he searched and searched, he came upon Varuṇa's cow who was like the Kāma Dhenu, the cow which yields the fruits of all desires. Kaśyapa thought that the milk from that cow would be the best with which to offer to the Gods in sacrifice. Therefore, he took the cow. When Varuṇa came home, he noticed the cow was missing, and began to search for his cow. He found the cow near the howan kuṅḍa, the sacrificial fire, where Kaśyapa was performing sacrifice along with his two wives, Aditi and Diti. Varuṇa became angry, and taking some water in his hand he cursed all three of them: "You have such greed for cows that you have become thieves! Go down to the world of men and give birth to a cow-herd!" With that Varuṇa threw the water at them, and the curse became binding upon all three of them.

Some time later Aditi gave birth to the noble Indra, who grew stronger and stronger until he was recognized as the King of the Gods. Then Diti said to her husband Kaśyapa that she too would like to have a son. Kaśyapa Muni told Diti to practice a very sincere vow of discipline, and when Diti undertook the vow she became pregnant. She began to grow in a motherly way, and her body radiated the light of her purity.

Then Aditi told her son Indra, "My son, if you desire my welfare find some way to destroy the fetus in your step-mother's womb. My son, I am very much afraid that her son will become more powerful then you, and also that our husband will love her more. Therefore, devise some plan by which we can cause the demise of her child.

One evening just after her meal, Indra went to Diti and

said, "Mother, I know you are extremely tired from the austerities that you have been keeping. Please let me rub your feet."

Diti replied, "You are very kind, but I have not yet completed all the functions of my vow. First I must wash my mouth after eating, and then I must clean before I can take a rest."

Indra said, "Mother, you look so tired from all of your privations. Just let me rub your feet a little while, and then you can complete your work."

Indra began to rub her feet, and after a short time Diti fell asleep. As she had not observed her vow, it became Indra's chance. He adorned himself with his subtle body and entered Diti's womb. Then he took his thunderbolt and cut the fetus into seven parts. Then he cut each of the seven parts into seven more parts. And thus the forty nine Maruts were born.

When Diti woke up she realized what had happened. She became very angry and cursed Indra that his dominion no longer would extend over the three worlds. From now on he would be lucky to maintain his sovereignty over the heavens. Even his pūjā would not be performed on the earth. Understanding that it was the fault of Aditi, she cursed Aditi as well, and said, "Your sons will die no sooner then they come out from your womb, and you will live in a prison experiencing fear and anxiety!"

The high souled Kaśyapa Muni consoled Diti by telling her that her sons would be very powerful and famous beings. They would become good friends with Indra, and would help him in protecting the realms of heaven. "Certainly your curse will come to fruition. Varuṇa Deva has ordered the three of us to earth, but you will be free while Aditi lives in a prison," said the Muni.

But the story of Kṛṣṇa's ancestry goes back even farther in time. From Brahmā's heart a son named Dharma was born.

He was truthful and always engaged in performing the rites and ceremonies of the Vedic Religion. Dharma married Dakṣa's ten daughters, and together they had four sons: Hari, Kṛṣṇa, Nara and Nārāyaṇa. All four were the manifestations of Viṣṇu. Hari and Kṛṣṇa remained in Divine Yoga, while Nara and Nārāyaṇa manifested upon the earth and went to Badrināth to practice tapasya.

### Nara and Nārāyaṇa and the Birth of Urvaśī

Nara and Nārāyaṇa engaged in such austerities that Indra became afraid. He sent the entire host of heaven to try break the meditation of the meditating sādhus. Spring went and caused a warm breeze to blow across the snow-capped mountains, while the host of heavenly Apsaras, celestial maidens, began to sing softly and to dance making amorous gestures. Love hid behind a tree waiting for the opportunity to shoot his arrows.

Nara and Nārāyaṇa awoke from their meditation and thought that it was very strange for the winter to have passed so suddenly. Then they saw ten thousand beautiful heavenly maidens coming towards them making seductive gestures, and Nārāyaṇa immediately recognized this to be the work of Indra. He became angry and he slapped his thigh, and out from the thigh came the most beautiful Urvaśī. Seeing the radiant beauty of Urvaśī, the heavenly ladies were put to shame. "You tell Indra," called Nārāyaṇa, "that if we were interested in physical pleasures, we could arrange our own! Thank him very kindly for thinking of us, but he can arrange seduction for others, not for us. Take this lady Urvaśī back to Indra as a present from two sādhus who are repulsed by his jealous behavior! To think this is the King of the Gods!"

The ten thousand ladies from heaven were extremely impressed by the power of the self control of the two sādhus.

"Oh Munis," they said. "We had no idea of the power of your tapasya. Indra sent us here to disturb your meditation, but please do not be angry with us. We take refuge in you, and ask for your mercy."

"I am not angry with you," replied Nārāyaṇa. "You are only doing your appointed task. You have no need to ask mercy from us. Ask for boons."

Then those ten thousand ladies said, "Oh Nārāyaṇa, never have we seen such generosity on the part of anyone. Not only are you strong and handsome, but you are fixed in self control and generous. If you will be so kind as to grant us boons, then all of us would like husbands like you. Will you please marry us all? What other boon could we request?"

Nārāyaṇa answered, "You can see that in this life we are busily engaged in performing tapasya. Therefore, we will be unable to fulfill your desires at present. But since I have already granted a boon, in the Dvapara Yuga in the form of Kṛṣṇa I will come to satisfy your desires. Now you return to heaven with this Urvaśī, and tell Indra that I will marry you sometime in history at my convenience. Tell him to leave me alone until then."

## The Curses of the Ṣaḍgarbha

Svāyambhuva Manu had six sons by his wife Urṇā. One day Brahmā looked at Sarasvatī very amorously and became filled with passion. Sarasvatī was somewhat taken aback to see her father in such a condition, and she started to run away. Brahmā forgot himself and ran after her. She saw that he was serious, and she began to run very hard. She ran right past those six sons of Svāyambhuva Manu, followed by her father, Brahmā, in hot pursuit.

When those six sons saw Brahmā's condition, they started to laugh: "Look at that old man filled with passion, chasing his own daughter around the heavens! Is there any limit to the egotism of man? Can you imagine an old man like that so enamored that he wants to enjoy his own daughter? Can there be anything more ridiculous than that?"

Brahmā was very embarrassed to have become the object of laughter of those boys. Then he said, "You don't understand what it is like to be under the dominion of desire. But you dare to laugh at an old man? I curse you. Be born in the form of aśuras!"

Brahmā caught Sarasvatī, and, among other distinctions, he was the first to marry his own daughter. Creative Consciousness married Knowledge. And the six sons of Svāyambhuva Manu were reborn in the home of the demon Kālanemi. In their second birth they incarnated in the home of the demon King Hiraṅyakaṣipu. In this life they remembered their curse by Brahmā and performed severe austerities. Brahmā became pleased with them and blessed them with invulnerability to Gods, humans, nāgas and gandharvas. Because they received that boon from Brahmā, their father, the demon King Hiraṅyakaṣipu, felt that his children had dis - regarded him. He became angry and cursed them, "You will be born one after another from the womb of Devakī. And your father from your previous birth, Kālanemi, will be reborn as the wicked Kamsa. He will be a very wicked man and will kill you as soon as you take birth!"

## The Birth of Kṛṣṇa

Surasena, Ugrasena and Devaka were three cousins, born in Mathura from the lineage which had been established by the King Śatrughna, the brother of Rāma. Ugrasena became the King of Mathura. He had a son named Kamsa, the incarnation of evil itself, the wicked demon Kālanemi. Kamsa grew to be hated and feared throughout the kingdom. Even though the King Ugrasena was completely pure and a lover of dharma, the people prayed for protection from the violations of his son Kamsa.

Surasena had a son named Vasudeva, the incarnation of Kaśyapa Muni, and Devaka had a daughter named Devakī, the incarnation of Aditi.

By the time Kamsa had come of age, he had developed sufficient power to imprison his father and usurp the throne, and then his suppression of dharma began in earnest. Kamsa prohibited the worship of the Gods and all Vedic rites and ceremonies. He imprisoned many ṛṣis, killed many others, and in many ways made his antagonism to religion well known. At this time there were many other evil kings born upon the earth, and Kamsa made alliances with them all. Together they oppressed the people of the earth, until even the Goddess Earth herself appealed to Lord Viṣṇu to incarnate upon the earth in his form as Kṛṣṇa to relieve the sufferings of humanity.

One day Kamsa came to Vasudeva and said, "I would like you to marry Devakī."

Vasudeva replied, "I am already married to Rohiṇī."

"That doesn't matter," said Kamsa. "You will take Devakī also, and make our house strong."

Vasudeva married Devakī. When they had completed the marriage ceremony, a voice cried out from heaven, "Kamsa, the eighth son of this union will be the death of you."

Kamsa drew his sword and was about to kill Devakī. "You can't kill an unarmed woman, your own relative, especially on her wedding day!" called Vasudeva. "I will give you all the children from our union, but spare the life of my wife."

Then the King Kamsa ordered that Devakī and Vasudeva be put into prison, and all the children born from their union be delivered to him immediately. No sooner was a child born, then the wicked Kamsa was informed. He would come, accompanied by his soldiers, and forcibly take the newborn child from its mother, and dash its head against the wall. In this way the six children were slain, much to the anguish of the imprisoned parents, in accordance with the curses of Varuṇa Deva and the demon King Hiraṅyakaṣipu.

At the end of the Rāmāyaṇa, Lakṣman, who was the incarnation of Ananta, the serpent upon whom Lord Viṣṇu reposes in the Ocean of Purity, said to his older brother Rāma, "Respected Brother, in this incarnation I have caused you so much pain and suffering, so much trouble by reason of my being your younger brother. Because I was the younger, you always had to look out for me and save me from the foolish behaviors I would commit. In our next life grant me the boon that I will come as your older brother, so I can serve and protect you as you have performed for me."

Rāma agreed, and now the very pure Devakī became pregnant with her seventh child. But Devakī feared for the conduct of her cousin Kamsa, killing all of her children as he was, and through the Māyā of Yoga, she transferred the fetus to her co-wife, Rohiṇī. Thus Rohiṇī gave birth to the very noble soul, Bālarāma, while Kamsa rejoiced at the knowledge that Devakī had miscarried her womb.

Rohiṇī was staying with great fear of Kamsa in the home of Nanda Rao and his wife Yaśodā in the Village of Gokula, along with her baby Bālarāma. At that time the Divine Mother Yoga Māyā entered into the womb of Yaśodā. At the same time, the incarnation of the Supreme Lord Viṣṇu entered as Kṛṣṇa into the womb of Devakī.

It was the eighth day of the dark fortnight of the month of Śrāvaṇa, when Devakī, bound in the prison, gave birth to the beautiful child Kṛṣṇa. When the child came out from her womb, both the mother and the father saw that He was in fact the Lord Viṣṇu. Then Vasudeva took that child in his arms, whereupon he heard a heavenly voice proclaim, "The gates are open, Vasudeva. The guards have fallen asleep. Take the child to the home of Nanda Rao in Gokula. Yaśodā has just given birth to an incarnation of the Divine Mother. Exchange your baby with hers, for your son is destined for greatness. Run, Vasudeva, run!"

Vasudeva wrapped the child in pure white linen, and ran to the bank of the Jamuna River. It was storming rain, and the Ananta snake held open its hood as an umbrella in order to shield the fleeing child. Vasudeva reached to Gokula and entered the house of Nanda Rao. He exchanged his baby Kṛṣṇa for the female child which Yaśodā had given birth to. Then he returned to the prison cell in Mathura. Immediately the guards awoke, and ran to tell Kamsa of the birth of Devakī's eighth child, a girl. Kamsa began to laugh. Then he thought of the heavenly voice and decided that even this girl child must be slain. He proceeded to the prison cell and grabbed the baby child from Devakī's arms. Then that infant child flew up into the air and took the form of the eight-armed Goddess Durgā. She said, "Foolish Sinner, why try to kill me? Your slayer has already taken birth. No one can escape the will of karma." Then she disappeared into the heavens.

Kamsa was overcome with fear. He sent his soldiers to kill all the babies born on that day in Gokula, but miraculously the child Kṛṣṇa escaped. Then he sent many demons with tremendous powers to kill the baby Kṛṣṇa, but the child killed all of the demons that came. So Kamsa decided to wait until the time was more favorable.

## The Incarnations of the Gods and Aśuras

In playing the līlā of the history of Śrī Kṛṣṇa, many Gods and aśuras came to manifestation to take part in this drama. Śrī Kṛṣṇa was himself the manifestation of Nārāyaṇa, the son of Dharma and representative of the Supreme Lord Viṣṇu. Bālarāma was the incarnation of Ananta. Vasudeva was the manifestation of Kaśyapa Muni; Devakī of Aditi and Rohiṇī of Diti.

Yudhiṣṭhira was born of Dharma, Bhīm from Vāyu, the mighty Arjuna was the son of Indra and incarnation of Nārāyaṇa's younger brother, Nara. Nakula and Sahadeva were born of the Aśvin twins. Karṇa came from the Sun, Vidura from Yāma, Droṇācārya from Bṛhaspati, and his son Aśvatthāmā was the partial incarnation of Rudra Deva. Śantānu was the incarnation of Mahā Biṣa who had come from Sāgar, the Ocean, and Gaṅgā came herself as his wife. Their son Bhīṣma was actually the oldest of the Vaśus named Dyau; Virāta, known as Matsya Rāj, was the part incarnation of the Maruts; Dṛtarāṣṭra was born from the Daitya Hamsa, the son of Ariṣṭanemi. Kṛpācārya came from the Maruts, Duryodhana from Kali (Darkness), and Ṣākūṇi from Dvāpara. Dhṛṣṭadyumna was an incarnation of Fire, Śikhaṇḍī of Rākṣasa, Pradyumna from Sanāt Kumāra, and King Draupada was an incarnation of Lord Varuṇa. Draupadī came from Lakṣmī, her five sons from the Viśvadevas, Kuntī from Siddhī, and Mādrī from Dhṛtī. Gandhārī came from Matī, and the ten thousand wives of Kṛṣṇa were the Apsaras who were promised marriage by Nārāyaṇa.

Among the aśuras Śiśupāla was the incarnation of Hiraṅyakaṣipu, Jarāsandha of Viprachitta, Śalya of Prahlād; Kamsa was born from Kālanemi, and Keśī from Hayaśirā. Many other aśuras had taken manifestation during the time of Śrī Kṛṣṇa for the impending battle between dharma and adharma.

## Kṛṣṇa Raises Govārdana Mountain

One day all the citizens of Nandagaṃ, which was the village in which Kṛṣṇa was raised, gathered together to perform a great pūjā. The young child Kṛsna asked, "What pūjā are you making?"

They said, "We are going to make pūjā to Indra because he brings the rain."

Kṛṣṇa said, "Why should you make pūjā to Indra? Make pūjā to someone who is worthy to be a recipient of pūjā. Why Indra? The rain comes from the seasons. The rain doesn't come from Indra. Make pūjā to the cow. The cow is always giving food to us. Make pūjā to the Tulasi plant. Tulasi plant is always so sweet and fragrant to us. Indra is sometimes happy, sometimes sad, constantly putting obstacles in the path of sādhus, who are striving to perfection in meditation. Why make pūjā to Indra?"

The citizens of Nandagaṃ couldn't argue with Kṛṣṇa, so Kṛṣṇa organized a pūjā and showed them how to make worship of the cow and worship of the Tulasi plant.

Indra was offended by this insult and said, "I'll show those citizens of the forest! I'll show that Kṛṣṇa!" And he caused it to rain. And it rained so hard that there was no place to take shelter. All the citizens came to Kṛṣṇa and said, "Kṛṣṇa, what will we do? It is raining so hard. We have offended Indra. Indra is angry with us. What shall we do? Where shall we seek refuge?"

With one finger the child Kṛṣṇa lifted up Govārdana Mountain and held it aloft in the sky, making a huge umbrella out of the mountain. All the citizens of the forest came and stood under the mountain along with their cattle, their cows, and all their pets and animals. Kṛṣṇa said, "Okay, let it rain. But we are not required to bow to Indra." And he held aloft the Govārdana Mountain while it rained for forty-eight hours continuously, causing great floods all around. But all the citizens were dry, and they experienced no difficulties at all.

No matter how hard Indra caused it to rain, he couldn't move Kṛṣṇa from his position. Finally Indra recognized that all his powers were nothing compared to the powers of Kṛṣṇa. Then Indra appeared to Kṛṣṇa with folded hands and said, "I am sorry for this offense. Please excuse me. I realize my power is nothing in comparison to your own."

Kṛṣṇa replied, "I am pleased with your humility. Stop the rain." And Indra made the rain stop. Then Kṛṣṇa said, "Choose some boon from me."

Indra replied, "Kṛṣṇa, always protect my son, Arjuna. Always be with him and make sure that he has no difficulty on this earth."

Kṛṣṇa proclaimed, "Tatā-stu! I grant you that boon."

Then all the citizens came out from underneath the mountain and looked at the freshness of the forest, while Kṛṣṇa put the mountain back in its original place.

## The Death of Kamsa

By the time Lord Kṛṣṇa and his older brother, Bālarāma, had become young men, Kamsa had become crazed with fear as to when his death would come. No longer could he stand the anxiety of waiting. Finally he sent for the boys from Gokula, and invited them to be present in the royal arena in Mathura.

When the two young boys arrived, Kamsa had prepared all manner of treachery in order to secure their death. A mad elephant was to attack them, the strongest warriors in the country were to fight with them, and many devious means were employed to slay the two young cow-herds. But the two young boys were invincible to every deception. They defeated the elephant and all the other warriors. Then Kṛṣṇa lifted Kamsa from the royal throne and threw him into the air, causing the wicked King to fall to his death.

The nation cheered at the death of Kamsa, and Kṛṣṇa immediately moved to the prison where he freed his parents, freed the King Ugrasena and restored him to his throne, and freed all of the sādhus who had been imprisoned. Once again the rule of dharma was established in the Kingdom of Mathura.

Some time after reunion with their parents, Kṛṣṇa and Bālarāma were sent to the Guru Sannidhāpaṇi's house. They grew up in their Guru's aśrama and received training in all the branches of knowledge of the traditions of kings and ṛṣis.

## The Pāṇḍavas in Indrapraṣṭa and the Rājaśuya Sacrifice

Now the five Pāṇḍava brothers were in their new kingdom in the middle of the desert. Bhīm became very angry and said, "What is this? What shall we do with this desert? They've got the kingdom. They've got the palaces and treasuries full of gold. They've got the city full of citizens and taxes. And they give to us this lonely, desolate desert, with no water, no vegetation. Let's go back to Hastinapura and fight."

Yudhiṣṭhira, the son of Dharma, said, "Stop! There will be plenty of fighting to do. Now let us devote our energy to constructive purposes. Let's build ourselves a kingdom."

So they sat down with the ṛṣis and munis of the forest and enkindled the sacred fire, and began the sacrifice for purifying the land. Then Kṛṣṇa along with his brother Bālarāma came and offered to help build their kingdom. Kṛṣṇa told Bālarām to take his plow and plow the fields. He told Viśvakarma, the architect of the Gods, to join in the effort, and instantly the fields were plowed, the seeds were sown, streams and rivers flowed, the crops and trees were growing, and a magnificent palace grew up out of the land, and a city with beauty beyond compare. This most beautiful city was called Indraprașța.

The brothers moved into the city, and then Kṛṣṇa said, "Now, Yudhiṣṭhira, conquer all of India. Perform the Rājaśuya sacrifice."

So Yudhiṣṭhira sent Bhīm, Arjuna, Nakula and Sahadeva across the length and breadth of India. And all the Kings of India recognized Indraprașța as the supreme authority of all the Kings, and Yudhiṣṭhira as the Emperor of all the Kings. The victorious armies marched back to Indraprașța, and then invitations were sent out all over India inviting all the Kings to crown Yudhiṣṭhira as the King of kings, the Rājaśuya sacrifice. The messengers came to Hastinapura, and they invited Dṛtarāṣṭra, Bhīṣma, and Vidura, Droṇācārya, Kṛpācārya, and Duryodhana and others of their family, who all came to witness the splendor of Indraprașța, and to participate in the Rājaśuya sacrifice. All the Kings of India acknowledged Yudhiṣṭhira as the King of kings.

## Arjuna Marries Subhādra and the Birth of the God of Love

After the Pāṇḍava brothers performed the Rājaśuya sacrifice, Bālarāma, Kṛṣṇa's older brother went to their parents, Vasudeva and Devakī, and said, "You know, I have been thinking about our sister, Subhādra. She is an excellent gem among women, and I was thinking that the Crown Prince of Hastinapura, Duryodhana, would be a fitting husband for her. So, if you are in agreement, let us go ahead and fix the wedding."

Vaśudeva and Devakī, the parents, agreed with him.

Then Kṛṣṇa sent an urgent message to Arjuna: "Arjuna

come quickly and go directly to the temple of the Goddess Gaurī outside the city gates. I'll make sure Subhādra is there, and take her away with you. I don't want Subhādra to marry Duryodhana. She will be happy with you." And Kṛṣṇa added one little anecdote. He said, "When you drive off in your chariot, make sure Subhādra holds the reigns."

Arjuna got the message and mounted his chariot, and proceeded directly to the temple of Gaurī, outside the city gates. It was the morning just before the proposed wedding, and Subhādra, dressed in her fine wedding clothes, went to worship the Goddess and pray for salvation. She didn't want to marry Duryodhana.

When she was returning from prayer, she had just stepped outside from the temple, when she saw Arjuna drive up in his chariot pulled by white horses. Arjuna looked like salvation incarnate. In her hands she held the wedding garland, which had just been blessed by the Goddess, and she looked him straight in the eye and put it around his neck.

Arjuna said, "Subhādra, let us go back to our City at Indraprașța."

With great joy Subhādra mounted the chariot and Arjuna said, "Here are the reigns, Subhādra. You drive the horses."

Subhādra took the reigns and she started to drive off, while the guards who were attending the princess could do nothing. They ran back to the palace and told Bālarāma that Arjuna came and stole away the bride. Bālarāma became extremely angry. "That Arjuna will never stop his enmity with Duryodhana. Every time the two of them come together, there is always going to be a conflict of some sort. Now he has stolen away the bride. I am going along with the army and we will overtake them, and we will teach that Arjuna a lesson."

Just then Kṛṣṇa came and asked, "Guards, who was driving the chariot when they left?"

The guards replied, "The princess was driving the chariot."

And Kṛṣṇa said, "Bālarāma, it seems like Subhādra has stolen away Arjuna, rather than Arjuna stealing away Subhādra! Put your army at rest. Put down your weapons. There is no fight here. Our sister has chosen her groom. She has exercised her right as a royal princess to choose her own husband herself."

Arjuna's child by Subhādra was Abhimanyu. And Abhimanyu was blessed by Lord Śiva, for Abhimanyu was Kāmadeva, the God of Love.

## The Dice of Deceit

Duryodhana burned with jealousy and anger. "Those people took my half of the kingdom and made it even better than my own." He couldn't think of anything other than plotting how he could deprive his cousins of their kingdom. He decided, along with his uncle Ṣākūṇi, that they would invite the Pāṇḍava brothers to play dice. Ṣākūṇi was a master of trickery and deceit, especially playing with loaded dice, and it was a tradition among the Kings of India never to refuse an invitation to dice. Just as a warrior would never refuse an invitation to battle, similarly the Kings of India could never refuse the invitation to dice.

Bhīm said to his brother, "Don't go. They are cheaters and will certainly be cheating us."

Yudhiṣṭhira said, "Hastinapura is our family home. How can we doubt our own family? We must go. It is the honor of Kings. Where Bhīṣma is present, where Droṇācārya is present, where Kṛpācārya is present, where Vidura is present, will they allow us to be cheated? We are their own family!"

Thus speaking, the five Pāṇḍava brothers along with Draupadī, went to Hastinapura, and entered into the dice game. Ṣākūṇi, that cheater, cheated on every roll of the dice. And one roll after another, it was double or nothing. The stakes grew and grew until Yudhiṣṭhira wagered the Kingdom of Indraprasṭa. And when he lost the kingdom, he wagered his brother Nakula. When he lost Nakula, he wagered his brother Sahadeva. When he lost Sahadeva, he wagered his brother Arjuna. And when Arjuna was lost, he wagered his brother Bhīm. And when Bhīm was lost, he wagered his own Self. And when he lost his own Self, he wagered Draupadī. And when Draupadī was lost, there was nothing left to wager.

Vidura said to Dṛtarāṣṭra, "Oh King, a daughter of our family, the Queen of Indraprasṭa, is not an item to be wagered. She is not some thing, a property, that can be traded, purchased, or sold. She is the Queen of the land."

But Karṇa remembered the day when he lifted up the bow in the assembly of her marriage, and she said, "I am not going to marry any son of a charioteer." Remembering that insult, he said, "Any lady who is married to five men, is not a lady. She is a prostitute, and she deserves no greater respect than any other prostitute. We won her fair and square! Why don't we bring our winnings into our presence!"

Duryodhana thought that was a very good idea and he commanded, "Duṣāṣāṇa, bring Draupadī here into the assembly. We won her fair and square. Bring her here! She now belongs to me!" Duṣāṣāṇa immediately went to Draupadī's apartment and said, "Draupadī, you are being summoned to the hall of audience in front of the King, Bhīṣma, Vidura, Droṇācārya and Kṛpācārya. You were just lost in a game of dice, and now you are the property of Duryodhana. Come before your master!"

Draupadī said, "Duṣāṣāṇa, I have my period right now, and I am not allowed to go outside to meet any of our elders according to our family custom. So how can it be that I will go? I am not even allowed to touch the feet of the elder ladies. How will I go before the King?"

Duṣāṣāṇa said, "We don't have time for these kinds of

problems right now. You come with me, or I will drag you by the hair."

Draupadī said, "Duṣāṣāṇa, I am the queen of this country's Royal Family, and you are my younger brother. If you drag me by the hair, there are five Pāṇḍavas who will avenge this insult. Don't think you will get away with it."

Duṣāṣāṇa replied, "Those five Pāṇḍavas are now the slaves of Duryodhana. They, too, were lost in the game of dice! Now either you will come with me nicely, or I will drag you by the hair."

Draupadī said, "Duṣāṣāṇa, this not the way to talk to your older sister, nor to the queen. Don't think you will get away with this!"

Duṣāṣāṇa grabbed her by the hair and said, "Now stop talking and come with me."

She said, "I am not coming!" And he began to drag her by the hair. He dragged her right down the hall, and he dragged her right into the assembly of all the elders, where she fell on the ground. He continued to drag her, while the five Pāṇḍava brothers heard her scream for help, but they were powerless. Kṛpācārya looked on in disgust, but he was powerless to speak. Droṇācārya watched in complete repulsion, yet he was powerless to do anything. Bhīṣma grabbed his sword in anger, yet was powerless to speak out, because of his vow to protect the King of Hastinapura.

When Draupadī was dragged into the middle of the assembly, she said in pitiful tones, "Elders of Hastinapura, what has happened to Dharma in our country? Is this the way you treat the Queen of Hastinapura? Is this the way you treat a daughter of your family? Is this the way you treat any human being?"

Duryodhana answered, "You are now my property! You don't deserve any more respect than I wish to give you. You were wagered and lost in the game of dice, and now you belong to me."

And Karṇa said, "Well, if she is really a prostitute, let's see how she looks without any clothes on."

Duryodhana said, "That's a wonderful idea. Duṣāṣāṇa, take off her sāri!"

And Draupadī called out, "Will none of my five heroic husbands help me? Bhīṣma, the protector of Dharma? Vidura, the wise and able minister? Will no one come to my rescue?"

Duṣāṣāṇa grabbed the end of her sāri and he began to pull. Draupadī prayed, "Oh Kṛṣṇa, not one of my family members can help me. Kṛṣṇa, I take refuge only in you."

Duṣāṣāṇa pulled on her sāri and Duryodhana ordered, "Pull, Duṣāṣāṇa, pull! Take that sāri off from her."

As Duṣāṣāṇa pulled on her sāri, Draupadī turned around and around, and when she looked up, there was Kṛṣṇa standing in the balcony adding yardage to her cloth. He granted her the boon of infinite cloth. Duṣāṣāṇa pulled on the sāri and kept on pulling, and the cloth was piling up and up until it filled half the room. Everyone stared in disbelief. From where has all this cloth come? No matter how hard Duṣāṣāṇa pulled, he couldn't remove the cloth. The cloth just kept getting longer and longer, until he dropped to the floor in exhaustion.

Gandhārī, Duryodhana's mother, hearing the commotion, came into the assembly hall with haste and asked, "What is this? You want to take off the clothes of a woman of the royal family in public? Is that the way my son was raised? Are you trying to insult the women of this household? Here, take off my clothes! This is an outrage! Don't you know if this woman of our family wishes, she could curse you? With one word from her lips, she could stop the rain! She could dry up all the vegetables, all the crops of all the farms in the kingdom with one word from her lips! And here you are insulting her? Dṛtarāṣṭra, you are the King, sitting on your throne. Your duty is to protect the citizens of our country. And here, right before your throne, this outrage is taking place?"

Dṛtarāṣṭra called Draupadī, "Come here, come to me." Draupadī, in tears and sorrow, came to the foot of the throne. Dṛtarāṣṭra said, "Draupadī, don't curse us. Please hold your anger. Don't curse the throne of Hastinapura. I will give you three boons. Anything you want!"

Draupadī with sobs said, "I won't curse you. First, what I want is that I will not be the slave of Duryodhana."

Dṛtarāṣṭra said, "I grant you that wish. You are free."

Then she said, "I want the five Pāṇḍavas to be free as well."

The King said, "I grant you that wish. They are free."

And then Draupadī said, "Please give them their weapons back."

He said, "I grant you that wish. They can have their weapons back. Choose something else. Take back your Indraprașṭa."

Draupadī said, "No, you gave me three boons. I have taken the three boons. We are free, and we have our weapons. We don't need to accept our kingdom as charity. We will take back our kingdom ourselves -- by force of arms. Kṣatriya warriors don't take a kingdom as a gift. The Pāṇḍava heroes will take their kingdom with the blood of these deceitful scum!"

The five brothers were freed and went with Draupadī to their Mother Kuntī's apartment.

Meanwhile, Duryodhana went to Dṛtarāṣṭra. He said, "Father, I won that kingdom fair and square. Everyone was present. Nobody spoke out. Nobody said Yudhiṣṭhira has no authority to gamble. Bhīṣma was there. You were there. Vidura was there. Droṇācārya was there. Kṛpācārya was there. Everyone saw. Nobody spoke out so long as they hoped that Yudhiṣṭhira would win. Nobody said anything. But when I won and became victorious, then they said, 'No, this is not fair!' Yudhiṣṭhira never complained at any time. He kept wagering and wagering. Now you have given all my winnings back. Why should they not be my slaves? I am the eldest son of the rightful King! I am the rightful heir to the kingdom and I won! And you gave back all my winnings. It wasn't your winnings you gave back. What kind of a father are you?"

Then Dṛtarāṣṭra summoned Yudhiṣṭhira and said, "Yudhiṣṭhira, rightfully my son won. Even though they cheated in the dice game, no one spoke out against it. Therefore, I pronounce that the Pāṇḍava brothers will spend twelve years in exile in the forest, and they will spend a thirteenth year in hiding. If they are not found out in that thirteenth year, that one year in hiding, then they can come back and ask for their half of the kingdom and they will receive their share. This is my proclamation."

Yudhiṣṭhira said, "King Dṛtarāṣṭra, you are the King of our nation. You are the oldest member of our family, and it is our duty to obey anything you say. We accept your order."

The brothers went back to their mother Kuntī, and said, "Mother, you stay here in Hastinapura. We are going to the forest along with Draupadī." Then Arjuna sent Abhimanyu with his wife, Subhādra, to Kṛṣṇa's house in Dwārka. There, with the blessings of Lord Śiva, Abhimanyu grew into the strongest, most heroic incarnation of the God of Love.

And with the greatest of sorrow, the five brothers, along with Draupadī, bereft of their kingdom, wealth and families departed into exile in the forest.

## Arjuna's Tapasya

Bhīm was always filled with anger. "Why should we wait twelve years in the forest, spend one year in hiding, and then go back to beg from Duryodhana? Do you think that he will give us the kingdom in thirteen years, when he will not give it to us now? Will anything be different then? Come, let us attack!"

Yudhiṣṭhira, the son of Dharma, said, "No! Attack we will. But we must do it as the last resort. When all else has failed we may resort to force of arms. Now we have this excellent opportunity to spend our time in the forest performing sādhana. Let's go visit all the sages and munis and learn the wisdom and practice of our Dharma with which we can cultivate the capacity to govern our kingdom with wisdom."

So the brothers went into the forest to sit at the feet of the ṛṣis and munis in order to learn wisdom. Oh how those days passed in the delight of sat sangha. One day Kṛṣṇa came to the hermitage where the Pāṇḍava brothers were staying and said, "My brothers, you are doing such a wonderful study of tapasya and sādhana while living here in the forest. How much patience you have cultivated. But there will be a war, and now is the time to prepare. Arjuna, you will need divine weapons to fight in this war. Propitiate Lord Śiva. Do pūjā for Śiva. Bhīm, you will need divine strength to fight in this war. All of you brothers perform sādhana."

Arjuna went to sit under a tree and began to chant: "Oṃ Namaḥ Śivāya, Oṃ Namaḥ Śivāya." After some time of intense meditation, one day a wild boar came rushing across the horizon directly towards where he was sitting. That boar was gaining speed and looked like it was going to run right into him to gore him with his tusks. When Arjuna saw the boar, he jumped up, grabbed his bow and his arrow, and let the arrow fly....whsssh! And the boar fell down dead. Arjuna walked over to where the animal was lying and saw that there were two arrows in the animal.

Over there in the bushes, a native huntsman from the forest called, "Oh Prince, why are you claiming my trophy?"

Arjuna said, "Native Hunter, you must be mistaken. This is my trophy."

The village hunter said, "Prince, please look at the animal. I believe you will find my arrow sticking into it."

"Oh yes, Native Hunter, I see your arrow just beside my own. The trophy is mine. I am Arjuna, the disciple of Droṇācārya. I never miss my mark."

"But," called the huntsman, "I'm sure this time you must have missed the mark, because it is my arrow that is sticking in that boar."

Arjuna said, "Native Huntsman, perhaps you have never heard of Droṇācārya, and you don't know his disciple, Arjuna, the greatest archer that walks the earth today."

The native huntsman said, "You have a big ego for being a little disciple."

Arjuna said, "I am not going to stand your insult," and he raised his bow.

The native huntsman split the bow with one arrow, and with more arrows he made his complete silhouette just behind on the tree in front of which Arjuna was standing.

Arjuna said, "There are only three people in existence who could have done that. The first is Droṇācārya, my Guru. The second is Bhīṣma, and the third is Mahādeva. And I know you are not Droṇācārya, and I know you are not Bhīṣma. Oṃ Namaḥ Śivāya! I bow to your lotus feet."

Arjuna bowed down while Śiva took his real form and said, "Arjuna, I am pleased with your tapasya. Choose from me a wish."

Arjuna said, "Mahādeva, Śiva, there is going to be a fight. Kṛṣṇa told me we must get divine weapons and he told me to pray to you."

Śiva replied, "Arjuna, I give you the Paśupati weapon, my own divine arrow. But I suggest you go to Indra to get more divine weapons. I bless you. You will be victorious!"

Receiving Śiva's blessing, Arjuna sat in the deepest meditation and ascended to the Indraloka, where he met Indra and said, "Indra, my Father, Mahādeva has sent me. I am to receive the divine arsenal of weapons. There is going to be a fight."

Indra said, "Stay here and study for some time."

And Arjuna began his study.

## Bhīm Invites Hanumān

Meanwhile, down on earth, one day Bhīm and Draupadī were out picking flowers for the family's pūjā. Draupadī found a lotus that was so beautiful. She said, "Bhīm, look at this lotus! Have you ever seen a lotus like this? Isn't this the most beautiful lotus you have ever seen? Bhīm, see if there are any more lotuses like this. I'm going to take this lotus back to the hut where we are living and offer it in the pūjā. You go on ahead and see if you can find some more lotuses like this one."

Bhīm said, "Okay," and went off to search for more. Draupadī took the lotus along with the other flowers and went back to the hermitage, while Bhīm followed the trail up the mountain in search of more lotuses of the same quality. Bhīm kept moving up the trail higher and higher into the mountains until he came to a clearing in an area where there was a large shade tree. Underneath the shade tree an old monkey was sitting with a long tail, and the tail was lying across the path. Bhīm said, "Hey Monkey, move your tail! I am looking for lotuses for Draupadī."

And the monkey replied, "Sing the name of Rāma. I am an

old monkey. I am tired."

Bhīm said, "Hey Monkey, don't give me any of that business, 'Sing the name of Rāma.' I'm busy. I'm looking for a special lotus for Draupadī. Will you move your tail, so I can cross the path?"

The monkey said, "What has this world come to? An old monkey can't even find a place to rest in peace. I climbed this mountain thinking I could be left alone, and here I am being disturbed again. I am tired and I am old, and I don't have the strength to move that tail by myself. Would you please move the tail for me? If it's bothering you, and you don't want to go around it, move the tail yourself. And sing the name of Rāma."

Bhīm got angry. He said, "Hey Monkey, I am sure you don't know who I am. But I just want to let you know that I am Bhīm, the son of Kuntī, the son of the Wind, and I have the strength of ten elephants. Move your tail out of my way."

The monkey said, "Bhīm, one day you will get old and you will know what it is like to be tired and without any strength. But I am telling you, I am just too tired to move that tail myself. You please move it out of your way. Sing the name of Rāma, brother, sing the name of Rāma!"

Bhīm replied with anger, "All right, I warned you, and now I am going to move your tail myself." He reached down with his one hand and started to lift that tail, but the tail wouldn't budge. So he took both of his hands and he started to lift the tail...but he couldn't move the tail an inch!

The old monkey looked at him and said, "Hey, please lift the tail. Come on, you are so strong! Ah, lift the tail, brother, come on! Lift the tail, come on and help me out. Move it out of your way."

"Grrrrrr..rrrr," Bhīm was struggling with the tail, but he couldn't move that tail. Then he looked at that old money and said, "You are no ordinary monkey."

The monkey looked at him and said, "I told you to sing the name of Rāma, sing the name of Rāma, brother."

Bhīm asked, "Who are you?"

The old monkey answered, "I am your older brother. I, too, am the son of the Wind. Now see my real form." And he became Hanumān!

Bhīm bowed down to his older brother, Hanumān, and said, "Hanumān, there is going to be a fight. We were cheated out of our kingdom and we are going to get it back. Come and help us."

Hanumān said, "Bhīm, this isn't my Yuga for fighting. I already did my fighting against Rāvaṇa, but I will be with you. I will sit on Arjuna's flag and I will bless you all. You will be victorious. But remember my words, Bhīm, sing the name of Rāma! Sing the name of Rāma! Go with the name of God! I will ride on Arjuna's flag, and I will bless your armies. But sing the name of Rāma!"

Bhīm found a bunch of lotuses and brought them back to Draupadī, and she was so happy to make pūjā with such beautiful lotuses. The other brothers also were happy to hear that Hanumān would be blessing their army.

## Arjuna Completes his Course

Meanwhile, up in heaven, Arjuna went to Indra and said, "Indra, I have completed the course of study, and have become a master of all the divine weapons. Please bless me and let me return to the earth. My brothers will certainly be concerned for me."

Indra said, "No, not yet. I want you to learn how to dance, first. This is Citragupta, the divine gandharva musician of the heavens, and he will be your dance teacher."

Arjuna said, "Indra, there is going to be a war. I came here for divine weapons. Why do I need to learn how to dance?"

Indra said, "It will come in handy."

Citragupta began dance lessons with Arjuna, and Arjuna became a master of dance. He was so graceful. One day Arjuna was dancing all the divine rhythms so beautifully. Urvāṣī, the divine Apsara, saw him dancing and her heart was stolen away. She danced along with him and the two of them dancing together, looked like grace incarnate.

After dancing with Arjuna, she said, "Arjuna, my heart has been stolen away. Come make love with me."

Arjuna replied, "Mother, you are a Divine Mother to me. I have been sent here on a very specific mission to get divine weapons to prepare for the war that is going to take place. Indra has told me to learn how to dance, but I am afraid that I don't have time to enter into a love affair and have romance at this time. Please excuse me, Mother."

She said, "I'm an Apsara. I am lust incarnate. Don't call me Mother. I am not your mother."

Arjuna said, "Mother, when Nārāyaṇa slapped his thigh, you were born from that thigh. That is why your name is Urvāṣī. Uru means thigh and vaṣī means the resident - she who resides in the thigh. And therefore, you were born from Nārāyaṇa, you are part of God, and you exemplify mother-hood to all creation. You are a Mother to me. You are not lust incarnate to me. So Mother, please excuse me. This is not my time to have a relationship."

Urvāṣī became very insulted. She said, "I curse you. You have denied my overtures. You've insulted me and rejected my invitation, the invitation which is so much longed for by all the men of the universe. You shall become a eunuch!" And she threw some water at him.

When the water splashed on him, Arjuna said, "For such a small fault you have given me such a terrible curse?"

Indra came and said, "Urvāṣī, that's not very divine behavior. Even your terrible curse should have some limit."

She said, "Yes, Indra, I know that, but I got very insulted and very angry."

He ordered, "Well then, put a limit on your curse."

Urvāṣī asked, "What should the limit be?"

"Make him a eunuch for one year," Indra answered.

Then Urvāṣī agreed, "Okay, he can be a eunuch for one year."

So Indra gave Arjuna all the divine weapons and the knowledge of dance and abundant blessings, and Arjuna returned to the earth. When he returned home to his brothers, they were so happy to have the whole family together again.

When their twelve years were complete, they were required to find a place to hide for one year. They went to the King of Cheddi, Matsya Rāj, the brother of Matsyagandha, who had become Satyavatī. Arjuna, the eunuch, dressed as a lady, became the dance teacher, Priyānela. Bhīm became a cook. Yudhiṣṭhira became a minister and advisor. Nakula and Sahadeva worked in the stables and took care of the cows, while Draupadī became Sarendrī, the chief servant to the queen. And in this way one year passed.

## Arjuna the Dance Teacher

Arjuna's dance pupil was the King's daughter, and her name was Uttarā. Uttarā was the incarnation of Ratī, whose husband was Kāmadeva, the God of Love, who had been burnt to ashes by the anger of Śiva. Uttarā was a beautiful girl and an excellent student. Therefore, Arjuna taught her all the rhythms that he had learned from Citragupta, when he was studying with the Master in heaven. Uttarā surrendered to her Guru with great devotion, and she learned every movement with tremendous grace.

Sometimes when Priyānela would talk with Uttarā, Uttarā would say, "Priyānela, when I grow up I want to have a husband just like you. There is no one else who exhibits such understanding, such grace, and such compassion, and yet is so firm and strong in knowledge."

Priyānela replied, "You know that's quite impossible for you to marry me. But I know one man who will be just perfect for you." And Arjuna thought of his son, Abhimanyu, the God of Love.

## Draupadī and the Death of Kitchat

One year's time passed for the Pāṇḍavas in hiding and working in menial jobs in the palace of Matsya Rāj, the King of Cheddi. The King of Cheddi's brother-in-law was commander in chief of his armies. He was a very demonic man named Kitchat. One day Kitchat came into the Queen's quarters, where he saw Draupadī, head servant of the Queen's helpers. Then he went to his sister, the queen, and he said, "Sister, who is that beautiful maid you have?"

The queen said, "That's my new servant."

Kitchat said, "Send her to me tonight."

The queen said, "That's not right, my brother. She's my servant."

Her brother said, "I will be very happy to have that lady wait on me. Send her to me. Otherwise, I will not be pleased with you."

So the queen called her servant, Draupadī. She said, "I want you to bring some wine to the commander in chief of the army this evening."

And Draupadī replied, "Do you understand what the result of this is going to be?"

The queen said, "No, I know nothing of results. My brother has requested you to come. I am only fulfilling his request. Go to him and don't argue with me."

Draupadī did as she was instructed, and took the wine to

Kitchat's apartment. When she arrived Kitchat was in a drunken stupor, and when he saw the beautiful Draupadī enter, he grabbed her and tried to attack her. She struggled and ran away from him. She ran to the cook's apartment, where Bhīm was staying, and seething with anger she said, "You must avenge this insult."

Bhīm replied, "Tell the commander of the army to meet you at midnight in the dance instruction room."

Draupadī was standing in the garden when Kitchat came to her and said, "You are the most beautiful of all the servants in the palace. I want you to be mine."

And Draupadī replied, "Come to meet me in the dancing room at midnight."

Kitchat was very happy.

That night at midnight Bhīm sat in the dance room with a very beautiful cloth over his head. Kitchat was quite drunk when he entered and said, "Oh my beloved, you are waiting here for me."

Bhīm made no response. Then Kitchat came up from behind and put his hand on his beloved's shoulder, and Bhīm turned around and punched him in the nose. Arjuna began to play the drums so that no one could hear the noise of the struggle, while Bhīm with his own bare hands strangled the commander in chief to death.

News of the death of Kitchat spread throughout India like wild-fire, and when that news was received in Hastinapura, Duryodhana thought: "There are only three people in the world who could have killed that general: Bhīṣma, Droṇācārya, and Bhīm. Bhīṣma is here in Hastinapura, and Droṇācārya is here as well. That means it must have been Bhīm who killed him. Now we know where the Pāṇḍavas are hiding. They are hiding in the palace of Matsya Rāj, the King of Cheddi. Quickly let's take our army and attack."

Then Ṣākūṇi advised, "If we take our army and attack,

Bhīṣma will never allow it. Let's tell Bhīṣma that because they have no commander of their army, their territory is weak and we will go to protect them."

Then Duryodhana went to Bhīṣma and said, "Bhīṣma, Kitchat, the commander in chief of the armies of the King of Cheddi, has just been killed. We must go to protect their country."

Duryodhana along with Bhīṣma, Droṇācārya, Kṛpācārya, Karṇa and Duṣāṣāṇa mounted on their chariots along with the huge army of Hastinapura, and proceeded to the northern borders of the Kingdom of Cheddi.

Some other wicked Kings also heard the news that Cheddi had no commander in chief, and they came to attack from the South. Matsya Rāj, the King of Cheddi, took his armies to the South to fight off those vicious enemies.

Then the guards of the boundary to the North sent news to the palace that the entire army of Hastinapura had assembled on the northern border. The Crown Prince was a young boy and he proudly proclaimed, "I will march off myself to face the enemy alone to protect our northern border."

Yudhiṣṭhira said, "That's fine, Crown Prince, defend the honor of your country. But take dear Priyānela as your charioteer."

He said, "What? That eunuch of a dance instructor is going to be my charioteer?"

Yudhiṣṭhira said, "Yes, please, just trust me. Take the dance instructor as your charioteer."

The Crown Prince consented, and Arjuna mounted the chariot and began to drive the chariot right into the face of the enemy. When the Crown Prince saw numerous soldiers led by Bhīṣma, Droṇācārya, Kṛpācārya, Karṇa, Duryodhana, and Duṣāṣāṇa, his heart sank into his stomach and he said, "I am getting out of here! I am not going to face that whole army by myself. Even the whole armies of Cheddi can't face those warriors. Come on Priyānela, drive the chariot. Let's get out of here!"

Priyānela replied, "No, Crown Prince, we've come to defend our borders, and defend them we must! There is no turning back for us. Let's drive to that tree over there." They went over to the tree, and Arjuna said, "Okay, Crown Prince, climb up into the tree and you will find some divine weapons."

The Crown Prince climbed up into the tree and found the weapons, and brought them down. Opening up the bundle, he exclaimed, "My goodness, this looks like Gandīva, the bow of Arjuna! These look like the weapons of the Pāṇḍavas! These are divine weapons. How did they get into that tree?"

Priyānela said, "Never mind! You drive the chariot and I will stand on top." Arjuna took his bow and his arrows and they drove off right into the face of the enemy. Arjuna sounded the string of his bow and it rumbled through the heavens. Everyone knew that Arjuna had come!

Duryodhana said, "That is Arjuna's bow! Ah, we have found the Pāṇḍava brothers! We have discovered them in their hiding and according to the rules of their exile, they must remain in the forest for twelve more years."

Bhīṣma replied, "No, Duryodhana, we didn't come here to find the Pāṇḍava brothers. We came here to defend the borders of Cheddi. Besides, the thirteenth year is over today."

Duryodhana replied, "I don't accept that. My astrologers say the year is not over yet. They have to go for twelve more years in exile."

Bhīṣma said, "We'll discuss that later. Let's protect the borders of Cheddi and not....."

Duryodhana said, "No, I'm going to kill Arjuna right now!" And he commanded his troops to attack.

Arjuna fired arrow after arrow and no one could cut his arrows. Then he summoned one divine arrow and he put the entire army of Hastinapura to sleep. He said, "Now, Crown

Prince, go take the neck-scarves from Duryodhana, Karṇa, and Duṣāṣāṇa and bring them back. They will make an excellent presentation to the princesses of Cheddi."

The Crown Prince went and removed the scarves from those warriors, which he took back to the princesses. Then Priyānela told everyone, "Look at the heroism of the Crown Prince! He defeated the entire army of Hastinapura by himself."

Everyone was so amazed at this feat of the Crown Prince, to display such heroism in his first battle. But the Crown Prince couldn't take credit for the victory all by himself, and he revealed the identity of the Pāṇḍavas.

The one year of hiding was over. The Pāṇḍavas resumed their real identities, took up their divine weapons, and sent messengers to Hastinapura. "Our thirteen years have been completed, twelve years in exile and one year in hiding. Give us back our kingdom."

Duryodhana said, "I am not giving back the kingdom. I found your hiding place, and therefore you return for twelve more years in exile, and then come back and beg from me. And then, maybe, I will give you the kingdom."

All the allies of the Pāṇḍavas began to assemble and the friends of Duryodhana assembled, and the stage was set for war.

The counsellors advised: "Let us fight."

Kṛṣṇa stepped forward into the council of the Pāṇḍavas and said, "Let us fight only as a last resort. When we go to war, we are going to be fighting Bhīṣma, your grandfather, Droṇācārya, your Guru, Kṛpācārya, the Guru of this family. Don't you see that brother will be fighting against brother, uncle against uncle, relative against relative, friends against friends. Let's try everything we possibly can to avoid the war. Only then will we accept that we must fight. I will go myself to Hastinapura as the Ambassador of the Pāṇḍavas."

Kṛṣṇa went to Hastinapura and said, "I have come on behalf of the Pāṇḍavas. Their thirteen years are complete. Give them back their kingdom. Be true. Be fair. Avoid this horrible war."

Duryodhana said, "I am not giving back the kingdom!"

Then Kṛṣṇa said, "Give them five villages and on behalf of the Pāṇḍavas, I declare that there will be peace. Any five villages you like."

Duryodhana said, "I won't give one foot of space. I won't give one inch of the land of Hastinapura to those Pāṇḍavas!"

Then there was no recourse but to fight.

## War!

On that fateful day the armies of the Kauravas, led by Duryodhana, Duṣāṣāṇa, and their hundred brothers along with many heroic warriors such as Bhīṣma, Droṇācārya, Kṛpācārya, Aśvathāma, Jayadratha, Karṇa, lined up facing the armies of the Pāṇḍavas led by Yudhiṣṭhira, Bhīm, Arjuna, Nakula and Sahadeva, with Kṛṣṇa driving the chariot of Arjuna. When Arjuna saw relatives, friends, cousins and uncles, all facing each other with weapons of destruction, ready to destroy the entire family for rights to real estate and property, he dropped his bow and said, "Kṛṣṇa, I was wrong. There is no need to fight. I'd rather that they have everything and we take nothing, than to enter into this battle of destruction. What good is the kingdom to us, if all of those whom we love will die in the battle to get it?"

Then Kṛṣṇa narrated the *Bhagavad Gītā*, the Song of God, and showed his universal form to Arjuna. Arjuna understood that everything that is, comes from Kṛṣṇa, and all Karma that is, is authored by God. Within each of us resides the spark of God. And every action we perform is demanded by God. Then Arjuna surrendered his will and said, "If God wills me to fight, make me an instrument of your will."

The fighting began and continued with a great struggle, and one by one the family members fell on the battlefield. There were so many momentous occasions in that war, but one very special fight was led by Abhimanyu. Just before Abhimanyu had marched off to war, his wife had conceived a child. And now on the battlefield Abhimanyu led the way for the Pāṇḍava armies to break open the Cakravyū formation. The Cakravyū formation is a series of concentric circles made by military might, in the center of which were assembled the cream of the Kaurava warriors. Abhimanyu drove his chariot right through the circle as a wedge, and pierced the center. One by one the Kaurava warriors faced Abhimanyu in battle, and one by one he cut down their weapons to pieces. No one could face him alone. He shot arrows at Droṇācārya, at Kṛpācārya, he defeated Duryodhana, Karṇa, Duṣāṣāṇa. There wasn't one warrior of the opposing army who could face him.

Then Duryodhana gave the command: "Let's all attack him at once!"

And Abhimanyu called out, "Wait, the rules of this war are one warrior will fight with one warrior! Why are you breaking your truth? You promised to fight a dharmic battle based on laws of military prowess. We have all taken an oath to maintain the code of military conduct that only one warrior will fight with one warrior."

Duryodhana replied, "My duty is to defeat my enemy any way that I can! I am here to win this war. I don't care about the ethics of military codes. Everyone attack him at once!"

Abhimanyu shot arrow after arrow and no one could pierce him. He wounded each of the warriors that faced him, and none could touch him. Then Karṇa shot an arrow which crippled his chariot. Abhimanyu fell from the chariot onto the ground. Each of the Kaurava warriors took his sword, and they all attacked him at once. Abhimanyu picked up the chariot wheel and spun it around so none could approach him. But while he was fighting in the front, they grabbed him from the rear, and they brought him down and stabbed him with their swords. And Abhimanyu left his body on the battlefield.

When Arjuna heard this news, he came to the battlefield to perform the rites of his fallen son. All the great warriors of both armies collected that night around the funeral pyre and Droṇācārya said, "Arjuna, if it were not for Abhimanyu, we would have won the war today. There was never a hero in any battle who was like your son. Single-handedly he defeated all the commanders of the Kaurava army, and it was only by deceit that he fell in battle." And that day Arjuna took the solemn vow that he would defeat those forces of deceit.

And he did. One by one the Pāṇḍava warriors killed each of the generals of the Kaurava armies. Bhīṣma, Droṇācārya, Kṛpācārya, Aśvathāma, Jayadratha, Duṣāṣāṇa and Karṇa, all met their deaths in the battle. Ultimately Bhīm met Duryodhana in direct combat with the mace. Having slain Duryodhana, the Pāṇḍavas regained their kingdom. But there was no joy in having such a kingdom, taken at such a cost.

Dṛtarāṣṭra, Gandhārī, Kuntī, and Vidura left for the forest to practice meditation. Ultimately they left their bodies. Kṛṣṇa was mistaken for a peacock and was killed by a hunter's arrow. And the last of the Dvāpara Yuga was coming to its completion.

The Pāṇḍava brothers no longer had any desire to maintain the kingdom. When Parikṣit, the son of Abhimanyu who came forth from Uttarā's womb, became thirty six years of age, the Pāṇḍava brothers crowned him as the King, and they, too, departed to perform tapasya in the Himalayas, and ultimately left their mortal bodies.

## Parikṣit and the Coming of Kali

What a mighty King was Parikṣit! He wouldn't let any enemy of Dharma reside anywhere in his kingdom. When Parikṣit was an old man, his wife conceived a son. But before the son was born, a most amazing thing happened. One day the King was out hunting in the forest, and when he came just near to the edge of his kingdom, he saw Kali Yuga approaching. He said, "Kali, what are you doing here? You can't come into my kingdom!"

He took out his sword and he began to chase Kali. Kali ran in fear. Wherever Kali ran, Parikṣit chased behind, until Parikṣit finally reached out and grabbed Kali by the hair and holding that hair, he took his sword and said, "I am going to cut off your head. I am not allowing Kali to live in my kingdom!"

And Kali said, "Wait King! I take refuge in you. You can't kill a being that has taken refuge in you. That is not the Dharma of Kings. I surrender to you. Don't kill me."

"Why shouldn't I kill you?" asked Parikṣit.

"I have some good qualities too," said Kali.

Parikṣit said, "Name one."

Kali replied, "Whatever Karma an individual performs in my age, he shall receive the fruits of it immediately."

Parikṣit agreed, "That is a good quality. If noble souls perform pure actions they will quickly advance in spiritual life. But I will not allow you to live in my kingdom while I am King."

And Kali asked, "Then where shall I live?"

Parikṣit replied, "I will give you three places to live. You can live in lust, you can live in deceit, and you can live in gambling."

Kali said, "Those places are too limited. Give me one other place to live."

And Parikṣit said, "You can live in gold."

Kali said, "Thank you, my King. I promise I will not enter into your kingdom so long as you are alive, but I will only inhabit those four places."

But the King forgot that the crown on his head was made of gold, and Kali moved on to the golden crown.

As the King pursued his hunt throughout the forest, he became very tired and thirsty, when he came to the hermitage of a ṛṣi. The ṛṣi was sitting deeply in meditation. King Parikṣit said, "Ṛṣi, I am extremely perplexed by thirst. Could I please have some water."

The sound of Parikṣit's words did not enter into the ṛṣi's ears. He was deep in meditation. Parikṣit cleared his throat and said again, "Hm, hm, Ṛṣi!" in a much louder tone. "Ṛṣi, please wake up! I am deeply perplexed by thirst. Please give me some water."

But the ṛṣi was absorbed in samādhi and made no response at all.

From the golden crown on the top of the King's head Kali said, "Look at this insult. He is faking. Nobody can be so insensitive to ignore the King when he is thirsty. All you asked for was a glass of water. See if he is really meditating or if he is just being deceitful."

Then the King looked down on the ground and saw a dead snake lying on the earth. Under the influence of Kali, he picked up that dead snake, wrapped it around the ṛṣi's neck and walked away. When the ṛṣi's son, Śṛṅga, returned to the aśrama, he saw his father meditating in the deepest samādhi, pure intuitive absorption, with a dead snake hanging around his neck. The son said, "What is this insult! Can you imagine that someone would do that to my father, who is meditating in the purest absorption of divine consciousness?"

He took some water in his hand, and pronounced a curse, "Whoever perpetrated this heinous offense, I curse him!

Within seven days, Takṣa, the King of Snakes, will bite him and that individual will die from snake poison." And he threw the water.

When King Parikṣit heard that he had been cursed to die by snake-bite within seven days, he called all his ministers together and said, "What shall we do?"

They said, "No one can avoid the will of God. Whatever God proclaims will happen. Still an individual should make every effort to act correctly. Quickly let us build a tower which is completely air-tight. On the very top of the tower, we will construct the King's quarters, and we will put sentries around so as to not allow even an insect to enter. And there let the King listen to the Bhagavāt, and we will all pray to God."

Immediately the immense tower with the King's quarters on the top floor was constructed, and all around sentries were stationed, so that even an insect could not enter. Parikṣit sat in the King's quarters and listened to Sanāt Kumāra recite the Bhagavāt and tell the stories of the history and traditions of Sanātana Dharma.

There was a very poor Brahmiṇ whose name was Kaśyapa. When Kaśyapa heard that the King had taken refuge in a high tower for fear of snake-bike, he thought, "I have a mantra that cures snake-bite. I will go to the King and teach it to him, so that when Takṣa bites him, he can pro - nounce the mantra and become cured immediately. Then maybe he will give me some money."

Kaśyapa set out for the King's tower, and on his way he met Takṣa, the King of Snakes. They started to walk down the road together towards the King's tower.

Takṣa started the conversation, "Oh Brahmiṇ, where are you going?"

Kaśyapa, the Brahmiṇ, replied, "I have heard that King Parikṣit has been cursed to die from snake poisoning within seven days. Takṣa, the King of Snakes, is going to bite him. I have a mantra that cures snake-bite."

Takṣa asked, "Really? What kind of a mantra is that?"

Kaśyapa said, "Oh, it's really a marvellous mantra. It works very well with all kinds of poisons."

And Takṣa said, "Do you see that tree? Do you think that if I put poison into that tree, you can cure it?"

Kaśyapa said, "Certainly!"

Then Takṣa injected poison into the tree through his venomous fangs, and the tree immediately shriveled to ashes. Takṣa said, "Do you think your mantra could cure that tree?"

Kaśyapa replied, "Surely it can!" He closed his eyes, rubbed his hands together a few times and said the mantra, and the tree came to life again.

Takṣa said, "That's marvelous! I have never seen anything like that in my life. What is it that you want?"

Kaśyapa replied, "I am a very poor Brahmiṇ and I need some money with which to feed my family. So I am going to give the mantra to the King. Maybe he will give me some wealth by which I can care for my family."

Then Takṣa said, "Well, I'll give you wealth right now. If you are going there just for money, you don't have to take the trouble to go all that way. Why don't you just go home. Here, take this money and return to your home."

Then Kaśyapa sat down in meditation and saw that it was the time for the King to leave his body anyway. So he said to Takṣa, "Okay, I'll take your money," and he went back home.

It was the evening of the seventh day, and Sanāt Kumāra had just finished reciting the Bhagavāt. Parikṣit was totally illumined with wisdom, and he said, "You know, my Guru, whatever God wills to be, will be. And I bow to the will of God. If God wants me to survive, I will survive; and if God wants me to leave my body, I will leave. No longer have I attachment to my own desire. I surrender to the will of God, and accept whatever is the Divine Will."

Just then Takṣa came to the base of that tower. He took on the form of a Brahmiṇ and other snakes with him all took on the form of Brahmiṇs as well. They said, "Captain of the Guard, we would like to see the King."

The Captain of the Guard said, "I am sorry, no one can go in. The King is not seeing anyone today."

Then Takṣa explained to the Captain of the Guard, "We are holy Brahmiṇs, and have been praying for the welfare of the King. We have been performing pūjā for his welfare, and we have brought some prasād from those offerings. Could you at least give this fruit to the King?"

The Captain of the Guard said, "Certainly." He took the basket of fruit and sent it up to the King's apartment.

The messenger said, "King, some holy Brahmiṇs from the forest have been making worship for your welfare, and they have sent some prasād from that offering. The sun is just about to set on the horizon, and you will be free from danger. Will you please accept an offering of their prasād?"

King Parikṣit said, "I am really not hungry right now. Take this prasād and divide it among the soldiers. Just leave me this one little apple." He took an apple from the basket and said, "Let's divide this apple amongst the ministers." He broke open the apple, where he saw a little spot. And the spot started to grow until it became a worm. And the worm grew until it became a snake. The snake grew and it became Takṣa, the King of Snakes, who bit the King Parikṣit injecting the deadly poisonous venom, and King Parikṣit gave up his life.

## King Janamejaya and the Great Yajña

After some time, the queen gave birth to a very beautiful son whose name was Janamejaya. Janamejaya grew up to be the King. After he had been crowned as the King and had taken over the duties of administering his nation, one day he turned to his ministers and said, "Tell me about my father. How did he die?"

The ministers said, "Your father was killed by a snake-bite from Takṣa, the King of the Snakes, because of the ṛṣi's curse."

Janamejaya said, "It is the duty of a son to avenge his father's death. Now I am declaring war on all snakes. I shall make one great snake yajña, in which I shall burn every snake in the fire of our sacrificial altar."

He sent out his soldiers in every direction rounding up as many snakes as they could find, and he invited the ṛṣis and Brahmiṇs, who sat around the sacred fire chanting mantras. One at a time he threw the snakes into the burning flames.

When Takṣa heard of the snake sacrifice, he ran and hid. Janamejaya called Garuḍa, the eagle who is Viṣṇu's conveyance, and ordered, "Find Takṣa. I am going to burn him in the fire!"

All of his soldiers brought many snakes, and as many snakes as were brought, Janamejaya would throw them into the fire. All the snakes that could escape, ran to take refuge with Mānasa Devi.

Mānasa Devi was the wife of Jarātkāru Muni, and they had a son named Aṣṭik Muni. When the snakes came to Mānasa Devi they said, "Mother, please save us! We are innocent. We didn't do anything. Is it fair to kill an entire race of this creation for the misdeed of one member? We are not responsible for the death of King Parikṣit. Save us!"

Mānasa Devi granted them freedom from fear and called

her son, Aṣṭik Muni. She said, "Muni, find a way to stop this snake sacrifice."

Aṣṭik Muni said, "Please give me your blessing, Mother, and certainly it will be stopped."

Mānasa Devi gave her blessings, and Aṣṭik Muni, shining with the radiance of tapasya, went walking into the sacrificial arena, where the snake yajña was taking place.

When the King Janamejaya saw the radiance of the muni coming into the sacrificial area to bless him, he stood up from his sacrifice and bowed down to him and welcomed him with great respect. He said, "Muni, ask some boon from me."

And the muni said, "King, I have one request for you."

The King replied, "Whatever it is, it will be done. I bow to the holy Brahmiṇ. I bow to the radiance of your tapasya, to the wisdom which you illuminate. Certainly I will fulfill your request. Please explain to me what is on your mind."

Then the muni said, "A King is the protector of the subjects of his kingdom. These innocent snakes have done harm to none. Also they are subjects of your kingdom. Therefore, you are transgressing your dharma by killing these innocent subjects. Your duty is to protect them. To protect the defenseless and the helpless, and to strive for the upliftment of the downtrodden is the duty of a King. Here you are persecuting the defenseless. You are using the powers of your warrior Dharma for evil rather than for good, and the effects of this will be adverse. Therefore, King Janamejaya, I request you to stop this sacrifice!"

The King said, "I have taken the saṅkalpa to avenge my father's death. How I can stop the sacrifice, when the slayer of my father is still at large, and my sacrifice is not yet complete?"

Aṣṭik Muni said, "Your father attained liberation through the ṛṣi's curse. The King of Snakes was merely the instrument. Now the greatest honor that you could pay to your father's memory is to change the nature of your sacrifice from one of destruction to one of construction. So King, if you will stop destroying this race of snakes, you can complete the sacrifice of all sacrifices by listening to the wisdom of the scriptures."

Janamejaya agreed. He set all the remaining snakes free, and then sat down and listened while Veda Vyāsa narrated the stories of the Swāmī Purāṇa. Ultimately he attained liberation.

Whoever will listen to these stories of the Swāmī Purāṇa with an open heart, and learn the Wisdom of our Dharma with Pure Faith and One-Pointed Attention, will certainly be blessed with Peace and Delight, Health and Prosperity, and the fullest harmony in every action performed.

www.ingramcontent.com/pod-product-compliance
Lightning Source LLC
Chambersburg PA
CBHW021054080526
44587CB00010B/245
* 9 7 8 1 8 8 7 4 7 2 6 1 6 *